Cambridge Studies in Applied Econometrics

NUMBER 1

MODELS AND PROJECTIONS OF DEMAND IN POST-WAR BRITAIN

WORKS OF THE CAMBRIDGE GROWTH PROJECT PUBLISHED FOR THE DEPARTMENT OF APPLIED ECONOMICS, UNIVERSITY OF CAMBRIDGE, BY CHAPMAN AND HALL

General Editor: RICHARD STONE

A PROGRAMME FOR GROWTH

1. A Computable Model of Economic Growth (July 1962). Richard Stone and Alan Brown.
2. A Social Accounting Matrix for 1960 (October 1962). Richard Stone and others.
3. Input–Output Relationships, 1954–1966 (September 1963).* John Bates and Michael Bacharach.
4. Capital, Output and Employment, 1948–1960 (April 1964). Graham Pyatt assisted by Patricia Hutcheson.
5. The Model in its Environment (July 1964). Richard Stone.
6. Exploring 1970 (July 1965). Alan Brown and others.
7. The Owners of Quoted Ordinary Shares (November 1966). Jack Revell and John Moyle.
8. The Demand for Fuel, 1948–1975 (November 1968). Kenneth Wigley.
9. Exploring 1972 (May 1970). Terence Barker and Richard Lecomber.
10. The Determinants of Britain's Visible Imports, 1949–1966 (December 1970). Terence Barker.
11. The Financial Interdependence of the Economy, 1957–1966 (October 1971). Alan Roe.
12. Structural Change in the British Economy, 1948–1968 (May 1974). Alan Armstrong.

CAMBRIDGE STUDIES IN APPLIED ECONOMETRICS

1. Models and Projections of Demand in Post-War Britain. Angus Deaton.

* *Out of print*

MODELS AND PROJECTIONS OF DEMAND IN POST-WAR BRITAIN

ANGUS DEATON

CHAPMAN AND HALL
LONDON

First published 1975
by Chapman and Hall Ltd
11 New Fetter Lane, London EC4P 4EE

Typeset by E.W.C. Wilkins Ltd, London and Northampton
and printed in Great Britain
at the University Printing House, Cambridge

ISBN 0 412 13640 6

Distributed in the U.S.A.
by Halsted Press, a Division
of John Wiley & Sons, Inc., New York

Library of Congress Catalog Card Number 74-19935

INTRODUCTION TO THE NEW SERIES

In the past twelve years the members of the group working on the Cambridge Growth Project produced twelve volumes in the series *A Programme for Growth* in addition to a large number of journal articles and other publications. Although the title of our former series expressed well enough our intentions when the project began, it has for some time given a rather restricted impression of the work on which we have actually been engaged. This work relates to the construction of a disaggregated model of the British economy designed to throw some light not only on questions of growth but also on questions of stability and on the likely effects of government policies for economic control. Further, while the size of the national cake is important, so is its distribution; and while we rely largely on technical progress to increase the size of the cake, we cannot ignore in these days its possible effect on the environment.

Because of these considerations and also because many of our studies are concerned not with conclusions derived from the model as a whole but with the detailed workings of some small part of it, we have decided to replace our old series with a new one: *Cambridge Studies in Applied Econometrics*. This new title is intended to give a truer indication of the nature of the work on which we are engaged.

The project continues to be financed jointly by the Social Science Research Council, the Treasury, the Central Statistical Office and the University of Cambridge.

July 1974 Richard Stone

FOREWORD

The first number of our earlier series, *A Programme for Growth*, carried a notice of forthcoming papers. Five were announced but eventually only four were published. The fifth, which was intended to deal with consumption functions, never appeared; now it takes its place as number one in the new series.

It is not that ten years ago we had nothing to say on the subject of consumers' behaviour. The crude estimation method that I had used in my original (1954) paper on the linear expenditure system gave interesting and in many respects satisfactory results, some of which were published outside our series, for instance in Stone, Brown and Rowe (1964). With this method the parameter estimates changed very little after the first few iterations. Nevertheless they did change, and with the computing resources then at our disposal we failed to reach convergence. It was mainly for this reason that we decided to wait.

As a consequence there has been a long delay in publishing a detailed account of our treatment of consumers' expenditure but the result is greatly superior to anything we could have produced a decade ago. Thanks in large measure to the work of Angus Deaton, it is now possible to see clearly the sources of the difficulties that arise in formulating and estimating coherent systems of demand equations, the strengths and weaknesses of the various models that have been proposed in the vast literature on the subject and the lines on which research must develop if these models are to be rendered economically more acceptable while remaining within the bounds set by available data and known techniques of estimation.

As regards applications, the results given here are geared to the needs of our model of the British economy and relate to projections for 1975 and 1980. The estimates are based on postwar data. A similar analysis based on the period 1900 to 1970 will be published shortly in *Econometrica*, Deaton 1974(b).

July 1974 Richard Stone

PREFACE

The work which is presented in this monograph began as a more or less routine attempt to estimate and project demand equations for the post-war British economy. It became clear quite quickly that this was not a straightforward task; there were considerable estimation difficulties in the way of applying what seemed to be theoretically satisfactory models, and, as these began to be solved and results to appear, numerous anomalies and difficulties of interpretation began to make themselves felt. Many of these had more to do with the theoretical basis of the model than with either estimation or data and they could only be clarified by questioning the underlying framework of the model. Consequently, work which began as a straightforward exercise in applied economics has trespassed into the preserves of both economic theory and econometrics. Even so, the original purpose remains; although much of the discussion is methodological, the fundamental aim is the empirical analysis of consumer demand.

I should like to record my gratitude to the many friends and colleagues from whose comments and discussion I have benefited in the writing of this book. In particular, I owe thanks to past and present members of the Cambridge growth project, especially Terence Barker, without whose help Chapters VII and VIII could not have been written. Anton Barten, David Champernowne, Michael Farrell, Terence Gorman, Louis Phlips and Henri Theil read earlier versions of much of this book and I am very grateful for their comments and suggestions. Nevertheless, none of the above should be held responsible for any of the errors or prejudices which remain.

To Richard Stone, the editor of this series and the director of the Cambridge Growth Project, my debt is a very special one. Without the example and inspiration of his own contributions to demand analysis, and without his continuous encouragement, help, and friendship, this book could not have been written.

Finally, I should like to thank the members of the assistant staff in the Department of Applied Economics, in particular Bobbie Coe who helped with data preparation and computation, and Christine Hudson who typed many drafts with unfailing skill, precision, and patience.

May 1974 Angus Deaton

CONTENTS

Chapter 1

INTRODUCTION

This book is concerned with the measurement of consumers' behaviour in the United Kingdom. It attempts to assess techniques of measuring, understanding, and thus predicting, the responses in the purchasing behaviour of households to the stimuli of changing prices and incomes. Since even the simplest of these responses may never be observed in isolation, it is necessary to use as tools of measurement more or less complex models of total consumer behaviour. The problem of measurement and prediction thus becomes a problem of estimation and evaluation of alternative models. In the chapters which follow, much attention is devoted to a critical assessment of one particular model, the linear expenditure system, and one of the aims of the book is to assess the applicability of this model to the analysis and projection of expenditures at a relatively high level of disaggregation. More generally, a considerable body of evidence will also be presented which is relevant to the broader issue of the role in applied analysis of models derived from the neo-classical theory of individual consumer behaviour. Such models yield complete systems of demand equations and one of the issues with which we shall be concerned is the advantages and disadvantages of these systems vis-à-vis the more traditional single equation methods.

These methodological issues, although they are an important part of the substance of the book, are in the final analysis only an intermediate step in the modelling of economic phenomena. The ultimate aim is a concrete set of relationships describing the behaviour of consumers' behaviour in the United Kingdom in the post-war period. One of the principal methodological conclusions of this work is that the models which have so far been proposed and which can be implemented have more serious deficiencies than has usually been supposed. Even so, it is hoped that the results and projections presented here have considerable practical application. A large number of empirical demand equations is presented and their strengths and weaknesses are fully explored from a number of different points of view. Thus, while the use of these models is only partially satisfactory from a purist point of view, the results together with a full knowledge of their weaknesses, provide a good substitute for the possession of the currently unobtainable ideal model.

The book falls into four parts; the first sandwiching the other three. In the first part, which consists of Chapters II and IX, the relationship between the theory of demand and the practice of empirical measurement is discussed. This is done first in an historical context and it is shown that it is only in the last twenty years or so that models based directly upon the theory have become popular tools of demand analysis. The basis and justification of such an approach are discussed in the second half of Chapter II and, at the end of the book in Chapter IX, this theme is revisited in the light of the theoretical and empirical evidence of the intervening material. This final chapter, which summarises the principal methodological results of the book, brings together our own empirical results with those of other studies in an assessment of the achievements to date of the theory-based models. Suggestions are also made as to the directions which future research might usefully follow.

In Chapters III and IV, which make up the second part of the book, we pass from the general to the particular. In Chapter III, the genesis and interpretation of the linear expenditure system is discussed with particular emphasis on how the structure of the model influences the measurement process. Most importantly in comparison with previous work, it is shown how, in common with other models derived from a directly additive utility function, the linear expenditure system enforces an approximate proportionality law between income and own-price elasticities. This relationship plays a vital part in determining the model's performance, and its consequences appear as a recurrent theme in the discussion of the later empirical results. Chapter IV presents a unified discussion of estimation problems associated with the model; these problems have occupied considerable energies in the past and here we present an efficient and rapid algorithm which is an important prerequisite for the computation of the empirical results. Although this chapter was written with the linear expenditure system in mind, it is hoped that the treatment may be found useful as a more general discussion of the problems involved in the estimation of large non-linear models.

The second of the central sections comprises Chapters V and VI; here the model is applied to the analysis of thirty-seven categories of expenditure using post-war British data. In Chapter V, the model is applied simultaneously to the full disaggregation; while in Chapter VI a hierarchic budgeting and estimation procedure is examined. The contrast in the results between the two chapters provides important information on the properties of the model and its applicability to the data. A simple single equation model is also estimated and is used to provide an alternative explanation of the data for comparison with that offered by the linear expenditure system.

Finally, in Chapters VII and VIII, the models are used for forecasting. Chapter VII is in the nature of an experiment; relative prices are generated for 1975 and trial forecasts by the alternative models are used to assess their relative performance. Using this information, and having updated the models on the most recent data available, Chapter VIII presents a set of compromise forecasts for 1975 and 1980, the latter on a range of assumptions about the development of total consumers' expenditure. Consequently, for those readers primarily interested in results for the British economy, Chapters V and VIII will be of the most specific interest.

Chapter 2

UTILITY AND DEMAND ANALYSIS

2.1 The historical background

It is now well over a century since utility functions were first introduced as tools of economic analysis. Since, then, they have achieved wide currency and play an essential role in the neo-classical economics in which most present-day economists were, and are, brought up. However, neither this long pedigree, nor the central place of utility analysis in the dominant orthodoxy of economics, can alone justify applied work which uses the theory as a basis of empirical observation. The long association of utility analysis with economics has left strong associations between the study of consumer preferences and particular propositions of economic theory, especially welfare propositions. Many of these associations are neither necessary nor useful in empirical work and yet it is not always made clear exactly what the empirical investigator is or is not assuming in constructing demand functions from mathematical preference relations. Conversely, much empirical work has made no use of consumer theory, believing utility analysis to be useless for the purpose. This view has received support both from those commentators who believe the theory to be completely vacuous, for example, Clarkson (1963), Mishan (1961) and Robinson (1960), and from those who believe it to be impossibly restrictive, for example, Kornai (1971).

In the belief that these issues are important and have not been adequately discussed by quantitative investigators, this chapter, which is introductory to the main material of the study, is devoted to a review of the relationship between the analysis of consumer preference and the empirical observation of demand behaviour. This is meant to establish the foundation for much that follows. Let us first consider how utility analysis was seen by its founders.

A number of distinct unifying themes appear in the early works of the 'marginalist revolution'. Not the least significant of these is the desire to put economics on a new footing, not as *political economy*, which was clearly identified with the body of Ricardian doctrine as represented by Mill, but as *economic science*. On this basis, economics could take her place as an equal with the physical sciences. We find Jevons removing all references to political economy, except in the title, in the second edition of his *Theory* . . . , adopting instead the contemporary Cambridge expression 'economics'. In the preface to that edition, he comments on the need to "discard, as quickly as possible, the old troublesome double-worded name of our science" and hopes "that *economics* will become the recognised name of a science, which nearly a century ago was known to the French economists as *la science économique*." Amongst other writers of the period, the references to physics and especially to astronomy become almost universal. Gossen, who in 1854 published almost certainly the first account of the marginal utility theory of demand, is described by Jevons as commencing "by claiming honours in economic science equal to those of Copernicus in astronomy". Walras too is said to have been much impressed as a youth by a treatise on 'Celestial Mechanics' and was determined to demonstrate the 'Harmony of the Spheres' in a utility and profit maximizing economy. But few went quite as far as Edgeworth who in 1881 could write:

> 'Mécanique Sociale' may one day take her place along with 'Mécanique Celeste', throned each upon the double-sided height of one maximum principle, the supreme pinnacle of moral as of physical science.
>
> Edgeworth (1881) p. 12.

Though even today, the 'maximum principle', whether of the Edgeworth or Pontryagin variety, is embodied in much of economic theory, this alone cannot accord full scientific status upon the subject. For although the mathematical methods which Jevons and his successors were so determined to introduce into the subject have flourished, much that is expected of a science is absent from economics. For although science may require mathematical techniques, the mere use of mathematics does not create science. The introduction of mathematical standards of rigorous argument, though of immense value from many points of view, does not guarantee any correspondence between theory and reality. Indeed in economics, by enforcing extreme simplicity or unreality of assumption, the inappropriate use of mathematics can do exactly the opposite. And since much of the mathematical development of economics has been incomprehensible to those who make political decisions on economic matters, political economy, far from having been destroyed or replaced by economic science, lives on in an untidy and heterodox state largely divorced from the mainstream of economic theory.

The dominance of mathematical developments in economic theory since the introduction, by Jevons and others, of constrained maximization, not only as an instrument, but also as the central subject matter of economic analysis, has greatly hampered the study of the empirical issues. Not only has the main body of mathematical economics paid but scant and casual attention to such empirical evidence as was available, but there has also been only sporadic interest in the descriptive, as opposed to prescriptive, content of the theory. Much as Jevons supported and encouraged the use of mathematics, he would, I think, have been distressed by the lack of application of the science which he believed himself to be pioneering. For Jevons was as distinguished as an applied economist as he was as a theorist. Not only did he make important contributions to the theory of price index numbers but he also constructed long time series going back into the eighteenth century. And of his pamphlet, *A Serious Fall in the Value of Gold*, published in 1863, J.M. Keynes was to write:

> For unceasing fertility and originality of mind applied, with a sure touch and unfailing control of the material, to a mass of statistics, involving immense labours . . . . this pamphlet stands unrivalled in the history of our subject. The numerous diagrams and charts which accompany are also of high interest in the history of statistical description.
>
> Keynes (1936b)

And it is clear from numerous passages in the *Theory*, that he regarded his theory of consumer demand as seriously incomplete without the empirical data to back it up, or to use his own words 'so that the formulae could be endowed with exact meaning by the aid of numerical data'.

Just how the data were to be used to make the theory more exact is none too clear from what Jevons writes. It is clearly realised that measurement must be indirect. But, as the following quotation illustrates, though this is clear enough in principle, there is not much practical help either for the testing of the theory or to guide its use as a basis of observation and quantitative analysis.

> I hesitate to say that men will ever have the means of measuring directly the feelings of the human heart. A unit of pleasure or of pain is difficult even to conceive; but it is the amount of these feelings which is continually prompting us to buying and selling, borrowing and lending, labouring and resting, producing and consuming; and *it is from the quantitative effects of the feelings that we must estimate their comparative amounts.* We can no more know nor measure gravity in its own nature than we can measure a feeling; but, just as we measure gravity by its effects in the motion of a pendulum, so we may estimate the equality or inequality of feelings by the decisions of the human mind. The will is our pendulum, and its oscillations are minutely registered in the price lists of the markets. I know not when we shall have a perfect system of statistics, but the want of it is the only insuperable obstacle in the way of making economics an exact science.
>
> Jevons (1871), Introduction

Yet even with the system of statistics we have at our disposal now, and this would appear almost perfect by the standards of Jevons' time, the marrying of the theory with the data still presents severe problems. And for most of the century since the publication of the *Theory*, with but a few distinguished exceptions, the indifference of theorists to empirical results has been mirrored by the lack of interest in the theory evinced by empirical investigators. It is only in the last twenty years or so that more than tentative attempts have been made to incorporate the utility theory of consumer behaviour into the body of statistical demand analysis.

Historically, there were a number of reasons why the impact of the new theory of demand on empirical analysis should have been so long delayed. In the first place, however important the statistical aspects to some writers, the main import of the theory lay in its normative conclusions. The model, with its explicit maximization of the social good, yields policy conclusions directly, without the need for quantification; and the question of its descriptive validity, though much more important from the policy point of view, was not something which could be usefully assessed by the statistical methods then available. But this last would have been very difficult for quite other reasons. For it is not at all clear from the original statements of Jevons and other writers of the period exactly what are the positive predictions of the theory, or indeed whether there are any. A nineteenth century reader could forgivably deduce that the theory was without refutable content; merely attaching to the everyday actions of the market-place a somewhat dubious utilitarian framework, the whole project being engineered for equally dubious political ends. Such deductions are, of course, much less forgivable now but continue to be made; see the works cited on page 4 above. But political consequences apart, certainly the statement that prices are in proportion to marginal utilities is unlikely to generate a spate of data collection and investigation similar for example to that following J.M. Keynes' (1936a) statement of a relationship between consumption and income. And though the theory did indeed have directly measurable predictions, these were not to be stated comprehensively for another thirty years until the now famous paper by Slutsky, published in 1915. Even then, little attention was paid and Slutsky's paper went largely unnoticed until 'rediscovered' by Hicks and Allen in the mid-1930's. By this time, half a century or more had passed since the first appearance of the marginal utility theory of demand.

Even if its implications had been more widely understood, it is doubtful whether much use could have been made of the theory by the methods of quantitative analysis then available. For, although there was a considerable tradition of empirical demand study, progress in statistical methodology was slow. There is at least one empirical study as early as the late seventeenth century: that on the demand for wheat published by Davenant (1699) and attributed to Gregory King. But it was not until two hundred years later that anything more than descriptive analysis was attempted. The impetus to this came from the invention by Marshall in 1881 of the concept of *elasticity of demand*; this, while not adding to the theory, contributed greatly to clarity of thought, and gave to empirical analysis a quantity upon which the task of measurement could be focused. In 1907, Benini measured the elasticity of demand for coffee in Italy allowing also for the effects of the prices of tea and of sugar. In England in 1914, Lefheldt estimated the elasticity of demand for wheat. This work makes little use of the theory over and above taking it as a prior basis for selecting which variables to include in the equation, and this *ad hoc* approach was to continue right up to the Second World War. Nevertheless, in the intervening years, considerable progress was made on a number of other issues. For example, the problem of disentangling demand from supply reactions was faced for the first time by Lenoir (1913) and Moore (1929) and work was done on the relationship between the statistical techniques of correlation and models of demand, especially when time series data were to be used, see for example, Yule (1926), Working (1927), Schultz (1928) and Ezekiel (1930).

Mention must however be made of two important exceptions. The first is Pigou's 1910 'indirect' method for estimating elasticities of demand. This is an elegant and sophisticated attempt to use the theory of demand to predict the relative price elasticities of two broadly defined categories of consumption from budget data, and is still one of the best examples of indirect measurement by use of theory to be found outside of the physical and biological sciences. Nevertheless, perhaps because Pigou's argument was misunderstood, or because his assumptions of additivity and constant marginal utility of money were found unacceptable, his method attracted no imitators. A later, and somewhat similar, attempt was made by Frisch in his book *New Methods of Measuring Marginal Utility*, published in 1932. Here, too, independent wants are assumed, and on this basis Frisch derives observable expressions for the income elasticity (or more properly, since a price is the dependent variable, the flexibility) of the marginal utility of money. This comes very close to Jevons' aim of measuring feelings by their effects in the price lists of the market. And yet once again, though the book attracted more attention than Pigou's article, the method had no lasting influence. This may have been due to the narrow basis of many of Frisch's observations which led him to some rather implausible estimates. Alternatively, it may have been that many economists of the period found the concept of income flexibility unnecessarily obscure, though, paradoxically enough, it has come to play an important part in modern empirical analysis. But it seems to me that the fundamental reason for the limited appeal of this type of analysis lies in its basic methodology. The use of observed data to infer propositions about human welfare and motivation is less interesting and fruitful than its converse, the use of utility analysis to help measure and observe actual behaviour. We must turn Jevons' ideas on their heads and use utility analysis not as the basis for a *laissez faire* social policy, but as a vehicle for the measurement of consumers' reactions. I shall return to these issues at greater length in the second section of this chapter.

To return to developments in the subject during the 1930's, we may see in retrospect that, by the end of that decade, independent progress on both statistical and theoretical fronts had prepared the way for first attempts at a synthesis. On the one hand, the positive predictions of the theory had been published accessibly and, on the other, the statistical estimation of demand equations by multiple regression analysis was a reasonably well understood activity. There are three important works which fulfil this role and, not only do they provide a restatement and systematisation of the subject as a whole as it then stood, but they also lay the foundation for much of what was to follow. These books are first, Henry Schultz's *Theory and Measurement of Demand* published in 1938, and then, after the hiatus of the period of the Second World War, Hermann Wold's *Demand Analysis*, and Richard Stone's *The Measurement of Consumers' Expenditure and Behaviour in the United Kingdom, 1920–1938, Volume 1*, published in 1953 and 1954 respectively. These books are of great importance because, for the first time, they firmly juxtaposed the theory and measurement of demand and between them put the combination before a wide readership of economists. Schultz's book, as one might expect from its date of publication, is the most retrospective of the three. He discussed at length the various techniques of measurement which had been suggested up to that time, yet there is room for empirical work and, in common with the other two authors and in spite of the early date of his studies, Schultz makes some attempt to test explicitly the empirical validity of the theory. At the other extreme, Stone's treatise looks boldly into the future. Many of the econometric techniques which are today commonplace are discussed for the first time and the book achieves the first full statement in modern terms of the basic results of econometric theory. It is here too that we find the original use of the matrix notation of econometrics which has done so much to make the subject accessible and which has contributed greatly to its rapid expansion and development in recent years. As has so often been the case, the exercise of synthesis and consolidation had led to the creation of very much more.

This then is the foundation for much of the fruitful interchange between theoretical and applied analysis which has taken place in the subject since the war. Perhaps the first step in this direction came from the discovery of the model which is the main subject of this book, the *linear expenditure system*. This model was not only consistent with demand theory but was computable even by the modest standards of twenty years ago and could thus be applied to actual data. The first statement of the system appears in a paper by

Klein and Rubin in 1948 and elaborations of its properties were discussed in contributions by Samuelson (1947–8) and by Geary (1950–1). In 1954, the model was restated by Stone who demonstrated a simple estimation technique and applied the model to inter-war British data. Here then, was a model which bridged the century-old gap between the theory and practice of modelling consumer behaviour. From an empirical viewpoint, it is a model which could not have existed without knowledge of the properties of the theory, something which, with the exceptions of the contributions by Pigou and by Frisch, cannot be said of the previous, more pragmatic, models. From a theoretical point of view, it is an opportunity to observe how well a theoretically-based model can conform to the actual data.

In this context, the historical primacy of the linear expenditure system could perhaps be challenged by Leser's (1942) invention of what was to become the indirect addilog system. However, Leser's contribution is more in the tradition of Pigou and Frisch in attempting to measure price elasticities from budget data by extending the theoretical restrictions so as to generate sufficient prior information. The completion of the model, in the sense of the confirmation that the additional restrictions are consistent with the theory and the derivation of the utility function itself, had to await the model's rediscovery by Houthakker, (1960a) and (1960b), nearly twenty years later. Incidentally, the story is further complicated by Houthakker's (1960a) attribution of the model to Konüs as Konüs (1939), and this attribution has been accepted by others, for example, Katzner (1970). However, the model developed by Konüs, though apparently similar, is quite different from the Leser–Houthakker model.

In the period since the mid-1950's, much progress has been made in the empirical analysis of theoretically plausible models. The linear expenditure system itself has had an enormous progeny of variants and generalisations and there now exists a number of other models which can be compared and evaluated alongside it. Other developments include attempts to formulate satisfactory dynamic models and a great deal of energy has gone into the construction and use of 'general' models which can be used to test formally the validity of the theory. There is not space here to discuss the results of these enquiries in detail nor is a knowledge of the majority of them necessary for what follows. In the meantime, we must consider the implications and justification of this new methodology.

2.2 The methodology of demand analysis

It is best to begin by making clear exactly what are the refutable propositions of utility theory. The proofs of these results are easily available elsewhere; for example the recent text by Malinvaud (1972) contains an excellent discussion, and I shall confine myself here to their statement, commenting only where necessary. The first point to emphasize is that the theory is a theory of the single consumer acting without error; he may be thought of as the representative or average of a cohort of consumers identical in all economically relevant respects. If his preference structure is sufficiently well behaved, and if he is capable of infinitely fine adjustment of a budget spent on a large number of homogeneous goods, then four propositions about his behaviour may be deduced. These are as follows:

(1) *Aggregation*: the sum of his individual expenditures is equal to total expenditure. This is a matter of assumption rather than deduction; the data used in most studies will satisfy the proposition by construction and thus cannot be used to test it. Note that total expenditure is *not* identified with income; an income constraint would not be binding in the single period and even over longer time spans would rarely be entirely inflexible. The force of the total expenditure constraint is twofold. In the first place, it ensures that the form of the demand functions is such that the sum of each expenditure comes to the predetermined total under all circumstances. In the second place, it defines the problem so that the allocation of the budget is included while the consumption function itself is not. Such a procedure can be justified on plausible behavioural assumptions (for example temporal additivity of preferences) but is perhaps best defended on the practical principle of attempting, as far as is possible, to study things one at a time.

(2) *Homogeneity*: the demand functions are homogeneous of degree zero in income and prices: a proportional change in income and all of the prices has no effect on the quantities purchased or, *a fortiori*, on the budget allocation. This proposition is often referred to as 'absence of money illusion'. It is clearly refutable by observation and indeed is so for each commodity separately, so that it can be tested or applied in a piecemeal fashion without the necessity of working with a complete system of equations. In consequence it is often used as a basis for writing demand functions in terms of *real*

income and *relative* prices and attempts have been made to test its validity at least since Schultz (1938).

(3) *Symmetry*: the matrix of compensated price derivatives, or substitution matrix, must be symmetric. These derivatives are calculated after the individual has been compensated for changes in real income brought about by the price change being considered. For example, the compensated cross price derivative between eggs and butter is measured as the number of extra eggs bought per unit increase in the price per pound of butter given that the consumer is simultaneously provided with enough extra cash to buy the original quantities at the new prices. The proposition then states that this number of eggs is equal to the number of extra pounds of butter that would have been bought had there instead been a similar compensated increase in the price of eggs. As in the case of homogeneity, and provided there are more than two goods in the budget, this proposition is refutable against the data. But in this case its intuitive basis is perhaps harder to explain. If it does not hold, the consumer can easily be cheated; for it is possible to lead him through a series of stages, each preferred to the next, which take him to a final point where he consumes less of everything. The symmetry condition can thus be regarded as a guarantee of *consistency of choice*. For a further illuminating discussion the reader is referred to Samuelson (1950).

(4) *Negativity*: relates also to the substitution matrix and states that the elements should be such that the matrix as a whole should be negative semi-definite. Among other things, this means that compensated price increases lead to lower demands for the goods involved, and more generally, that the same must be true for any constant-weighted bundle or index of goods. This condition derives from the assumption of maximization of utility; if, for example, aggregation, homogeneity, and symmetry all hold but the substitution matrix is *positive* semi-definite, the consumer would be minimizing rather than maximizing utility.

The validity of these four propositions, deduced from the theory, also guarantees, at least locally, the validity of the theory itself. By this it is meant that, at a particular budget allocation with a particular configuration of income and prices, if the consumer behaves according to propositions (1) to (4), he may be thought of as obeying the theory; indeed, utility surfaces can be drawn for him which would lead to the exact replication of his actual behaviour.

On the other hand, these propositions do not exhaust the predictive power of the theory. For utility analysis provides a possible tool for the organisation of prior knowledge about how commodities interact in consumption. It may be possible to separate the utility function into branches, each associated with particular groups of commodities or activities in consumption, and this separation leads, via the theory, to further restrictions on behaviour. As with the case of the propositions already discussed these can be held up against the data either to be refuted or else to help in the estimation of parameters.

Note, however, that so far all of this is of very limited use. For we are still in the world of the individual consumer and to make use of the model we should need data on individuals and on a highly disaggregated commodity basis. But even given this, it could be argued that the theory is still of no consequence. This has been done on a number of grounds: that preferences change over time, invalidating the propositions: that indivisibilities prevent small equilibriating movements, with similar results: that small finite changes are no substitute for the infinitesimals of the theory: or, finally, that the theory is too restrictive altogether, omitting reference to the really important determinants of consumer behaviour. From a positive empirical point of view it is hard to have much sympathy with these criticisms. They could equally, *pari passu*, be directed at any theory in the natural sciences. The parallel is quite fair since the theory is being used positively to attempt to explain reality, and may be rejected or modified if the attempt fails. If it is necessary to allow for changes in preferences, there is no reason why this cannot be done. The theory is not being used to derive political propositions and so is unaffected by several possibilities which could seriously harm a normative version. For example, the notion of consumer sovereignty is quite irrelevant to the empirical issue; it is a matter of no importance where preferences come from, whether they are truly exogenous or whether they are entirely determined by manipulation or by advertisement.

The more serious difficulties remain: aggregation over commodities and aggregation over consumers. The former is the easier and I shall deal with it first. The problem is essentially one of index number theory; how is it possible to define *composite* commodities and price indices which behave in all respects identically to the individual commodities of the original statement? In earlier studies, up till the late 1950's, this was dealt with by use of the Hicks–Leontief 'composite-commodity' theorem, see Hicks (1936) and Leontief (1936). This allows goods to be combined into composites if their relative prices remain unchanged. The problem is solved essentially by avoiding the weighting problem; if all the prices move in proportion, changes in the weights cannot influence the index. However, this is of limited usefulness since the goods that we wish to group together, indeed which most available data forces us to group together, are very unlikely to satisfy the condition. The more modern approach derives from the work of Strotz (1957), Gorman (1959) and Green (1964) and works, not by restricting the prices, but by restricting the weights. This is done by restricting the utility function in such a way that all expenditures within the grouping remain in fixed proportion as group expenditure changes with prices constant; this requires the use of a utility function which can be weakly separated into homogeneous parts, each part relating to the goods in a single group. Now, while it is unlikely that all prices within a group should happen to move proportionately it is almost equally unlikely that consumers do not change the structure of their purchases within a group in response to changes in total group expenditure. And to block further loopholes, we are assured that, if prices are not to be restricted in any way, this solution is the only one.

Fortunately, however, there exists an approximate solution which has all the appearances of being quite exact enough; this has been provided by Barten and Turnovsky (1966) and Barten (1970). It also relies on the commonsense method of grouping, of putting together those goods which have some inherent relationship in consumption (e.g. tea, sugar, coffee) and keeping apart those that do not (e.g. cigars, underclothes, petrol). It turns out that separating the utility function only weakly with respect to these groups allows the construction of two price indices for each group, one of which is used for analysing income effects of price changes, the other for substitution effects. As one might expect, the indices only coincide exactly in the case of separable homogeneity discussed above. In practice, when relative prices do not diverge very much, the two are almost indistinguishable, and can in practice be replaced by a single series. This method then relies on some of the restrictions from each of the previous two methods; behaviour is weakly restricted in a way which does not contradict casual experience, and while relative prices are required not to diverge greatly there is no insistence that they do not move at all. This is a remarkable result, combining as it does the virtues of the more exact methods without their accompanying vices. So this problem is unlikely to be a serious difficulty except in pathological cases.

Aggregation over consumers is less easily brushed aside. Although the problem is similar in principle and the conditions for an exact solution are equally restrictive, see Gorman (1953) and Green (1964), no acceptable approximate solution has yet been devised. I write 'yet' because it seems likely that such exists given the theoretical similarity of the two problems. In outline the problem is as follows: even if every single consumer in the economy behaves according to the theory, there is no guarantee that their aggregate behaviour will likewise conform. This is partly because changes in aggregate income will in general involve changes in the distribution of income and even when this is not so, differences in utility functions between consumers can cause apparent inconsistencies in aggregate behaviour. Such examples are not at all hard to construct and simple examples have been constructed by a number of writers: see, for example, Hicks (1956). More surprisingly perhaps, the converse proposition also holds and this has been shown in recent papers by Sonnenschein (1972), (1973) and by Debreu (1973). According to this, it is possible to construct individual preferences and a distribution of income so that *any* demand function, however apparently unreasonable, is the sum of individual demand equations, each conforming to the theory. None of this necessarily removes the basis for the use of the theory in aggregate; for it may be that, if changes in the distribution of income are limited in some way, the aggregation goes through. In fairness, the opposite may equally be true.

Pure theory is of little help here. For perfect aggregation over consumers, like perfect aggregation over commodities, requires highly implausible restrictions. In order that all consumers taken together, or alternatively the average consumer, should behave as the single consumer of the theory, it is necessary that all consumers' Engel curves be parallel straight lines. Thus, under all circumstances, increases in income must be spent in fixed proportions on each of the goods and these fixed proportions are not only constant for each individual through time but are also the same for all individuals. A consequence of this is that every consumer buys all of the goods.

At best, this could only hold for broad categories of goods and even so, it requires a quite unreasonable degree of uniformity between individuals. A more practical solution may perhaps be effected through restrictions on the permitted range of income distribution. In the commodity aggregation case, an optimal balance was struck between restrictions on behaviour on the one hand, and restrictions on relative prices on the other. Here, the role of prices is played by the income distribution and, as we have seen, imposing no restrictions on this, leads, as before, to impossibly stringent restrictions on behaviour.

First steps in this direction have been taken by I.F. Pearce in his book *A Contribution to Demand Analysis*. He shows that if the income distribution is held constant, in the sense that changes in income are proportional to the level of income for each individual, more general Engel curves can be allowed. In particular they need no longer be linear and may have different parameters for different consumers. He also suggests that even when his special Engel curves do not hold, the application of the aggregate theory will lead only to small errors. Note however that the income distribution is held constant and once again the result only applies to broad groupings of commodities, though this latter may not be a problem in itself since these groupings can be constructed for each of the individuals. However, more recently, Muellbauer (1974b) has shown that even in the most favourable case when all preferences are identical and only proportional changes in the distribution of income are allowed, aggregate demand functions will only mirror individual demand functions if the Engel curves exhibit what he calls 'generalised' linearity. For this to hold, all budget shares must be linear functions of one another, and this is not greatly more likely than strict linearity. All these results agree in that the use of aggregate demand functions derived directly from a utility function is wrong; what they do not tell us is how large the errors of misspecification are likely to be. If we had a reasonably credible model of income distribution, it would be possible to integrate explicitly over consumers allowing for covariances between income and tastes and this must surely be the most satisfactory approach. Although it has been applied in production theory, see Houthakker (1955–6) and Johansen (1972), I know of no similar application to the analysis of demand.

Pending the results of such an enquiry, we should for the present adopt an agnostic position on these issues. Nevertheless it is not impossible, and it may not even be unlikely, that changes in the income distribution since the war have been modest enough to allow the approximate aggregation, for empirical purposes, of preference relations defined over categories broad enough to enter the budget of each income group. By aggregation of preference relations, I refer, of course, not to the construction of a social welfare function, but to the aggregation of demand functions in such a way that the aggregate equation is itself derivable from some preference ordering over the commodity space. This latter has no welfare connotations whatsoever. There is a certain amount of empirical evidence to support this proposition; I have shown elsewhere, Deaton (1974b), that the aggregate historical experience for the United Kingdom tends to conform to the propositions of the theory, and other studies have shown similar tendencies in other countries. This evidence is of course indirect, and is a poor substitute for an explicit solution of the aggregation problem based on direct knowledge of the distributional structure.

Most empirical analysis based on the theory of demand has simply ignored this problem. Fundamentally, such a procedure may or may not be useful quite independently of the validity of its assumptions, but there is certainly no justification for the often repeated contention that such models are 'theoretically' superior to alternative demand equations derived on a more casual basis. Indeed such claims often seem to be used to bolster poor empirical results presumably in the nonsensical belief that there exists some objective standard of theoretical perfection, whatever the evidence might say to the contrary. The important problem is whether aggregate models derived directly from utility functions do or do not provide a viable empirical methodology and whether such a methodology is in some respects preferable to more traditional single equation methods. The examination of this question will occupy much of this book. In accordance with these terms of reference, whenever models are described as being derived from theory or as utility-based, this should be taken to imply that the derivation is done in aggregate *ab initio* and that no allowance is made for aggregation errors. Clearly any criticisms which are levelled at such an approach do not necessarily imply criticisms of the theory at the micro-economic level, nor do results which support it imply anything about the behaviour of individual consumers. Both the question of the validity of utility theory at the micro-level and the question of what aggregate demand functions should look like if it were valid, are clearly important: but they are not the subject matter of this book.

Alternative approaches, which explicitly repudiate the theory, have usually little constructive to offer. In consequence, investigators who do not make use of the theory can face considerable difficulties of model formulation and selection. It is easy enough to select models which appear quite plausible on the surface but which, on closer inspection, turn out to have quite unexpected and undesirable consequences. There is the well-known example of the double-logarithmic demand function which yields direct estimates of elasticities and which can fit quite well; yet such demand equations lead inevitably to a violation of the budget constraint. And though this can be allowed for in practice, confidence in such a model is naturally diminished. There is another quite different problem associated with such methods. In nearly all applications of demand analysis, and especially when time series are used, there is only a limited amount of independent variation in the observations on purchases, prices, and incomes. In consequence, only a limited number of responses can be measured and it is necessary either to define many responses to be zero or to use a sufficient number of restrictions to make up for the limited number of degrees of freedom. Either one of these courses of action is open to criticism unless explicit reference is made to a theoretical model; indeed, without such reference, it is difficult even to think of appropriate restrictions. The usual recourse is to specify many cross-price responses to be zero *a priori*, not because it is believed that they really are zero but because it is clear that without the assumption it will be impossible to measure the effects which are of the first order of importance. Use of theory in this context is surely more satisfactory; the second-order effects are not assigned arbitrarily or ignored, but are derived by plausible connection with the first order measurable effects.

If it is only the smaller responses which are affected by the choice of methodology, the position can perhaps be regarded with equanimity. It would be comforting to know that the differences between two sets of coefficients, one derived from the estimation of a theoretical model and one from more *ad hoc* considerations, were confined to the measurement of second-order effects, typically cross-price responses. It would only be with respect to these that assumption and model selection would predominate over exogenous information in the final determination of the estimates. Otherwise, the model would only act as a vehicle for the transmission of undistorted messages from the data.

In later chapters we shall see that reality is not quite so co-operative. The choice of alternative models leads to major differences in the interpretation of the evidence, even in cases where the models differ little in principle. We shall attempt to quantify the extent of these differences in a practical context and to contribute towards a critical assessment of the application of alternative models and alternative methodologies.

Chapter 3

THE LINEAR EXPENDITURE SYSTEM

3.1 The derivation of the model

In this chapter I shall discuss the theoretical basis of the linear expenditure system. Before going on to empirical analysis it is convenient to gather together here the general properties of the model, that is those which do not depend upon the data. It is important to make the basic structure clear at this early stage for only thus can a clear distinction be made between those aspects of behaviour which are measured by the estimation of the model and those which are preordained by the assumptions of its construction.

I shall proceed in three stages. In this section we consider the mathematical derivation of the model. First, it is derived by imposing the constraints of consumer theory on a general linear model and, second, the resulting demand equations are integrated to give the underlying preference function from which the model can be deduced. In the second section, 3.2, the mathematical formality is relaxed and the properties and interpretation of the model are discussed. In particular I shall discuss the derivation of the elasticities and the relationships between them; these relationships are important for the interpretation of the empirical results for it is through these that the structure of the model makes its presence felt. Finally, in section 3.3, I shall present some variants of the basic model; these allow some relaxation of the very stringent requirements of the unmodified equations.

I shall follow here the derivation of the model given by Stone (1954); some minor notational changes have been made and there is an attempt further to elucidate one or two points in the argument.

The starting point is a general linear formulation; the expenditure on each good is a linear function of income and of each of the prices.

Thus, if we denote the vector of prices by p, the vectors of quantities bought by q, and income, or total expenditure by the scalar μ, we may write

$$\hat{p}q = b\mu + Bp, \tag{3.1}$$

where b is a vector and B is a matrix, each of constant parameters. A superimposed circumflex denotes a vector diagonalized into a matrix whose off-diagonal terms are zero. Referring back to Chapter II, we have four constraints which must be satisfied by the equations (3.1), aggregation, homogeneity, symmetry, and negativity.

The first two of these pose little difficulty. We may add up the equations by pre-multiplying by the transpose of the unit vector ι; thus, if expenditures sum to μ,

$$\iota'\hat{p}q = p'q = \iota'b\mu + \iota'Bp = \mu. \tag{3.2}$$

If (3.2) is to hold for any value of the price vector p, we must have

$$\iota'b = 1 \tag{3.3}$$

and

$$\iota'B = 0'. \tag{3.4}$$

Homogeneity requires no further restriction since the equations (3.1) are already linear homogeneous; proportional changes in p and μ clearly involve no change in q. To derive the restrictions imposed by symmetry we differentiate the model (3.1) with respect to p to give

$$\hat{p}\frac{\partial q}{\partial p} + \hat{q} = B, \tag{3.5}$$

giving,

$$\frac{\partial q}{\partial p} = \hat{p}^{-1}B - \hat{p}^{-1}\hat{q}. \tag{3.6}$$

The substitution matrix S is defined by the Slutsky identity

$$S = \frac{\partial q}{\partial p} + \frac{\partial q}{\partial \mu}q' \tag{3.7}$$

and so, for the linear model,

$$S = \hat{p}^{-1}B - \hat{p}^{-1}\hat{q} + \hat{p}^{-1}bq' \tag{3.8}$$

and it is this expression which must be symmetric and negative semi-definite.

Since the second term on the right-hand side of equation (3.8) is a diagonal vector, and is thus symmetric, the symmetry condition may be stated,

$$\hat{p}^{-1}B + \hat{p}^{-1}bq' = B'\hat{p}^{-1} + qb'\hat{p}^{-1}, \tag{3.9}$$

or, more simply, pre- and post-multiplying by $\hat{p}$,

$$B\hat{p} + bq'\hat{p} = \hat{p}B' + \hat{p}qb'. \tag{3.10}$$

If we substitute for q in (3.10) and delete the symmetric terms, the symmetry condition becomes

$$B\hat{p} + bp'B' = \hat{p}B' + Bpb'. \tag{3.11}$$

It is not immediately obvious what equation (3.11) implies in terms of restrictions on B and b. However, realising that, once again, the equations must hold for all values of p, we may set the vector p to be any value we choose. First we rewrite (3.11) in the form, for all i, j

$$b_{ij}p_j + b_i \sum_k b_{jk}p_k = p_i b_{ji} + b_j \sum_k b_{ik}p_k. \tag{3.12}$$

If we take a particular case where $i \neq j$ and we select p such that p_j is unity and otherwise p_k is zero, then (3.12), becomes

$$\frac{b_{jj}}{1-b_j} = -\frac{b_{ij}}{b_i}, \quad \text{all } i \neq j, \tag{3.13}$$

and we denote this ratio, which is clearly independent of the index i, as c_j. It follows immediately from (3.13) that

$$B = \hat{c} - bc'. \tag{3.14}$$

Note that B as given by (3.14) satisfies the restriction (3.4) if (3.3) holds. This happens because the constraints of aggregation, homogeneity and symmetry are not independent.

Using (3.14), the original model may be rewritten

$$\hat{p}q = \hat{c}p + b(\mu - c'p), \tag{3.15}$$

and this is the usual way of writing the linear expenditure system. It only remains now to show what restrictions are necessary for the substitution matrix to be negative semi-definite. From (3.7) some manipulation gives

$$S = -(\mu - p'c)\hat{p}^{-1}(\hat{b} - bb')\hat{p}^{-1}. \tag{3.16}$$

We see immediately that the rank of S is, in general, less than the number of commodities, since

$$p'S = Sp = 0. \tag{3.17}$$

For negativity, the condition

$$\mu - p'c > 0, \quad b > 0 \tag{3.18}$$

must hold, since the alternative possibility with $b < 0$ is ruled out by the aggregation restriction (3.3). Note also that (3.18) when substituted in (3.15) implies that $q > c$.

This completes the derivation of the model; equations (3.15) with the restrictions (3.3) and (3.18) define the system and we are guaranteed by construction that this is the *only* set of *linear* demand equations consistent with the theory. Note the considerable force of the linearity assumption: this may be assessed by computing the number of restrictions implied by each of the other assumptions. If the number of commodities is denoted by n, there are $n + n^2$ degrees of freedom in the original unrestricted model (3.1). Aggregation imposes $n + 1$ constraints; homogeneity imposes none; symmetry involves $\frac{1}{2}n(n + 1)$ constraints in principle but this must be reduced to $\frac{1}{2}n(n - 1)$ since n of these are already accounted for by the combination of aggregation and homogeneity. This would leave $(n - 1)(\frac{1}{2}n + 1)$ free parameters as compared with $(2n - 1)$ in the final model (3.15); if $n = 40$, this is the difference between 819 and 79 degrees of freedom. This difference is entirely due to linearity and gives some idea of how specialized the system is. Indeed, in the next section we shall see that the system imposes many more constraints on behaviour than does the theory in general.

The utility function underlying the linear expenditure system was first described by Samuelson (1947–8). The integration process proceeds by first deriving the cost function or constant utility price index. This can be regarded as giving that level of income which, given the prices as arguments, keeps utility at a given constant level; this function defines the utility surfaces in the dual price–income space and these can then be converted via the demand functions to give utility as a function of quantities consumed. Writing the cost-of-living function as $\mu(p)$, the equation to be integrated is, from (3.15)

$$\frac{\partial \mu}{\partial p} = c + \hat{p}^{-1} b(\mu - p'c) \tag{3.19}$$

Writing $x = \mu - p'c$, gives the simplification,

$$\frac{\partial \log x}{\partial \log p} = b, \tag{3.20}$$

which has the solution, after substitution

$$\log(\mu - p'c) = \alpha + b' \log p, \tag{3.21}$$

where α is a constant of integration. This gives μ as a function of p and the parameters c and b and defines the constant-utility price-index for the linear expenditure system. From this we can thus write the *indirect* utility function as

$$\psi = \psi\{\log(\mu - p'c) - b' \log p\}, \tag{3.22}$$

for an arbitrary function ψ. But from the demand functions (3.15),

$$\log p = \log b + \log(\mu - p'c) - \log(q - c), \tag{3.23}$$

so that, after substitution, we may write the *direct* utility function v as

$$v(q) = f\{b' \log(q - c)\}, \tag{3.24}$$

for an arbitrary function f. The function is often given the exponential form and the utility function written

$$v(q) = \prod_k (q_k - c_k)^{b_k}. \tag{3.25}$$

Once again we have reached the standard result and indeed it would have been equally acceptable to have proceeded in reverse order, using the utility functions above to derive the system by constrained maximization. Or less conventionally perhaps, we could have used the indirect function (3.22) and Roy's identity, Roy (1942),

$$q = -\frac{\partial\psi}{\partial p} \Big/ \frac{\partial\psi}{\partial\mu},$$

to go directly to the demand equations. The interested reader can check that all these alternatives lead to the same set of demand functions, those given by equations (3.15).

It is of some interest to look at these utility functions in the light of the convexity restrictions (3.18) derived above to see exactly what is implied by their violation, for example, by the presence of negative b's. If the b-vector is negative, the indifference curves corresponding to (3.24) will be *concave* to the origin. This is not necessarily impossible and a consumer possessed of such preferences will still have negative substitution responses and a cost function concave in the prices even though his demand functions will be discontinuous. Even so, these demand functions would not be those of the linear expenditure system, nor would the cost function and indirect utility functions be (3.21) and (3.22). Conversely, if the b's are negative, the cost function implied by (3.21) will not be concave in the prices rendering it completely invalid. Consequently, violations of convexity through negative b's, do not mean that the direct utility function is necessarily wrong, but that the demand equations derived by solving first-order conditions can no longer be regarded as consistent with it.

3.2 The interpretation of the model

The linear expenditure system is an extremely simple and elegant formulation of demand behaviour. The basic equations (3.15) can be described in a number of ways; the most obvious of these is the division of expenditure into 'committed' and 'supernumerary' categories. The constant c's have the dimension of quantities and it is thus perhaps natural to regard these as committed or necessary purchases. The expenditure $\mu - p'c$, is thus the residual once these quantities have been purchased, and this total, or 'supernumerary expenditure' is allocated according to fixed proportions b. The interpretation derives some extra force from the fact that, if $\mu - p'c$ is close to zero, i.e. if purchases of each good are close to the committed levels c, utility, as defined by (3.24), becomes large and negative, approaching minus infinity as supernumerary expenditure approaches zero. This facet of the model is clearly consistent with an interpretation of the c's as necessary or subsistence quantities. The difficulty with this is that the model does not require that the vector c be positive, indeed, as we shall see below, all price elastic goods must have negative c's, and the existence of negative subsistence levels rather stretches the interpretation.

Some other general points should be made. Note in particular that quantities are *not* a function of income and of *all* prices as in the general linear model (3.1). Each purchase in the linear expenditure system can be written as a function of three quantities only: the own price of that commodity, total expenditure, and a constant weight index of all other prices. In consequence, cross-price effects between commodities are extremely limited in scope and we shall see below that this restrictiveness of the model extends also to the own-price responses. Note too the extremely simple formulation of reactions to changes in income. An increase in total expenditure is always shared out in fixed proportions between the goods, i.e. there are constant marginal propensities to spend for each good.

The analysis of income responses

Since the b parameters are independent of income all the Engel curves are linear. These curves plot the relationship between quantities purchased and total expenditure with prices taken as fixed. Thus, from equations (3.15), if the prices are absorbed into the constants, we may write

$$q = f + g\mu, \tag{3.26}$$

for some vectors of constants f and g. This is a very convenient form for the relationship in some respects; for example, if the g's are the same for each consumer, this relationship can be aggregated exactly over the population. Nevertheless, there is considerable doubt about the empirical validity of such a simplistic treatment and in section 3.3 below I shall discuss various ways in which it might be modified.

Income elasticities are perhaps more familiar concepts than marginal budget shares and the other aspects of income response in the model may be discussed with reference to them. Differentiating the demand equations with respect to μ gives,

$$e = \hat{q}^{-1}\frac{\partial q}{\partial \mu}\mu = \hat{p}^{-1}\hat{q}^{-1}b\mu, \tag{3.27}$$

where e is the vector of total expenditure elasticities. This may be written more simply by defining w, the vector of budget shares, i.e.

$$w = \hat{p}q\mu^{-1}, \tag{3.28}$$

giving

$$e = \hat{w}^{-1}b. \tag{3.29}$$

Clearly, if the convexity conditions are to be satisfied, each of these income elasticities must be positive. This precludes inferior goods and this prohibition is likely to be serious in dealing with all but the broadest classification of expenditures. This conclusion must, in practice, be treated with some care. For although it is possible to restrict estimates of b to be positive, it is not particularly useful to do so. This is not so much because of the econometric difficulties, but rather because of the consequences elsewhere in the model. The violation of convexity is not important *per se*; difficulties arise only because it causes an abrogation of the sign conditions on the substitution elasticities. In the case of the linear expenditure system an inferior good will have *positive* compensated and uncompensated price elasticities. While this is clearly nonsense, the real practical question is whether a nonsensical income response is better or worse than a nonsensical price response. In a world where income information is dominant and price information often barely exists it is clear that to allow inferiority is of greater importance than to prohibit non-convexity. It could of course be argued that it is better to abandon the model altogether than to be faced with such a choice. I shall reserve judgement on this wider issue until a broader selection of the evidence has been presented. For the time being, the difficulty is noted but in the empirical work I shall make no attempt to restrict the elements of b to be positive.

The general behaviour of the income elasticities is not immediately obvious from the expression (3.29) since the budget shares w themselves depend on the parameters as well as on income and the prices. However, since the value share of a good increases if the income elasticity of that good is greater than unity, we can see that w_i will be increasing with income if w_i is less than b_i and *vice versa*; thus as income increases all income elasticities tend to unity. This can be seen more formally by deriving an alternative formula for the elasticities. From (3.15) the value shares w_i may be written

$$w_i = \frac{p_i c_i}{\mu} + b_i \frac{(\mu - p'c)}{\mu}, \qquad (3.30)$$

so that from

$$e_i = b_i w_i \qquad (3.31)$$

we may deduce

$$e_i = \mu/(\mu + a_i), \qquad (3.32)$$

where a_i is a quantity dependent on prices but not in income, i.e.

$$a_i = \frac{p_i c_i}{b_i} - \sum_k p_k c_k . \qquad (3.33)$$

Thus if prices are constant, as income increases each of the income elasticities tends to unity and the budget shares w tend to the marginal budget shares b. Once again these properties tell us something about the type of expenditure which the system can hope to analyse successfully. Here too there are difficulties for detailed disaggregation since it has often been noted in the analysis of specific commodities that the income elasticity tends to follow a general pattern which would preclude the relationship (3.32). Goods start their lives as highly income elastic, they become less so as they become more commonplace, and eventually their consumption approaches saturation or even falls off, giving zero or negative elasticities. Thus it is only for broader categories of wants that we should expect demand to be so little subject to changes in fashion and the technology of consumption that a tendency of unitary elasticity could be the rule rather than the exception.

The analysis of price effects

It is clear from what has already been said that there is little scope for a wide range of price responses in this model. This is not necessarily a negative attribute of the system since restrictiveness is always necessary to compensate for a lack of complete information. Whether restrictions are helpful or repressive depends very much on one's point of view. Most of the constraints discussed in this section stem from the fact that the utility function underlying the system is *additive*; in other words, it may be written as the sum of n functions, one relating to each good. Clearly the utility function (3.24) is of this form. It has been shown by Houthakker (1960b) that the use of a functional form of this type implies generally that the off-diagonal terms in the substitution matrix are proportional to the product of the corresponding income derivatives. Formally, for $i \neq j$,

$$v = f\{\Sigma g_k(q_k)\} \Leftrightarrow S_{ij} \propto \frac{\partial q_i}{\partial \mu} \cdot \frac{\partial q_j}{\partial \mu}. \tag{3.34}$$

It is a simple matter to check that the matrix S given by (3.16) is of this form. Now, since the uncompensated price responses can be derived via the Slutsky equation (3.7) from the substitution and income derivatives, equation (3.34) plus the homogeneity restrictions on S, (3.17), determines, but for a multiplicative constant, all price responses in terms of income responses. We shall see below how this works out in detail for the linear expenditure system.

The matrix of uncompensated price elasticities, E, can be derived directly from the demand equations (3.15),

$$E = -I + \hat{q}^{-1}\hat{c} - \hat{p}^{-1}\hat{q}^{-1}b\hat{c}p'. \tag{3.35}$$

Pre-multiplying (3.15) by $\hat{q}^{-1}$ gives

$$\hat{q}^{-1}\hat{c} = I - \hat{q}^{-1}\hat{p}^{-1}\hat{b}(\mu - p'c). \tag{3.36}$$

For notational ease, we define the negative of the 'supernumerary ratio', by

$$\phi = -\mu^{-1}(\mu - p'c), \tag{3.37}$$

and (3.36) becomes

$$\hat{q}^{-1}\hat{c} = I + \phi e. \tag{3.38}$$

Substituting in (3.35) gives finally

$$E = \phi\hat{e} - ew' - \phi eb', \tag{3.39}$$

and from the Slutsky identity, the compensated elasticities E^* are given by

$$E^* = \phi(\hat{e} - eb'). \tag{3.40}$$

The quantity ϕ has an important rôle in the analysis of preference independence and is the inverse of Frisch's income flexibility of money as discussed in Chapter II. The reciprocal of ϕ may be interpreted as the income elasticity of the marginal utility of money if utility is expressed by (3.24) with the function f taken to be unity. Though this interpretation is superficially cardinal, the relationships involving it are not and in no way depend upon the choice of f.

Looking first at the own-price elasticities which might be expected to be quantitatively the most important, we may write

$$e_{ii} = \phi e_i - e_i(w_i + \phi b_i). \tag{3.41}$$

From (3.38) it can be seen that if $c_i < 0$, $e_i\phi < -1$ and substituting this in (3.41) gives $e_{ii} < -1$. Thus, as stated above, goods with negative c's are price elastic. Similarly, if convexity holds, all income elasticities are positive and, since ϕ is negative, all own-price elasticities are negative. The prohibition of inferior goods rules out Giffen goods, *a fortiori*. But it is here that negative b's come home to roost. For all inferior goods, by (3.41), turn out to be Giffen goods; this is because of the perverse sign of the substitution effect which, instead of helping to cancel out the perverse income effect, reinforces it. But although it is unfortunate that the system should force us to choose between treating an inferior good as normal or taking it to be a Giffen good into the bargain, it is still true that by estimating the system simultaneously the *data* are allowed to choose which of the alternatives is closest to reality. And though negative b's are no evidence for the existence of the Giffen paradox, even in this bastard form, neither is it obviously true *a priori* that inferiority will necessarily enforce negative b's in the presence of strongly normal price behaviour.

Equation (3.41) can be used to explore another aspect of the model. For any single commodity, and even for a broad group of commodities, w_i and b_i, being of order n^{-1}, are small compared with e_i which is of order 1. The quantity ϕ tends to be somewhere between $-\frac{1}{4}$ and -1 and so the first term of (3.41) is nearly always dominant over the others. This gives, as an approximation

$$e_{ii} = \phi e_i. \tag{3.42}$$

This relationship I shall refer to throughout the book as *Pigou's Law* since it was first put forward by A.C. Pigou in 1910. I have discussed elsewhere, Deaton (1974a), the theoretical basis of the law. What is important here is that, under only the assumption of additivity, (3.42) is an excellent approximation. And in Chapters V and VI, where empirical results are discussed, we shall see that the existence and relative inflexibility of this relationship limits the model perhaps more than any of the other aspects so far discussed. This is because in general, there is more information in the data relating to own-price responses than can be absorbed within the law.

This is much less true of the cross-price elasticities; the information available is slight and so the restrictions implied by the system become less onerous. Here the restrictions are *expected* to do most of the work and a highly specific model comes very much into its own. In addition, this prevents, what can easily happen in more general models, the existence of a chance correlation giving a large, perhaps dominant, but nonsensical response. By the same token, genuine interrelationships between commodities are also forbidden and this once again is likely to restrict the application of the model to broad groupings of commodities.

From (3.39–3.40) we have for $i \neq j$,

$$e_{ij} = -e_i(w_j + \phi b_j) \tag{3.43}$$

and

$$e_{ij}^* = -\phi e_i b_j = -\frac{\phi b_i b_j}{w_i} \tag{3.44}$$

This second equation means that, if convexity holds, all goods are substitutes, or worse, if a good is inferior, it is a complement to all normal goods and a substitute to other inferior goods. It is clear from this nonsense that we need a much more sophisticated model to deal satisfactorily with such detailed interaçtions. But in my view, these are secondary difficulties. The crucial issue is not one of complementarity or the structure of substitution responses, but rather whether the system can overcome the difficulties over inferiority and the over-rigid relationships between own-price and income elasticities. This is further connected with the question of the degree of disaggregation which can be handled by the system. These issues will be discussed again later when the empirical as well as the theoretical evidence has been presented.

3.3 Variants of the model

Many variants of the model have been suggested in order to try to repair its most obvious deficiencies while retaining some of its original structure and simplicity. These have most often been directed towards allowing greater sophistication in the income response though there have been a number of attempts to allow greater substitution possibilities. This emphasis in favour of the former is natural since most investigators have worked with a relatively small number of commodity groups on data where income responses were much better defined than price responses and where the theoretical deficiencies of the system in dealing with cross-price effects were of little significance. Though in this study the number of commodities with which I shall work extends up to nearly forty, I share this order of priority. The cost of improving the structure of price effects, in terms of both intellectual and computer resources, is very high, and the return relative to that from improving the income responses, very low. This is not to say that the price problem should be neglected. I have reported results elsewhere, Deaton (1974a), (1974b), which indicate otherwise, but I believe that the most important problem should be dealt with first.

The simplest way of modifying the model in this direction, and the one which interferes least with its interpretation, is to allow for steady changes in preferences by introducing time trends in the parameters. This has been suggested on a number of occasions by Stone, e.g. (1965). In this book, I shall work with time trends in the b's only, omitting those in the c's. Of the two sets of parameters, the b's are certainly the most important; as can be seen from 3.2 above, all of the elasticities depend crucially on the b's while the c's appear only incidentally. Undoubtedly it would improve the fit to allow for both but for reasons which will appear subsequently I am very doubtful as to whether this can be done in a satisfactory manner. The basic equation of much of the subsequent work is thus, writing θ for time,

$$\hat{p}q = \hat{p}c + (b^0 + b^1\theta)(\mu - p'c) \tag{3.45}$$

Clearly a much more satisfactory method of modifying the income response is to make the model genuinely dynamic, permitting behaviour to depend on past decisions via stocks of durable goods or via habits formed by past consumption activities. While a number of such models now exist, e.g. Houthakker and Taylor (1970), and there even is a variant of the linear expenditure system of this type proposed by Phlips (1972), for this book such developments must, regretfully, be left aside. We shall see that achieving a full understanding of even the modified static model is, in itself, a considerable task.

Chapter 4

THE ESTIMATION OF THE LINEAR EXPENDITURE SYSTEM

4.1 General considerations

From the point of view of consumer demand theory the *linearity* of the linear expenditure system is one of its most attractive and interesting features. But when estimation problems are discussed, the descriptive adjective is more notable for its irony than its accuracy. Indeed the *non-linearity* of the model in terms of its parameters presents formidable estimation problems especially when a large number of goods is being considered. Although it is true that many econometricians are now prepared to deal with non-linearity as an everyday occurrence, the successful and convincing estimation of large non-linear models is still a comparative rarity. And since the time, now twenty years ago, when Stone (1954) first calculated parameter estimates for the linear expenditure system, a considerable amount of both human and machine intelligence has been devoted to the development and improvement of viable estimation techniques for the model. In this chapter I shall review the techniques which have been suggested for the estimation of the parameters of the linear expenditure system, from Stone's method to the application of modern algorithms of non-linear estimation. I shall also put forward a particular modification to the latter which results in a considerable increase in efficiency when dealing with the linear expenditure system and which thus permits the estimation of much larger systems than has been possible to date. These matters are dealt with in section 4.3. Before this, in section 4.2, the theory behind the estimators is discussed; in particular, various types of maximum likelihood estimation are discussed, as well as that specification which leads to ordinary least squares. First, however, some notation must be introduced.

Referring back to equation (3.45) we introduce a stochastic disturbance term to write the model

$$y_t = \hat{p}_t c + (b^0 + b^1\theta_t)(\mu_t - p_t'c) + e_t \tag{4.1}$$

where y_t is the vector of expenditures on the n goods in year t, p_t is the price vector, μ_t is total expenditure, θ_t is time, e_t is the vector of errors and b^0, b^1 and c are the n-vectors of parameters. We have in addition the two constraints corresponding to (3.3),

$$b^{0\prime}\iota = 1; \qquad b^{1\prime}\iota = 0. \tag{4.2}$$

We also make use of the following notation; for the predicted values of y_t, f_t, i.e.

$$f_t = \hat{p}_t c + (b^0 + b^1\theta_t)(\mu_t - p_t'c), \tag{4.3}$$

and for supernumerary income, ξ_t, i.e.

$$\xi_t = \mu_t - p_t'c. \tag{4.4}$$

We also drop the time suffix t from now on whenever this is unlikely to cause confusion: note that θ_t is the measure of time attached to t and is not necessarily equal to t, e.g. $\theta = 0$ in a base year, say 1963.

Clearly, if n is at all large the estimation problem is of considerable difficulty. Since I wish to be able to handle up to 40 commodities, 120 parameters must be dealt with (or 118 if we take the constraints into account) and if we are to estimate the variance–covariance matrix of the disturbances e_t, we add another 780. In such a situation an efficient computational technique is of paramount importance.

4.2 Derivation of the estimators

The most direct way to proceed is via the formulation of a likelihood function for the model and its stochastic specification. From this, several variants can be deduced. Full information maximum likelihood arises from the maximization of the likelihood function not only with respect to the parameters of the model but also with respect to the elements of the variance–covariance matrix. We shall also require estimators for the case where the structure of this matrix is known while its scale is unknown and these also can be derived from the original likelihood function. Finally, we show under what circumstances the maximum likelihood estimation of the linear expenditure system reduces to an ordinary least squares problem. This leads to the derivation and statement of the set of non-linear first-order conditions (4.35–4.37) below, the solution of which leads to the estimators required.

Much of the original work on maximum likelihood estimation of models of this type was done by Barten (1969), and the unified treatment given here owes much to his presentation. Specifically for the linear expenditure system, and independently of Barten, estimators were formulated by Solari (1971), and by Parks (1971). As far as the full information estimators are concerned, the formulae presented here are identical to theirs. Though the notation f refers to the linear expenditure system (4.3), the treatment is quite general and may be applied to any system of equations.

We write the model in the form

$$y_t = f_t + e_t, \tag{4.5}$$

with the stochastic specifications

$$\mathcal{E}(e_t) = 0, \quad \mathcal{E}(e_t e_t') = \Omega, \quad \text{for all } t. \tag{4.6}$$

Contemporaneous covariances only are recognized, there is no serial correlation either within or across commodities. From the adding-up property, we have

$$\iota' y_t = \mu_t = \iota' f_t, \quad \text{giving} \quad \iota' e_t = 0. \tag{4.7}$$

Thus $$\iota'\Omega = \iota'\mathcal{E}(e_t e_t') = \mathcal{E}(\iota' e_t e_t') = 0. \tag{4.8}$$

In other words the variance–covariance matrix of the residuals is singular, and this causes some problem over the formulation of the likelihood function. This is dealt with in the first instance by deleting an arbitrary element of e_t; without loss of generality we may order the goods so that it is taken as the last or nth element. This truncated vector of residuals is denoted e_n, and the corresponding part of the variance–covariance matrix is denoted Ω_n. The likelihood for a single observation is thus written

$$L = 2\pi^{-\frac{1}{2}(n-1)}(\det \Omega_n)^{-\frac{1}{2}} \exp(-\tfrac{1}{2} e_n' \Omega_n^{-1} e_n). \tag{4.9}$$

We now define the matrix V,

$$V = (\Omega + \kappa i i'), \tag{4.10}$$

for some positive constant κ, where i is the normalized vector of units, i.e. $i = \iota/\sqrt{n}$, and we proceed to show that the likelihood may be written entirely in terms of V. Clearly, $V^{-1} - \kappa^{-1}ii'$ is the Moore–Penrose generalized inverse of Ω, e.g. Theil (1971a), and it is the properties associated with this that allow us to use V to replace Ω. This substitution will give a value of the likelihood independent of which element is deleted and thus yields an analytical and computational method which preserves the symmetry of the original problem.

Define E_n to be the $n \times n$ identity matrix with the last row and column replaced by minus ones. Then we have immediately

$$E_n \begin{pmatrix} \Omega_n & 0 \\ 0' & \kappa/n \end{pmatrix} E_n = V. \tag{4.11}$$

Thus, taking determinants

$$|E_n^2| \cdot |\Omega_n| \cdot \kappa/n = |V|. \tag{4.12}$$

To find the determinant of E_n, we may expand by the first row

$$|E_n| = |E_{n-1}| - (-1)^{n+1} \begin{vmatrix} 0 & I_{n-2} \\ -1 & -\iota' \end{vmatrix} = |E_{n-1}| + (-1)^{n-1}(-1)^n |I_{n-2}|. \tag{4.13}$$

Thus
$$|E_n| = |E_{n-1}| - 1, \tag{4.14}$$

and since $|E_2| = -2$, we have $|E_n| = -n$, and from (4.12)

$$|\Omega_n| = (\kappa n)^{-1} |V|. \tag{4.15}$$

Clearly (4.15) also implies that V is non-singular. We may thus also write

$$e_n' \Omega_n^{-1} e_n = (e_n' \; 0) \begin{pmatrix} \Omega_n & 0 \\ 0 & \kappa/n \end{pmatrix}^{-1} \begin{pmatrix} e_n \\ 0 \end{pmatrix}$$

$$= (e_n' \; 0) E_n V^{-1} E_n \begin{pmatrix} e_n \\ 0 \end{pmatrix} = e' V^{-1} e, \tag{4.16}$$

which can be substituted in equation (4.19). Multiplying up, for a sample of T observations and taking logarithms,

$$\log L = \tfrac{1}{2} T \{ \log \kappa + \log n - (n-1) \log 2\pi - \log \det V \} - \tfrac{1}{2} \sum_{t=1}^{T} e_t' V^{-1} e_t \tag{4.17}$$

Equation (4.17) gives a formula for the logarithm of the likelihood of a sample with the residuals e_t. The estimation problem thus reduces to seeking values of the parameters, in this case, b^0, b^1 and c, which will maximize the value of this expression. In general, however, precise values for Ω, and thus for V, are not known. In practice, the situation will vary from the case where nothing is known to the case where the structure of the matrix can be deduced from theoretical considerations.

Taking the second case first, let us assume that, according to our theory, the matrix Ω is known except for a scale factor σ^2. Thus we may write

$$\Omega = \sigma^2\Omega_0, \tag{4.18}$$

where Ω_0 is a known, singular matrix, the null space of which is spanned by the unit vector. Since κ is an arbitrary positive quantity, we may set it equal to σ^2 and define

$$V = \sigma^2\Omega_0 + \sigma^2 ii' = \sigma^2(\Omega_0 + ii') = \sigma^2 V_0, \text{ say,} \tag{4.19}$$

where

$$V_0 = \Omega_0 + ii'. \tag{4.20}$$

These expressions may be substituted in the likelihood function (4.17) to give

$$2 \log L = T\{\log n - (n-1) \log 2\pi - (n-1) \log \sigma^2 - \log \det V_0\} - \frac{1}{2\sigma^2} \sum_{t=1}^{T} e_t' V_0^{-1} e_t. \tag{4.21}$$

A conditional maximum of (4.21) can be derived with respect to σ^2; the resulting value of σ^2 can then be substituted back and a *maximum maximorum* reached with respect to the parameters. From (4.21)

$$\frac{\partial(2 \log L)}{\partial\sigma^2} = -\frac{T(n-1)}{\sigma^2} + \frac{1}{\sigma} \sum_{t=1}^{T} e_t' V_0^{-1} e_t, \tag{4.22}$$

So that a maximum-likelihood estimate of σ^2, $\tilde{\sigma}^2$, is given by

$$\tilde{\sigma}^2 = \frac{1}{T(n-1)} \sum_{t=1}^{T} e_t' V_0^{-1} e_t. \tag{4.23}$$

Given this, the likelihood function concentrates to

$$2 \log L^* = T\{\log n - (n-1)(\log 2\pi + 1) - (n-1) \log \tilde{\sigma}^2 - \log \det V_0\}. \tag{4.24}$$

Thus, under conditions where the structure of the variance–covariance matrix is known, maximization of the likelihood function reduces to minimization of the expression (4.23). This, in turn, may be interpreted as the minimization of a weighted sum of squares, the weights being given, *a priori*, from the theoretically specified variance–covariance matrix Ω. Note that the maximum-likelihood procedure reduces to ordinary least squares if the matrix V_0 is the identity matrix. Looking back at (4.20) and (4.18), this will occur if, and only if,

$$\Omega = \sigma^2(I - ii'). \tag{4.25}$$

This is the sort of result that might be expected. Usually, with a non-singular variance–covariance matrix, maximum-likelihood reduces to ordinary least squares estimation if and only if the variance–covariance matrix is a multiple of the unit matrix. This is a similar result taking into account the adding-up condition which must hold for Ω. The plausibility of (4.25) in economic terms is quite another matter. In general it would not be expected to be a sensible specification in view of its requirement that errors be homoscedastic across commodities; this is most unlikely to hold in the absence of some scaling device. We shall return to this problem in Chapter V, section 2, below.

First-order conditions for the minimum of (4.23) are easily derived. If we let β denote a representative parameter, differentiating (4.23) after substitution from (4.5) and setting to zero, gives

$$\sum_t \frac{\partial f_t'}{\partial \beta} V_0^{-1}(y_t - f_t) = 0. \tag{4.26}$$

These equations, normally non-linear in β, define the maximum-likelihood estimates of the parameters. Methods of solving them are discussed in the next section.

In some cases this procedure will not be suitable, either because there is no theoretical basis for supposing a fixed structure for Ω or, if there is, because it is not sufficiently convincing to be used as the sole basis for estimation. In these circumstances, full-information maximum-likelihood estimation can yield an estimate of Ω provided there are sufficient observations. Again the starting point is equation (4.17); this time conditional maximization is carried out with respect to all the elements of Ω. This must be done subject to the singularity constraint $\Omega\iota = 0$; for V, this takes the form $V\iota = \kappa\iota$. Ignoring the irrelevant parts of the likelihood, we may form the Lagrangian

$$\phi = -T \log \det V - \Sigma\, e_t V^{-1} e_t + m'(V\iota - \kappa\iota), \qquad (4.27)$$

where m is a vector of Lagrange multipliers. The first order conditions are

$$\frac{\partial\phi}{\partial V} = -T\tilde{V}^{-1} + \sum_t \tilde{V}^{-1} e_t e_t' \tilde{V}^{-1} + m\iota' = 0 \qquad (4.28)$$

$$\frac{\partial\phi}{\partial m} = \tilde{V}\iota - \kappa\iota = 0. \qquad (4.29)$$

From (4.29), $\tilde{V}^{-1}\iota = \kappa^{-1}\iota$, and thus post-multiplying (4.28) by ι and making use of $e_t'\iota = 0$, we have $m = T(\kappa n)^{-1}$. Using this and pre- and post-multiplying (4.28) by $\tilde{V}$ gives

$$\tilde{V} = \frac{1}{T}\Sigma\, e_t e_t' + \kappa\, ii' \qquad (4.30)$$

or

$$\tilde{\Omega} = \frac{1}{T}\Sigma\, e_t e_t', \qquad (4.31)$$

as maximum-likelihood estimators for V and Ω. The estimate of Ω is the one which usually occurs in multivariate problems, see for example the discussion in Goldberger (1964).

When these expressions are substituted back in (4.26) we have to evaluate $\sum_t e_t' \tilde{V}^{-1} e_t$, which may be done as follows:

$$\sum_t e_t'\tilde{V}^{-1}e_t = \sum_t \mathrm{tr}\,(e_t'\tilde{V}^{-1}e_t) = \mathrm{tr}\,(\tilde{V}^{-1}\sum_t e_t e_t')$$

$$= \mathrm{tr}\,\{\tilde{V}^{-1}(T\tilde{V} - T\kappa\, ii')\} = T\,\mathrm{tr}\,(I + ii') = T(n-1). \qquad (4.32)$$

where tr denotes the trace of a matrix. Thus the concentrated likelihood function in logarithmic form is given by

$$2 \log L^* = T\{\log\kappa + \log n - (n-1)(1 + \log 2\pi) - \log\det\tilde{V}\}, \qquad (4.33)$$

and it is now this expression that is maximized with respect to the parameters to give the estimating equations. Apart from the fact that $\kappa = 1$ in his analysis, (4.33) is identical to Barten's (1969) formulation. It is useful to have some flexibility in κ since an inappropriate choice may lead to V becoming ill-conditioned. If again we differentiate with respect to an arbitrary parameter β, we have

$$\frac{\partial \log L^*}{\partial \beta} = \sum_{\kappa} \sum_{l} \frac{\partial \log L^*}{\partial \tilde{v}_{\kappa l}} \frac{\partial \tilde{v}_{\kappa l}}{\partial \beta}$$

$$= \sum_{t} \frac{\partial f_t'}{\partial \beta} \tilde{V}^{-1}(y_t - f_t) = 0. \tag{4.34}$$

Note that equation (4.34) is formally identical to equation (4.26) with V_0 in the latter replaced by $\tilde{V}$ in the former. This is very convenient since we can deal with both forms of maximum likelihood estimation as well as with ordinary least squares estimation in terms of the same set of equations. We may rewrite these in terms of the actual parameters of the linear expenditure system as well as substituting for the derivatives to give

$$\frac{\partial \log L^*}{\partial b^0} = \sum_{t} \xi_t \tilde{V}^{-1}(y_t - f_t) = 0 \tag{4.35}$$

$$\frac{\partial \log L^*}{\partial b^1} = \sum_{t} \theta_t \xi_t \tilde{V}^{-1}(y_t - f_t) = 0 \tag{4.36}$$

$$\frac{\partial \log L^*}{\partial c} = \sum_{t} (\hat{p}_t - p_t b_t')\tilde{V}^{-1}(y_t - f_t) = 0. \tag{4.37}$$

Although the ordinary least squares and *a priori* maximum likelihood estimators are derived from these three conditions by substituting for $\tilde{V}$, it must be remembered that for full-information maximum likelihood the matrix $\tilde{V}$ is also a function of the parameters. Thus while (4.35)–(4.37) define the first two estimators completely (apart from the estimate of σ^2 defined by (4.23), which is not required in the procedure) for the full-information estimator they must be supplemented by equation (4.30) which defines $\tilde{V}$ in terms of b^0, b^1 and c. As can be imagined, this extra complexity adds considerably to the computational burden. It is also equation (4.30) which limits the applicability of full-information estimation. For if the estimate of V is to be non-singular, as required by the equations (4.35) to (4.37), the number of observations must be large relative to the order of the matrix. As we shall see in Chapter V, this condition is frequently not met and we are forced to consider some *a priori* specification for Ω so as to use one of the two other techniques.

4.3 Methods of solution

(i) *Stone method*

Inspection of (4.3) shows that if the c-parameters are known, the model is linear in the b-parameters while, *vice versa*, if the b-parameters are known the model is linear in the c-parameters. This is the basis of the iterative procedure employed by Stone in his early work with the model and this procedure is still a popular technique for estimating the system.

The method minimizes the residual sum of squares and so seeks a solution to the first order conditions (4.35)–(4.37) where the matrix $\tilde{V}$ is replaced by the identity matrix I. The equations, like the model, are bilinear in the parameters. Substituting yields

$$\sum_t \xi_t \{y_t - \hat{p}_t c - (b^0 + b^1\theta)\xi_t\} = 0, \tag{4.38}$$

$$\sum_t \theta_t \xi_t \{y_t - \hat{p}_t c - (b^0 + b^1\theta)\xi_t\} = 0, \tag{4.39}$$

and

$$\sum_t (\hat{p}_t - p_t b_t')\{y_t - (\hat{p}_t - b_t p_t')c - b_t \mu_t\} = 0. \tag{4.40}$$

Clearly, given c, (4.38) and (4.39) are a system of $2n$ linear equations in b^0 and b^1, while, given b^0 and b^1, and thus b_t, (4.40) is a system of n linear equations in c. The estimating equations are thus

$$\begin{pmatrix} b^{0\prime} \\ b^{1\prime} \end{pmatrix} = \begin{pmatrix} \xi_t\xi_t & \theta_t\xi_t\xi_t \\ \theta_t\xi_t\xi_t & \theta_t^2\xi_t\xi_t \end{pmatrix}^{-1} \begin{pmatrix} \xi_t(y_t - \hat{p}_t c)' \\ \xi_t\theta_t(y_t - \hat{p}_t c)' \end{pmatrix} \tag{4.41}$$

for the b's, and

$$c = \{(\hat{p}_t - p_t b_t')(\hat{p}_t - b_t p_t')\}^{-1}\{(\hat{p}_t - p_t b')(y_t - b_t\mu_t)\} \tag{4.42}$$

for the c's, where, for simplicity of exposition, the summation signs over the t's have been omitted.

From (4.41) given some arbitrary value for c, for example, the zero vector, estimates of b^0 and b^1 may be calculated; these are then used to form b_t and thus to yield a new estimate of c from (4.42). Since each estimating equation guarantees the minimization of the residual sum of squares for given values of the other parameters, a continuation of this process will always lead closer to the minimum and the procedure is convergent in the sense that the process will not stop until a minimum has been reached. Furthermore, each iteration is easily computed since it involves only the inversion of two matrices, one $n \times n$ and the other 2×2, and, in practice, after only a few iterations, the parameter estimates give equations which fit the data remarkably well. In consequence of this convenience the method still retains considerable popularity and a number of quite recent applications of the model have made use of it.

However there are a number of problems, perhaps the most serious in practice being difficulties over the speed of convergence. For, although the model very rapidly attains reasonable values for at least some of the parameters, subsequent iterations lead to very small changes which diminish hardly at all from iteration to iteration. Thus, even though the parameter estimates are altering only very slightly at each step, the cumulative effect over several thousand iterations may be large and the first estimates may be quite different from the values at the maximum. And although this difference may reflect a relatively modest decrease in the residual sum of squares, we may be interested in the point estimates in their own right as well as for their contribution to the sum of squares. In the next chapter, some results of using the method will be presented and discussed and we shall see that these comments are borne out in this particular case.

Perhaps the most crippling technical defect of this procedure as a computational algorithm is the fact that its search directions are fixed in advance and are always the same. Search is first carried out in the b-directions and is always followed by search in the c-directions. It is easy to imagine surfaces over which such a procedure will be far from optimal and indeed in the next chapter a detailed explanation of the performance of the method will be given in these terms. What is required is a much more flexible search procedure and we go on to discuss possible candidates below.

(ii) *Gradient and Newton–Raphson technique*

Since the first-order conditions (4.35)–(4.37) are derived from the differentiation of the logarithmic likelihood function, for any values of the parameters, the left-hand side can be used to evaluate the gradient vector of the function. This is useful information since it may be a good indicator of the direction of the maximum. One possible algorithm is then to proceed in this direction with a step length linked to the steepness of the slope. This is very valuable as a fall-back procedure since, except at the maximum itself, there will always exist a step proportional to the gradient which will increase the value of the maximand. As a general algorithm it is poor, however, since if the contours of the function are elongated ellipsoids – a case which often seems to occur – the gradient is frequently almost orthogonal to the direction of the maximum. If in addition, the maximum is not sharply defined, small steps will result while the optimum is still some way off. The method is thus very slow.

Newton–Raphson techniques are much more rapid though they have a tendency to get out of hand. Their basis may be outlined as follows. Let $\pi(h)$, a scalar function of a vector of variables h, be the function to be maximized. Then we seek a solution to the first order conditions,

$$\frac{\partial \pi}{\partial h} = 0, \tag{4.43}$$

and we take these to be non-linear in the h's. Selecting some arbitrary point h^0, hopefully close to the maximum, we may write approximately

$$\frac{\partial \pi}{\partial h} = \left.\frac{\partial \pi}{\partial h}\right|_0 + \frac{\partial^2 \pi}{\partial h \partial h'} \delta h. \tag{4.44}$$

Denoting the Hessian by H and setting the left-hand side of (4.44) equal to zero, we have a step δh, given by

$$\delta h = -H_0^{-1} \left.\frac{\partial \pi}{\partial h}\right|_0 = -H_0^{-1} g_0, \tag{4.45}$$

where g_0 is the gradient of the function at the point. Clearly an iterative procedure can be built up on this basis.

Such algorithms are frequently powerfully convergent, especially if the function π is not too far from quadratic. However if a starting point is selected at which the Hessian is not negative definite – and this is quite likely, since there is no reason to suppose that the likelihood function is uniformly convex – then the step δh calculated by (4.45) for that point will lead *away* from the maximum rather than towards it. In practice it is possible to pool the optimal qualities of the gradient and Newton–Raphson procedures by using the latter in most circumstances, reserving the former for rescue operations in tight situations. On this basis, it is not difficult to construct an algorithm which checks each Newton–Raphson step for movement in the right direction, replacing it where necessary by a step more directly up the slope. For example, the algorithm suggested by Goldfeld and Quandt (1972) works in this way.

Nevertheless the evaluation of the Hessian can be exceedingly laborious in large models and it is possible to modify the technique to allow much greater economy of computation. Retaining the notation, h, to denote the vector of parameters, maximizing likelihood involves solving first order conditions of the form

$$g = \frac{\partial \log L^*}{\partial h} = \sum_t \frac{\partial f'}{\partial h} \tilde{V}^{-1}(y-f) = 0. \tag{4.46}$$

The Hessian is thus given by

$$H = \sum_t \frac{\partial^2 f'}{\partial h \partial h'} \tilde{V}^{-1}(y-f) - \sum_t \frac{\partial f'}{\partial h} \tilde{V}^{-1} \frac{\partial f}{\partial h}. \tag{4.47}$$

Now, in an iterative method of this sort since further steps may well retrace some of the ground previously covered, great precision in the calculation of each step is largely wasted. Thus if some precision can be sacrificed to buy greater ease of calculation, the algorithm is likely to be more rapidly convergent overall. One such method based on (4.47) is the 'method of scoring' discussed, for example, by Rao (1952). This consists of replacing H by its probability limit at each step; thus

$$\operatorname*{plim}_{T \to \infty} H = \frac{1}{T} \sum_{t=1}^{T} \frac{\partial f'}{\partial h} \tilde{V}^{-1} \frac{\partial f}{\partial h}, \tag{4.48}$$

giving the modified step

$$\delta h = \left[\sum_t \frac{\partial f'}{\partial h} \tilde{V}^{-1} \frac{\partial f}{\partial h}\right]^{-1} \left[\sum_t \frac{\partial f'}{\partial h} \tilde{V}^{-1}(y-f)\right]. \tag{4.49}$$

This is considerably easier to compute than is (4.45), since the derivatives $\frac{\partial f}{\partial h}$ will always be calculated in any case. An algorithm using an optimal interpolation between (4.49) and the gradient method has been put forward by Marquardt (1963) for least-squares estimation and it may be adapted to this situation.

In the case of the linear expenditure system we have

$$h = \begin{pmatrix} b^0 \\ b^1 \\ c \end{pmatrix} \tag{4.50}$$

and

$$\frac{\partial f}{\partial b^0} = \xi I, \quad \frac{\partial f}{\partial b^1} = \xi\theta I, \quad \frac{\partial f}{\partial c} = \hat{p} - bp'. \tag{4.51}$$

The approximation to the Hessian is thus given by the matrix

$$\sum_t \begin{pmatrix} \xi\xi\tilde{V}^{-1} & \xi\theta\xi\tilde{V}^{-1} & \xi\tilde{V}^{-1}(\hat{p}-bp') \\ \xi\theta\xi\tilde{V}^{-1} & \xi\theta^2\xi\tilde{V}^{-1} & \xi\theta\tilde{V}^{-1}(\hat{p}-bp') \\ (\hat{p}-pb')\tilde{V}^{-1}\xi & (\hat{p}-pb')\tilde{V}^{-1} & (\hat{p}-pb')\tilde{V}^{-1}(\hat{p}-bp') \end{pmatrix} \tag{4.52}$$

It can be shown on the basis of (4.49) and (4.52) that, if b^0 and b^1 satisfy the adding-up criteria (4.2), the changes will add to zero. The proof of this proposition is tedious and will be omitted here; it is important only in so far as it obviates any need for further restriction of the step estimator (4.49).

This technique is generally considered the most satisfactory available and has now been used successfully in several applications which have estimated the linear expenditure system, for example, Solari (1971). It can be taken as representative of the current best practice techniques for dealing with large non-linear systems. Its main drawback is the expense involved if we are dealing with a really large model. In a 40 equation system we are repeatedly required to invert a matrix containing $120 \times 120 = 14\,400$ elements, and this is unlikely to be practicable even by modern computing standards. The problem is compounded by the tendency of the model to require more iterations as the size of the system increases and so if we wish to consider any but the smallest system we must devise some more radical method.

(iii) *Concentration of the first-order conditions: the ridge-walking algorithm*

This section describes a technique for modifying the methods of section (ii) above. It cannot be used in general since it requires that a subset of the first-order conditions be linear in some of the variables. And although this requirement is a strong one, in those cases where it is satisfied – and the linear expenditure system is an example – the use of the algorithm can make computation very much easier.

Let us return to the general function, $\pi(h)$, and now we shall assume that h can be partitioned in such a way that for one part of the partition, the first-order conditions are linear. The parameter vector and the corresponding partition of the Hessian H are given,

$$h = \begin{pmatrix} h_1 \\ h_2 \end{pmatrix}, \qquad H = \begin{pmatrix} H_{11} & H_{12} \\ H_{21} & H_{22} \end{pmatrix}, \tag{4.53}$$

and the first-order conditions are

$$\frac{\partial \pi}{\partial h_1} = 0, \tag{4.54}$$

$$\frac{\partial \pi}{\partial h_2} = 0. \tag{4.55}$$

Clearly, there are several possibilities which may arise for the solution of (4.54) and (4.55) linearly for some of the h's. To fix our ideas, assume that for given h_2, (4.54) can be solved as a system of linear equations for h_1. This solution is then used at each step of the iterative procedure so that maximization is carried out in the reduced dimensionality of h_2 – space.

The calculation thus begins by selecting a starting value for h_2 and using (4.54) to calculate a starting value for h_1. If (4.54) is to continue to hold, then

$$H_{11}\delta h_1 + H_{12}\delta h_2 = 0, \tag{4.56}$$

giving

$$\delta h_1 = -H_{11}^{-1}H_{12}\delta h_2. \tag{4.57}$$

The solution of (4.55), the remaining first-order conditions, is obtained iteratively, much as in the Newton–Raphson process, i.e. expanding,

$$H_{22}\delta h_2 + H_{21}\delta h_1 + \left.\frac{\partial \pi}{\partial h_2}\right|_0 = 0, \tag{4.58}$$

which, after substitution from (4.57), gives an estimating equation,

$$\delta h_2 = -(H_{22} - H_{21}H_{11}^{-1}H_{12})^{-1} \left.\frac{\partial \pi}{\partial h_2}\right|_0. \tag{4.59}$$

By this substitution, the minimization problem can be reduced in dimensionality by working directly only with those elements of h which do not appear linearly in the first-order conditions. If no elements appear linearly, then (4.59) reduces to the Newton–Raphson process and nothing is gained. On the other hand, if some do, the linearity is exploited to the full. Once again, of course, (4.59) is not evaluated as written; the probability limit of H is used rather than the Hessian itself.

Note that (4.59) resembles very closely the formula for partitioned inversion of a matrix. This must be so since it may be derived directly from the inversion of the Hessian in (4.53): the matrix on the right-hand side of (4.59) is the bottom right-hand corner of the partitioned inverse. The off-diagonal terms do not appear since the partition of the gradient corresponding to h_1 is always held to zero. But the method is much more than a mere partitioning of the Newton–Raphson process; here some of the first-order conditions are solved at each step of the iteration and thus always hold; the others, as usual, are only satisfied when the maximum is reached.

The method may now be applied to the linear expenditure system. Looking back to the first-order conditions (4.35)–(4.37), since the derivatives of f with respect to the b^0 and b^1 vectors are the same for all elements of those vectors, the $\tilde{V}^{-1}$ matrix may be cancelled out. This gives the ordinary least-squares first-order conditions (4.38) to (4.39), which, as we have seen from the Stone method, yield a linear estimator of b^0 and b^1 for a given value of c. Clearly then, b^0 and b^1 go into the first partition of h and maximization can be carried out in terms of c alone. The reduction of dimensionality is from $3n$ to n, allowing us to deal with three times as many commodities as we could using (4.49). And there is an extra bonus: from (4.41) we see that b^0 and b^1 are estimated from c by inverting a matrix which is only 2×2. The parallels with the Stone method are more than accidental. For the concentration method, like the Stone technique, depends on the bi-linearity of the first-order conditions, which in the linear expenditure system happen to be partially the same for ordinary least squares as for maximum likelihood estimation. What the new technique does is to combine the computational ease of the Stone method with the rapid convergence properties of the Newton–Raphson algorithms.

The algorithm can also be given a geometrical interpretation in its application to the linear expenditure system and this will be explored in more detail in the next chapter. In brief, it appears that the likelihood function of the model can be thought of as a long curving ridge with its base roughly parallel to the c-directions with a strong peak in the directions parallel to the b-directions. Concentration of the first-order conditions thus focuses the search in the neighbourhood of the top of the ridge, thus giving the algorithm its name.

To implement the algorithm, equations (4.41) are used to calculate the b^0 and b^1 parameters and the matrix (4.52) is partitioned to correspond to the general formula (4.59). The details are confined to Appendix I which also contains specifications of the computer program used to calculate the estimates in the next chapter. This program combines all the aspects discussed in this chapter allowing the various types of specification discussed in section 4.2 above. Equation (4.59) is used as a basis for calculating each step though a procedure similar to that proposed by Marquardt (1963) for least squares estimation is used to rotate the step towards the gradient whenever the likelihood threatens to decrease.

Finally, a note about standard errors. These will be given for all estimates and are evaluated using the Cramer–Rao minimum-variance bound, or at least its probability limit. This amounts to using as a variance–covariance matrix (minus) the inverse of the Hessian of the log-likelihood function which is given, to a degree of approximation, by the inverse of the matrix (4.52). Once again, by the use of partitioning, this can be obtained without having to invert matrices larger than $n \times n$.

Chapter 5

THE DISAGGREGATED MODEL

It is possible, using post-war time series data for the United Kingdom, to distinguish some forty separate commodities, and throughout this study I shall wish to be able to explain and predict the behaviour of each of these. One way of doing this, the application of the linear expenditure system to the full disaggregation treating all commodities simultaneously, is discussed in this chapter. This is not the only approach to the problem and, in Chapter VI, I shall present an alternative hierarchic methodology employing several different levels of disaggregation.

5.1 Data

The data used was taken from Tables 23 and 24 of the National Income and Expenditure Blue Book for 1971 and each of the categories distinguished in this chapter is directly available from that source. Consistent time series were built up from earlier Blue Books so as to give data from 1954 through to 1970; years before 1954 were not used, mainly because of the problem of dealing with the existence and influence of direct controls before that date. The series were deflated by mid-year estimates of *de facto*, or home population, taken from Table 6 of C.S.O. (1971b), so as to give *per capita* expenditures on each of 37 commodities at current and at 1963 prices. The income, or total expenditure variable μ, was computed by adding up these categories; the prices p_i used were the Paasche indices or implicit price deflators calculated by dividing current values by 1963 based values. The durable categories, motor cars, motor cycles, furniture and floor coverings, and radio and electrical goods were excluded. These goods can hardly be explained by a static model such as the unmodified linear expenditure system; moreover, their purchases have been specially affected in the post-war period by direct controls on hire-purchase borrowing and it would thus seem necessary to deal with them separately. They will not be further considered in this book.

Little would seem to be gained by describing the movement and behaviour of these series at this stage; each commodity is discussed in detail in section 5.6 in conjunction with the empirical results.

5.2 Stochastic specification

It is not possible to apply full information maximum likelihood (FIML) estimation as discussed in Chapter IV for data on 37 commodities over only 17 observations. It can easily be shown that these estimators are not defined over such a time span.

FIML estimation makes use of the variance–covariance matrix Ω; this is known to be singular because of the adding-up property but will in general have only the one zero eigenvalue corresponding to the eigenvector of units. In the formulation of the likelihood function, the matrix $V = \Omega + \kappa ii'$, is inverted and this matrix will in general be non-singular on the conditions for Ω discussed above. However, when Ω is unknown and FIML techniques are used, Ω is replaced by an estimator $\tilde{\Omega}$, given by

$$\tilde{\Omega} = \frac{1}{T} \sum_{t=1}^{T} e_t e_t',$$

where e_t is a vector of errors from maximum likelihood estimation, (see Chapter IV, equation 4.31). Clearly each matrix $e_t e_t'$ is of rank one, and the sum of T such matrices is at most of rank T. Thus, in the case of post-war data with $T = 17$ and 37 commodities, the maximum likelihood estimate of Ω will have rank 16 or less and will have 20 or more zero eigenvalues. These will carry through to V and neither its inverse nor the estimators will exist.

This is more than a mere technical problem; the information just does not exist to determine Ω as well as the parameters of the system so that to remedy this it is necessary to impose some structure on the variance–covariance matrix *a priori*. There are a number of possible ways in which this might be done; perhaps the most satisfactory is to develop a theoretical basis for the determination of these errors. This approach, which has been pioneered by Theil (1957–8), (1971b), (1973), is applied in the next chapter, but the model developed there is not easily used in this context and something rather simpler must be devised.

The most obvious method is to use ordinary least squares estimation but this really only evades the problem. As was shown on p. 39 above, this is equivalent to assuming a multivariate-normal distribution for the errors with zero mean and covariance matrix Ω given by

$$\Omega = \sigma^2(I - \iota\iota'). \tag{5.1}$$

Although this matrix is singular as required, it has few desirable properties other than its simplicity. The most obvious of its deficiencies relates to its assumption of homoscedacity *across commodities*; the variance of the errors of a small commodity, say fruit, which takes up 1.6% of the budget is required to be the same as that of, say meat, which takes up 7.0%. It seems more reasonable to assume a structure which allows for larger errors when budgeting for goods which occupy a large proportion of the budget than for goods which occupy only a small share. This can be accomplished by assuming the following structure

$$\Omega = \sigma^2(\hat{x} - xx') \tag{5.2}$$

where

$$x = \frac{1}{T}\sum_{t=1}^{T} w_t, \tag{5.3}$$

and the parameter σ^2 is to be estimated. This formulation makes the desired adjustment since the larger categories have the larger variances and the covariances between commodities are proportional to the product of their average value shares. The maximum likelihood estimates in this chapter are calculated on this basis and a branch of the program (see Appendix I) deals automatically with this alternative.

An interesting interpretation of this error structure has been pointed out to me by Professor A.P. Barten, who in an unpublished paper with Professor Theil, Barten and Theil (1964), used the formulation in estimation of what has since become known as the Rotterdam demand model. This runs in terms of a multinomial distribution; the consumer is modelled as selecting his purchases in the manner of coloured balls from an urn. The balls are of different colours in proportions determined by the non-stochastic part of the consumer's behaviour; thus if a good makes up 5% of the budget, 5% of the balls in the urn are of the colour corresponding to that good. Standard statistical theory then shows that the errors in behaviour will be characterised by a variance–covariance structure given by equation (5.2). This is perhaps one way of formalizing the ideas of the previous paragraph.

The selection of Ω must not however be accorded an undue importance in this context. Experience with different formulations has shown that from most points of view, the structure of the variance–covariance matrix has only a second-order effect on the results of estimation. This is certainly true in terms of noticeable alterations to parameter estimates, see for example the difference between ordinary least squares and maximum likelihood estimates in Tables 5.1 and 5.2. The exception, and it is an important one in general, is formal hypothesis testing, where the results can be very sensitive to the assumption about stochastic specification, see Deaton (1972). This is because the likelihood functions are defined by this assumption and it is these on which the tests depend. Once it is recognised that formal tests of competing hypotheses are impossible (or meaningless) at this level of disaggregation over this sort of time period, the issue becomes relatively unimportant and we can concentrate on the broader issues of parameter estimation and model performance.

5.3 Assessment of estimation techniques

In addition to the maximum likelihood estimates based on the specification (5.2), two other techniques were used to give parameter estimates for the post-war data. Both of these give ordinary least squares rather than maximum likelihood estimates and differ only in their approach to the computational difficulties. The first is the method employed by Stone in his 1954 paper and described in Chapter IV; the second is the ridge-walking algorithm as applied to ordinary least squares estimation. The comparison of these different techniques allows us to compare maximum likelihood with least squares estimation and thus permits assessment of the effects of the stochastic specification. In addition, in assessing the Stone methodology against the other techniques, we can discover the price that is paid by using a relatively simple estimation technique.

TABLE 5.1
Ordinary least squares estimates

Category no.	OLS – final			STONE (5)			STONE (15)			
	b^0	$b^1 \times 10^2$	c	b^0	$b^1 \times 10^2$	c	b^0	$b^1 \times 10^2$	c	R^2
1.	−.0108	−.0488	12.50	−.0155	−.0219	12.55	−.0139	−.0338	12.46	.9928
2.	.0491	−.1978	19.19	.0456	−.2171	20.34	.0442	−.2054	20.41	.9968
3.	.0083	−.0679	2.46	.0076	−.0820	2.68	.0069	−.0760	2.71	.9692
4.	.0037	−.0314	4.21	.0051	−.0522	4.22	.0038	−.0396	4.29	.8372
5.	−.0070	−.0337	9.46	−.0085	−.0297	9.41	−.0083	−.0316	9.40	.9771
6.	.0230	−.1043	11.28	.0166	−.0657	12.10	.0193	−.0909	11.96	.9947
7.	.0157	−.0813	4.16	.0140	−.0806	4.56	.0141	−.0815	4.56	.9753
8.	.0229	.0235	8.34	.0259	.0081	8.63	.0247	.0191	8.70	.9958
9.	.0122	−.0157	4.55	.0146	−.0373	4.67	.0133	−.0255	4.73	.9859
10.	.0101	−.0308	1.97	.0107	−.0426	2.15	.0100	−.0367	2.18	.9630
11.	.0235	−.0913	4.19	.0208	−.0853	4.84	.0209	−.0867	4.83	.9896
12.	.1257	−.3944	18.88	.1239	−.4331	21.52	.1202	−.3992	21.71	.9962
13.	.0511	.4715	28.80	.0724	.4280	28.55	.0697	.4436	28.69	.9996
14.	.0311	.1694	4.58	.0335	.1977	5.02	.0345	.1879	4.96	.9948
15.	.0001	−.2797	5.84	−.0181	−.2288	6.94	−.0151	−.2496	6.77	.8716
16.	.0735	−.0428	0.69	.0703	−.0031	2.27	.0729	−.0272	2.14	.9924
17.	−.0187	.4829	4.79	.0019	.3845	3.15	−.0011	.4142	3.31	.9943
18.	.0132	−.0810	1.00	.0094	−.0737	1.50	.0093	−.0723	1.51	.9840
19.	.0203	.2244	11.57	.0291	.2134	11.44	.0274	.2260	11.52	.9961

TABLE 5.1 continued

Category no.	OLS – final			STONE (5)			STONE (15)			
	b^0	$b^1 \times 10^2$	c	b^0	$b^1 \times 10^2$	c	b^0	$b^1 \times 10^2$	c	R^2
20.	.0625	−.0279	4.44	.0606	−.0208	5.72	.0621	−.0338	5.64	.9938
21.	.0479	−.4119	19.91	.0340	−.4219	21.68	.0323	−.4080	21.77	.9925
22.	.0097	.0801	2.44	.0129	.0754	2.45	.0123	.0794	2.47	.9980
23.	.1174	.5960	3.36	.1430	.5410	4.15	.1385	.5751	4.37	.9984
24.	−.0210	.0525	4.80	−.0107	.0069	3.75	−.0129	.0217	3.87	.9297
25.	−.0045	.0930	9.76	.0006	.0827	9.36	−.0547	.0908	9.42	.9952
26.	.0417	−.2013	2.58	.0317	−.1853	3.98	.0344	−.2060	3.83	.9317
27.	.0395	−.0666	4.59	.0391	−.0732	5.40	.0387	−.0703	5.42	.9961
28.	.0015	−.0012	3.73	.0031	−.0157	3.68	.0022	−.0076	3.73	.9940
29.	−.0015	−.0014	2.36	−.0007	−.0058	2.29	−.0012	−.0030	2.31	.9843
30.	−.0011	−.0645	3.15	−.0085	−.0422	3.54	−.0074	−.0476	3.48	.9851
31.	.0458	.0015	3.93	.0494	−.0234	4.63	.0478	−.0103	4.71	.9972
32.	.0338	−.0950	2.77	.0285	−.0703	3.73	.0306	−.0886	3.61	.9956
33.	.0297	−.1510	2.54	.0262	−.1656	3.33	.0273	−.1747	3.27	.9899
34.	−.0150	.0265	3.28	−.0129	.0280	2.86	−.0131	.0290	2.87	.9434
35.	.0841	−.4704	13.26	.0574	−.4356	16.47	.0601	−.4546	16.32	.9951
36.	.0210	.0603	4.64	.0176	.1122	5.20	.0209	.0823	5.03	.9868
37.	.0613	.7105	18.75	.0694	.8351	19.34	.0746	.7916	19.05	.9978

Maximum likelihood estimates of the system are presented in Table 5.2. These parameters were computed from starting values of zero for the *c*-parameters; this corresponds roughly to starting from average value shares for the *b*'s, the procedure adopted by Stone. Although problems of multiple solution cannot be ruled out in theory, they do not seem to arise in practice. This statement is based on fairly extensive experience with the linear expenditure system using a number of different algorithms and may take what validity it has from the fact that the model is not highly non-linear and thus may possess a likelihood function which is only a relatively slight distortion of that arising for linear models. Convergence in this case was reached after 25 iterations at the values listed; at this point the algorithm was unable to find any step with at least one element absolutely larger than 10^{-6}, even in the direction of the gradients of the likelihood function. The process required 17 seconds of computation time on an IBM 370/165 computer. While this is considerable, so is the task of estimating a non-linear model containing 111 parameters.

Table 5.1 lists the ordinary least squares estimates both from the ridge program and from the Stone method. The first three columns of the table give the converged least squares estimates from RIDGE; starting from zero values for c as before, a similar number of iterations and computation time was required and so there is no advantage to least squares estimation in terms of cost. Neither is there very much difference between the maximum likelihood and least squares parameter estimates; indeed, there is almost nothing to choose between the first three columns of Table 5.1 and the estimates in Table 5.2. Conversely, there is little difference between the R^2-statistics; the maximum likelihood values, which are not directly maximised, are not noticeably inferior to the ordinary least squares values which are.

The table also shows both the strength and weakness of the Stone method; strength, in that 'satisfactory' R^2-statistics are achieved very quickly and at no great cost, and weakness, in that the residual sum of squares and the parameter estimates are some way from their final maximized values. As a first attempt, the Stone method was started from the same point, $c = 0$, but the c's remained very small for a large number of steps so that some alternative had to be sought. This was found by adopting a procedure suggested by Paelinck (1964) and setting $c = q_0$, where q_0 is the first available observation (1954 in this case), since in many experiments with the linear expenditure system the c's have taken values close to this. The estimates in the table are based on this starting point. The first set of the Stone estimates, columns 4–6 in the table, relate to the position after 5 iterations; the second set, columns 7–10 in the table, to the position after a further 10 iterations, i.e. after 15 in all. The R^2-statistics are given only for the last case since they are very little different for the other two sets of estimates. Now clearly both sets of Stone estimates are very close to both the converged ordinary least squares values and indeed to the maximum likelihood values; this however reflects more the excellence of the starting values than it does the general feasibility of the method. When poor starting values were selected, such as $c = 0$, progress was painfully slow. And even in the estimates in Table 5.1, the values are changing only very slowly and will require many more iterations to achieve the converged values. The residual sum of squares for the converged estimates is 24.70 while it is 27.36 and 25.70 respectively for the Stone (5) and Stone (15) estimates; again there is considerable leeway to make up at an ever-diminishing rate.

Nor is the procedure particularly cheap; each complete cycle of the method requires 0.5 seconds compared with 0.7 seconds for the much more rapidly convergent Ridge procedure. Even so, if the q_0 values are good starting values – and with a few exceptions they usually are – the Stone procedure gives quite good estimates quite quickly though it is hard to see why it should be preferred.

These properties of the two estimation techniques correspond exactly to what might be expected from a likelihood function shaped as a long narrow curving ridge. That the likelihood function is indeed this shape may be seen by considering the matrix given by (4.52); since in the probability limit this matrix is the Hessian of the log-likelihood function, its elements give information about the slope of the function near the maximum. Comparing the appropriate diagonal terms, it can be calculated that a percentage change in one of the b^0-coefficients will have about one hundred times as much direct impact on the likelihood as a percentage change in one of the c-coefficients. Thus the ridge runs roughly parallel to the c-directions in parameter space and is sharply defined in the b-directions; it does however curve since cross terms in the matrix are not zero. A highly simplified schematic representation is given in Figure 5.1.

Figure 5.1: Schematic sketch and contour plan of linear expenditure system likelihood function

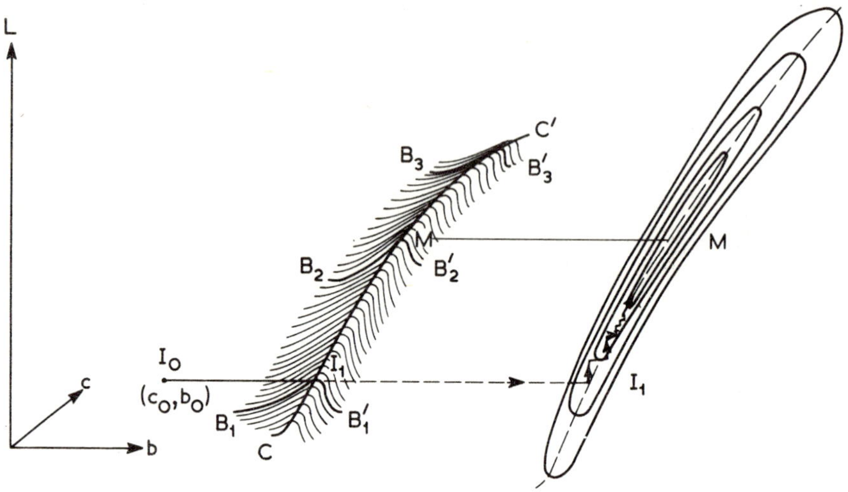

The top of the ridge is represented by the line CC′ and cross-sections by the lines BB′; suppose that the *maximum maximorum* is located at the point M on the line B_2B_2'. From the description of the likelihood function above, it is clear that the slope of the likelihood function is much steeper along the cross-sections BB′ than in the *c*-directions or along the top of the ridge CC′. Suppose iterations start from a point (c^0, b^0) given by I_0; maximization with respect to *b* leads to the ridge at I_1 and to a very large increase in likelihood since there is much less difference between I_1 and M than between I_1 and I_0. Indeed, at I_1, the likelihood may be very close to that at M. The second step will lead along the ridge but, since the ridge curves, it will lead only a very small distance towards M; further iterations can easily be seen to lead merely to a very slow zig-zag along the top CC′, and it is the results of this which cause progress using the algorithm to be so slow.

The choice between least squares and maximum likelihood estimators leaves rather more room for personal preference. I have not had either the time or the resources to conduct formal comparative tests of the two methods at this level of disaggregation, nor would the difference in results warrant such an investigation. Some points can however be made. In a pioneering study, Solari (1971) conducted Monte-Carlo experiments comparing OLS and ML techniques for both post-war and a long run of British data, though at a much less detailed disaggregation, distinguishing only 8 groups. In these tests, though neither method produced very comforting results, maximum likelihood performed much better than least squares. Such a difference overstates the difference between the estimators in this case. Since Solari had only 8 categories, the variance–covariance matrix Ω could be estimated and was not imposed *a priori*; thus if, as seems likely, the superiority of maximum likelihood depended on the ability to avoid an incorrect specification of the matrix, then the results are only relevant in so far as (5.2) is a better specification than the OLS specification (5.1). From the arguments advanced in the previous section, we might reasonably expect this to be the case and it is these maximum likelihood estimates on which I shall focus attention in the rest of the chapter.

5.4 *General assessment of the results*

Table 5.2 presents the main results for this chapter, the maximum likelihood estimates of the 37 commodity linear expenditure system. Listed in the table are the parameter estimates for b^0, b^1 (the time trends are based on 1963, so $b = b^0$ in 1963) and c, each accompanied by their asymptotic standard errors. It must be remembered that these last are evaluated from the Cramer–Rao minimum variance bound at the point of convergence and will thus tend to understate the true standard errors. In the fourth column the R^2-statistics are calculated, first R^2_{ex}, the statistic calculated from the predictions for expenditures, and then R^2_{q}, which measures the correspondence between the actual expenditures at 1963 prices and the values calculated by price deflation of the current price expenditure predictions. Finally, in the last two columns, the total expenditure and price elasticities, calculated from equations (3.29) and (3.41), are given for 1963. These elasticities vary from year to year and are not parameters of the system; they are calculated for the *predicted* values only, thus, in calculating the income elasticity e_i, the value for b_i in 1963 is divided by the predicted rather than actual value share for that year. Since the elasticities are not measured directly by the linear expenditure system, this seems the only consistent way to calculate them in practice.

TABLE 5.2
Maximum likelihood estimates of the linear expenditure system

	b^0	$b^1 \times 10^2$	c	R^2_{ex}/R^2_q	e_i^{63}	e_{ii}^{63}
1. Bread & cereal	−.0121	−.0442	12.47	.9931	−0.364	0.087
	(.0045)	(.0337)	(0.28)	.9182		
2. Meat & bacon	.0445	−.1867	20.00	.9969	0.680	−0.177
	(.0059)	(.0456)	(0.48)	.9413		
3. Fish	.0078	−.0741	2.59	.9682	0.863	−0.182
	(.0025)	(.0185)	(0.17)	.5014		
4. Oils & fats	.0041	−.0389	4.23	.8416	0.312	−0.067
	(.0021)	(.0204)	(0.13)	.3192		
5. Sugar & sweets	−.0074	−.0344	9.42	.9770	−0.293	0.068
	(.0034)	(.0265	(0.21)	.8481		
6. Dairy produce	.0213	−.1003	11.65	.9951	0.570	−0.135
	(.0040)	(.0344)	(0.29)	.9348		
7. Fruit	.0149	−.0820	4.38	.9763	0.959	−0.207
	(.0025)	(.0223)	(0.18)	.8798		
8. Potatoes & veg.	.0233	.0263	8.57	.9958	0.797	−0.182
	(.0036)	(.0311)	(0.26)	.9779		
9. Beverages	.0127	−.0193	4.66	.9855	0.796	−0.173
	(.0025)	(.0234)	(0.17)	.9510		
10. Other man. food	.0103	−.0360	2.08	.9631	1.277	−0.268
	(.0019)	(.0165)	(0.14)	.8515		
11. Footwear	.0224	−.0917	4.54	.9895	1.283	−0.278
	(.0030)	(.0246)	(0.26)	.9537		
12. Clothing	.1206	−.3784	20.60	.9963	1.454	−0.381
	(.0061)	(.0505)	(0.88)	.9897		
13. Rents, rates, etc.	.0584	.4767	28.84	.9997	0.625	−0.179
	(.0104)	(.0600)	(0.66)	.9890		
14. Household repairs	.0335	.1747	4.74	.9949	1.641	−0.356
	(.0334)	(.0256)	(0.22)	.9878		
15. Coal	−.0056	−.2827	6.26	.8917	−0.329	0.073
	(.0046)	(.0228)	(0.29)	.9615		
16. Electricity	.0741	−.0434	1.44	.9918	3.878	−0.805
	(.0028)	(.0240)	(0.44)	.9866		
17. Gas	−.0103	.4592	3.96	.9940	−1.163	0.250
	(.0053)	(.0300)	(0.42)	.9913		
18. Other fuels	.0112	−.0783	1.29	.9834	1.883	−0.390
	(.0025)	(.0167)	(0.21)	.8437		
19. Beer	.0236	.2300	11.55	.9961	0.622	−0.147
	(.0044)	(.0302)	(0.24)	.9735		

TABLE 5.2 continued

	b^0	$b^1 \times 10^2$	c	R^2_{ex}/R^2_q	e_i^{63}	e_{ii}^{63}
20. Wines & spirits	.0630	−.0367	5.06	.9940	2.316	−0.505
	(.0033)	(.0257)	(0.38)	.9845		
21. Cigarettes & tobacco	.0377	−.3995	21.11	.9929	0.564	−0.149
	(.0078)	(.0469)	(0.64)	.7442		
22. Postal, telephone	.0109	.0817	2.46	.9981	1.162	−0.245
	(.0026)	(.0198)	(0.16)	.9909		
23. R.c. of motor v.	.1274	.5979	3.93	.9985	3.435	−0.738
	(.0063)	(.0299)	(0.42)	.9973		
24. Rail travel	−.0176	.0448	4.32	.9290	−2.033	0.439
	(.0034)	(.0199)	(0.29)	.7883		
25. Other travel	−.0031	.0976	9.60	.9951	−0.120	0.028
	(.0043)	(.0298)	(0.28)	.6071		
26. Expenditure abroad	.0391	−.2141	3.22	.9350	2.290	−0.487
	(.0030)	(.0203)	(0.36)	.8112		
27. Textiles & hardware	.0392	−.0693	5.05	.9964	1.753	−0.382
	(.0030)	(.0249)	(0.30)	.9895		
28. Matches, soap etc.	.0018	−.0038	3.73	.9942	0.152	−0.033
	(.0026)	(.0227)	(0.16)	.5522		
29. Books & magazines	−.0011	−.0037	2.32	.9843	−0.182	0.038
	(.0022)	(.0134)	(0.14)	.2385		
30. Newspapers	−.0028	−.0649	3.25	.9875	−0.335	0.071
	(.0029)	(.0126)	(0.18)	.8354		
31. Recreational goods	.0465	−.0017	4.37	.9972	2.112	−0.458
	(.0030)	(.0243)	(0.30)	.9923		
32. Chemists' goods	.0329	−.0986	3.20	.9964	2.083	−0.443
	(.0026)	(.0209)	(0.27)	.9863		
33. Other goods	.0292	−.1684	2.91	.9911	2.052	−0.435
	(.0022)	(.0181)	(0.24)	.9674		
34. Domestic service	−.0135	.0254	3.02	.9380	−2.333	0.495
	(.0023)	(.0141)	(0.18)	.9207		
35. Catering	.0713	−.4679	15.03	.9953	1.255	−0.309
	(.0083)	(.0398)	(0.87)	.9139		
36. Entertainment	.0220	.0630	4.79	.9874	1.208	−0.262
	(.0227)	(.0225)	(0.18)	.9548		
37. Other services	.0700	.7417	18.76	.9973	1.030	−0.265
	(.0086)	(.0480)	(0.40)	.9888		

Predicted expenditures are very close to those actually observed over the sample period. Twenty-two out of the thirty-seven commodities have R^2-statistics greater than 0.99, and a further ten lie in the range 0.95 to 0.99. Thus only five commodities have less than 95% of their variance explained and only one of these – coal – has less than 90% explained. However, there is a strong common upward trend in each of the current price expenditures, and the performance of the model in predicting quantities is a more telling test since errors in predicting expenditure will tend to be magnified once the common price trend has been removed. In consequence, I have chosen to illustrate predicted against actual for quantities rather than expenditures, and these values are illustrated in the graphs which follow in section 5.6 below. These give a much more detailed idea of the performance of the equations than can the raw R^2-statistics in the table.

It is not only the absence of price trends which make these equations fit much less well than their current price counterparts. The linear expenditure system, and thus the likelihood function which is maximized by these estimates, is defined in terms of current price behaviour. The constant price predictions are thus not optimal with respect to any objective function since they are no more than the deflated current price predictions. They automatically share many properties with them; for example, the constant price estimate will lie above or below the actual whenever the current price estimate does so. The general impression from these diagrams is that the linear expenditure system is rather deficient in picking up off-trend movements, while it does relatively well in following the trend itself; in only a few cases does the model overestimate the cyclical effects, e.g. goods 16 and 23. This is reflected in the much lower R^2-statistics; here only 19 commodities have more than 95% of their variance explained by the model and only 24 more than 90%. The trends clearly account for much of the excellent fit in the current price model.

The standard errors of the parameter estimates are uniformly low. This is no doubt partly due to the underestimation already referred to; however, since the model contains a great deal of prior information, these parameters should be very well determined. For each quantity is being explained by two factors: a constant, c_i, and supernumerary income divided by own price and the supernumerary element of this term is the same for all commodities, i.e.

$$q_i = c_i + (b_i^0 + b_i^1\theta) \cdot (\mu - p'c)/p_i \tag{5.4}$$

To explain each quantity using so few exogenous variables is bound to result in high determination of the parameters. This, of course, means very little, since the standard errors are based on the presumption that the model is correct and this takes no account of any doubts about the validity of the structure of the system. And, as we shall see below, there are considerable grounds for doubts of this nature.

Turning to the parameter estimates themselves, undoubtedly the most immediately striking feature is the absence of any negative estimates for the c parameters. This implies that every good is price inelastic and so that, as price increases with income constant, expenditures will always rise. While this might be expected for a broad classification of commodities, where substitutes are scarce, or very imperfect, it is more surprising for a detailed disaggregation such as this. We shall advance an explanation of this phenomenon below: it is partly due to the absence of any genuine price elasticity in the data, but has also much to do with the use of a model which assumes independent wants and thus, by construction, rules out much possible substitutability.

The assessment of income elasticities calculated from the results presents certain difficulties due to the time trends in the b-coefficients. This is not merely because elasticities change over time so that, for example, a good may not be inferior throughout the period, but also because the time trends can in some cases obscure the usual meanings of 'inferiority' and 'normality'. If the time trend on a given coefficient is such that the overall value of b, though positive, is falling more rapidly than deflated supernumerary income is rising, then the quantity predicted will fall through time as income rises. Thus, because income rises through time, and although quantity falls as income rises in every period, the good is not classed as inferior in the usual sense because it has a positive income elasticity.. There are two quite separate issues. First, we might wish to classify a good as inferior when tastes are changing so that its consumption falls, though this does not correspond to the usual definition. Second, the data cannot always be relied upon to separate clearly the effects of changing income and changing tastes, especially when the latter are represented by time trends which are highly collinear with income. These issues only pose problems for a subset of commodities – generally those in which the time trend is doing much of the work of explanation. The general issue is raised here because, although time trends are one way of making the linear expenditure system fit well, their use raises problems of interpretation which are not confined to one particular model or to a particular collection of commodities.

We shall return to this difficulty explicitly at the level of the individual goods when the results are discussed in detail in section 5.6 below; for the time being, while being aware of the difficulties, we may take the elasticities as presented to classify the commodities into inferior goods, necessities and luxuries as they appear in the base year 1963. We proceed in order of ascending elasticity, beginning with the nine *inferior* goods. Starting with the lowest elasticities and indicating the direction of change given by the time trend by bracketed + or –, these are

34. Domestic service (+)
24. Rail travel (+)
17. Gas (+)
1. Bread and cereals (+)
30. Newspapers (–)
15. Coal (–)
5. Sugar and confectionary (–)
29. Books and magazines (–)
25. Other travel (+)

Of these, gas and other travel were normal goods after 1966 and indeed, by 1970, gas was classified as a luxury with an income elasticity of 1.6. The 'necessities', with income elasticity between 0 and 1, were in 1963

28. Matches, soap, and other cleaning materials (–)
4. Oils and fats (–)
21. Cigarettes and tobacco (–)
6. Dairy produce (–)
19. Beer (+)
13. Rent and rates (+)
2. Meat and bacon (–)
9. Beverages (–)
8. Potatoes and vegetables (+)
3. Fish (–)
7. Fruit (–)

The remaining 17 commodities have income elasticities greater than unity and may thus be classified as 'luxuries'. Again in ascending order of elasticity:

37. Other services (including insurance) (+)
22. Postal and telephone charges (+)
36. Entertainment (+)
35. Catering (–)
10. Other manufactured food (–)
11. Footwear (–)

12. Clothing	(−)	32. Chemists goods	(−)
14. Household maintenance and repairs	(+)	31. Recreational goods	(−)
27. Household textiles and hardware	(−)	26. Expenditure abroad	(−)
18. Other fuels	(−)	20. Wines and spirits	(−)
33. Other goods n.e.s.	(−)	23. Running costs of motor vehicles	(+)
		16. Electricity	(−)

While this list may not conform exactly to *a priori* beliefs, it still makes a good deal of intuitive sense. The foods appear low in the list, only one – other manufactured food – has an elasticity greater than unity, and they are accompanied by cigarettes, beer and the more necessary of household expenditures. Higher in the list appear the obvious luxury items such as recreational goods, expenditure abroad, wines and spirits, cosmetics, betting and gaming and so on. The four fuels pose something of a problem: there is obviously a high degree of substitutability between these which is not allowed for by the model and, in addition, there has been the introduction of a new commodity, North Sea gas, in the middle of the sample period. Problems with these four commodities will appear at many stages in the analysis.

Perhaps the major eccentricity of this list lies in the number of inferior goods and we shall see that this has as much to do with the choice of model as with the data. The point will be discussed more fully and formally in the next section, but one source of difficulty can be seen immediately. Looking at equation (5.4) it can be seen that for the quantity purchased to decline over time, one of three things must happen: either (a) the coefficient b is negative, i.e. the good is inferior; or (b) the coefficient b has a downward time trend great enough to offset the upward trend in its multiplicand, i.e. tastes are changing away from the good sufficiently fast to overcome the effects of rising income, a sort of 'technical' inferiority; or, failing these, (c) the price p_i rises faster than supernumerary income, thus allowing normal tastes and a normal income response. This last is very unlikely indeed as, in most circumstances, it would require the price index to rise faster than total expenditure. Thus if the quantity purchased of a good *is* actually declining because it is price elastic and its price is rising relative to other prices then, freak cases apart, the linear expenditure system will model it as being inferior in one of the senses above. This is, I think, the explanation for the large number of goods, almost a quarter, which the model treats as inferior.

As is perhaps inevitable, I have so far concentrated on the defects of the system. However, on a balanced assessment, the estimates and the model as a whole could not be said to be unsuccessful. A large percentage of the variation in both current and constant prices has been accounted for and the majority of the parameter estimates are quantitatively plausible. And while, in the sections that follow, I shall return to a more critical position, the achievements of the model must always be borne in mind. It is also true that it is no easy task to construct something which will do better empirically and which is in a form which can be trusted to give sensible results in a model which may well be asked to produce forecasts well outside the sample period.

5.5 Pigou's Law

Though Pigou's Law, the relationship of proportionality between income and price elasticities, holds only as an approximation for the linear expenditure system, for the elasticities given in Table 5.2, the approximation is very close indeed. This is illustrated in Figure 5.2 below where price elasticity and income elasticity are plotted against one another for the base year 1963.

The slope of the line is given by minus the supernumerary ratio i.e. $\phi = -(\mu - p'c)/\mu$ for 1963. Since this is not constant from year to year, but rather increases absolutely as income increases, the line will rotate through time; starting along the e_i-axis ('misery' – when income just covers committed purchases) and finishing at 45° below the axis ('bliss' – when income is infinite). Thus, though a linear relationship through the origin exists for each year, the actual slope will be different from year to year.

This is a very restrictive relationship. It is also so little supported by casual empirical observation that it would be surprising if it were universally valid. Indeed, we have already come across difficulties with the model which might be traced at least partially to this source; for example, the presence of large numbers of inferior goods and the inability of the system to track the cycle. Even so, it is perhaps surprising that such a strong relationship should not have had a much more drastic effect on the ability of the model to approximate reality.

Figure 5.2: Linear expenditure system income and price elasticities illustrating Pigou's Law

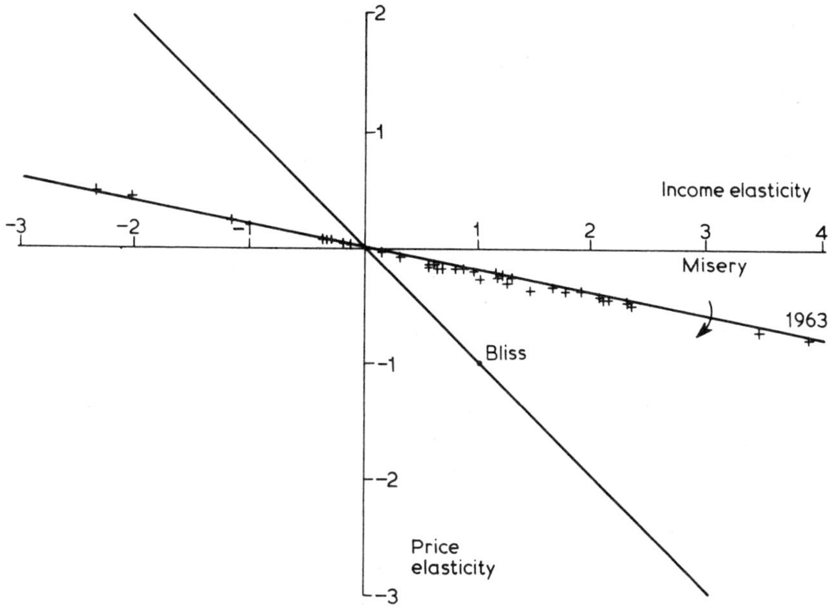

A formal assessment of the validity of the law is difficult in the circumstances. In the first place, a really satisfactory test would relate the empirical validity of the linear expenditure system to that of a system which contained it as a special case and which did not embody the law. Though such models exist (e.g. Nasse's (1970) generalization of the linear expenditure system) the extra parameters needed and the resulting computational difficulties would rule out their application to the data being considered. Secondly, even if the computational difficulties were to be overcome, the results of the tests would depend, probably crucially, on the selection of the variance–covariance matrix for the system. And again, given the size of the problem, FIML estimators cannot solve this problem for us. It is thus necessary to fall back on rather less formal methods.

The possibility followed here is the estimation of an alternative and competing system, the loglinear model which takes elasticities as parameters. As shown below, this model can be set up so that it may be estimated with and without the imposition of the law. This, while giving a direct test of the law in one context, does not necessarily tell us anything about its validity in another; i.e. in the linear expenditure system. Nevertheless, this disadvantage is compensated for in other ways. The estimation of a different model gives us an alternative way of describing the behaviour of the expenditures, and this gives a useful set of results to compare with those of the linear expenditure system. And while it will not always be possible to separate the effects of Pigou's law on the one hand and model structure on the other in their contributions to the difference between the two sets of results, by discussing each commodity separately we shall be able to get a fairly clear idea of what is happening. There is another advantage in comparing the two models and this refers right back to the discussion in Chapter I. The loglinear model is the 'pragmatic' model *par excellence*; it is the obvious tool to use if the investigator wants quick results in an easily assimilable form and is sceptical of, or unconcerned about the usefulness of, the theory in a practical context. The relative performance of the two models is thus of considerable interest towards a general assessment of the usefulness of theory in this context and we shall devote considerable attention to it at various points in this book.

The loglinear model in the desired form is written

$$\log q_i = \alpha_i + (\beta_i^0 + \beta_i^1\theta) \log \frac{\mu}{\pi} + (\gamma_i^0 + \gamma_i^1\theta) \log \frac{p_i}{\pi}, \qquad (5.5)$$

where π is a price index of all prices; for simplicity this is taken to be the implicit price deflator of total consumers' expenditure μ. The time trend in the income term is introduced to put the model on a par with the linear expenditure system as estimated and the time trend in the relative price term so as to allow a Pigou's Law restricted version to be tested within it. The coefficients β_i and γ_i will be interpreted as income and own-price elasticities respectively although γ_i differs from the actual price elasticity by an amount or order n^{-1} since changes in p_i affect the indices π.

Compared with the linear expenditure system with all its theoretical underpinnings, this may seem a very simple model with its cavalier treatment of prices other than that of the good being considered. However, the linear expenditure system can also be written as a function of real income and a price relative alone; defining the constant-weight price index $\pi^* = p'c$, equation (5.4) may be written

$$q_i = c_i + (b_i^0 + b_i^1\theta)\left(\frac{\mu}{\pi^*} - 1\right)\frac{\pi^*}{p_i} \qquad (5.6)$$

which, whether simpler or not than (5.5) is certainly more restrictive. However, the loglinear model does not share a number of other properties with the linear expenditure system; it does not in general give expenditures which add up to total expenditure, nor does it yield a symmetric negative–definite substitution matrix. Homogeneity is however shared since proportional changes in p_i, π and μ will leave (5.5) unchanged.

Figure 5.3: Price and income elasticities for unrestricted loglinear system (1963)

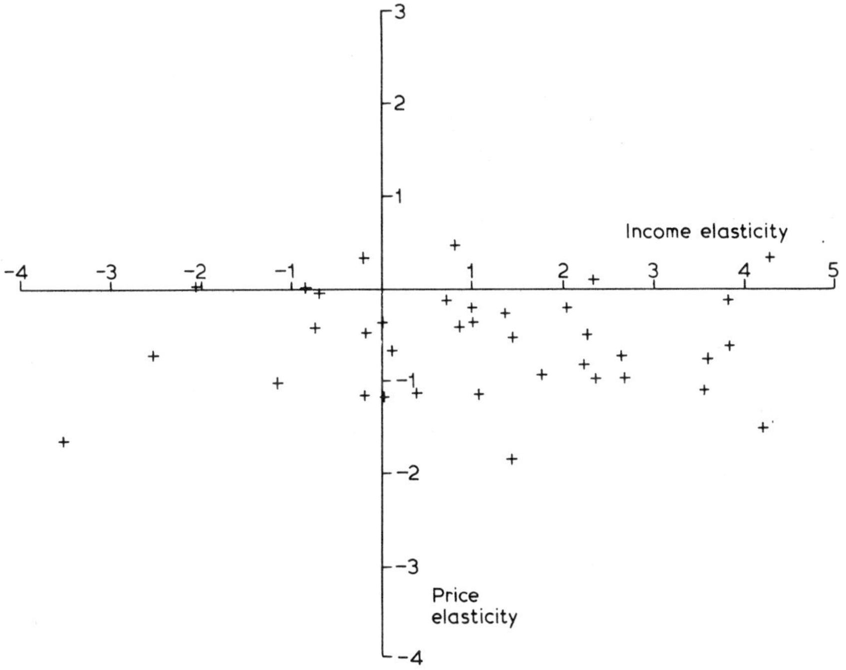

The double logarithmic model, equation (5.5), was estimated on a single equation basis for each of the 37 commodities by ordinary least squares and the parameter estimates are given in Table 5.3. Figure 5.3 shows the relationship between price and income elasticities for 1963 as given by this model while, as a comparison with the linear expenditure system, Figure 5.4 shows the relationship, again for 1963, of the two sets of income elasticities. This second chart, which

TABLE 5.3
Log–linear model unrestricted

	α	β^0	β^1	γ^0	γ^1	R^2
1. Bread and cereals	−1.759	0.719	−0.004	−0.120	0.010	.9704
	(2.084)	(0.356)	(0.001)	(0.378)	(0.043)	
2. Meat and bacon	−4.802	1.357	−0.003	−0.272	0.011	.9068
	(3.085)	(0.527)	(0.002)	(0.270)	(0.046)	
3. Fish	−3.694	0.820	−0.003	0.469	−0.157	.5600
	(7.851)	(1.342)	(0.004)	(0.417)	(0.066)	
4. Oils and fats	13.49	−2.046	0.007	0.021	0.034	.8068
	(4.18)	(0.714)	(0.003)	(0.095)	(0.007)	
5. Sugar and sweets	3.149	−0.168	−0.001	−0.484	−0.029	.9428
	(2.184)	(0.373)	(0.001)	(0.120)	(0.019)	
6. Dairy produce	−2.430	0.855	−0.003	−0.410	0.022	.9739
	(1.675)	(0.286)	(0.001)	(0.127)	(0.008)	
7. Fruit	−4.272	1.019	−0.003	−0.356	0.039	.8978
	(6.927)	(1.183)	(0.003)	(0.225)	(0.025)	
8. Potatoes and vegetables	−3.464	0.988	−0.001	−0.196	−0.036	.9795
	(3.085)	(0.527)	(0.002)	(0.093)	(0.021)	
9. Beverages	2.848	−0.193	0.004	0.324	0.015	.9640
	(4.266)	(0.729)	(0.003)	(0.187)	(0.013)	
10. Other manufactured food	2.172	−0.197	0.001	−1.163	0.104	.9110
	(10.07)	(1.718)	(0.007)	(0.913)	(0.046)	
11. Footwear	−10.208	2.052	−0.004	−0.217	0.051	.9487
	(7.385)	(1.260)	(0.005)	(0.530)	(0.032)	
12. Clothing	−12.318	2.678	−0.008	−0.989	0.005	.9926
	(3.211)	(0.548)	(0.002)	(0.345)	(0.013)	
13. Rents, rates, etc.	8.353	−0.829	0.006	−0.011	−0.003	.9966
	(1.377)	(0.235)	(0.001)	(0.066)	(0.004)	
14. Household repairs	−6.317	1.414	0.002	−1.855	−0.208	.9875
	(5.532)	(0.945)	(0.003)	(0.552)	(0.084)	
15. Coal	−20.63	3.820	−0.020	−0.137	−0.081	.9616
	(9.54)	(1.631)	(0.006)	(0.503)	(0.035)	
16. Electricity	−13.57	2.636	0.004	−0.737	0.117	.9902
	(14.89)	(2.542)	(0.007)	(0.491)	(0.055)	
17. Gas	21.802	−3.526	0.015	−1.646	−0.030	.9950
	(7.858)	(1.341)	(0.005)	(0.093)	(0.026)	
18. Other fuel	−12.96	2.339	−0.009	0.093	−0.201	.7624
	(15.87)	(2.707)	(0.008)	(0.791)	(0.102)	
19. Beer	2.506	0.016	0.004	−0.355	−0.095	.9665
	(4.347)	(0.743)	(0.002)	(0.201)	(0.043)	

TABLE 5.3 continued

	α	β^0	β^1	γ^0	γ^1	R^2
20. Wines and spirits	−18.52 (4.30)	3.551 (0.734)	−0.004 (0.002)	−1.120 (0.297)	−0.111 (0.036)	.9942
21. Cigarettes and tobacco	−10.00 (4.26)	2.250 (0.728)	−0.006 (0.002)	−0.823 (0.246)	−0.072 (0.047)	.6642
22. Post, telephone	7.872 (3.085)	−1.146 (0.528)	0.010 (0.002)	−1.019 (0.365)	−0.107 (0.047)	.9933
23. R.c. of m.v.	−19.790 (6.700)	3.814 (1.144)	0.003 (0.004)	−0.630 (0.417)	0.120 (0.045)	.9982
24. Rail travel	15.861 (10.754)	−2.521 (1.835)	0.006 (0.005)	−0.726 (0.291)	−0.047 (0.028)	.9394
25. Other travel	0.053 (2.688)	0.374 (0.459)	0.002 (0.002)	−1.132 (0.311)	0.044 (0.019)	.8751
26. Expenditure abroad	−22.90 (11.95)	4.214 (2.041)	−0.009 (0.007)	−1.516 (0.464)	−0.126 (0.068)	.9088
27. Textiles and hardware	−11.79 (3.33)	2.363 (0.570)	−0.004 (0.002)	−0.980 (0.242)	−0.005 (0.018)	.9931
28. Matches, soap etc.	5.317 (4.837)	−0.678 (0.826)	0.003 (0.003)	−0.049 (0.111)	0.042 (0.032)	.6031
29. Books and magazines	0.074 (7.664)	0.125 (1.309)	0.001 (0.004)	−0.680 (0.398)	0.008 (0.024)	.4057
30. Newspapers	5.379 (6.131)	−0.728 (1.047)	0.002 (0.004)	−0.426 (0.194)	−0.007 (0.009)	.9431
31. Recreational goods	−23.05 (7.78)	4.284 (1.328)	−0.006 (0.004)	0.332 (0.571)	0.054 (0.039)	.9916
32. Chemists' goods	−8.643 (3.634)	1.768 (0.621)	−0.002 (0.002)	−0.933 (0.188)	0.111 (0.028)	.9925
33. Other goods n.e.s.	−19.40 (4.95)	3.585 (0.845)	−0.010 (0.003)	−0.770 (0.143)	0.044 (0.021)	.9812
34. Domestic service	−7.714 (2.479)	1.442 (0.423)	−0.007 (0.002)	−0.528 (0.188)	0.121 (0.009)	.9956
35. Catering	2.864 (2.751)	0.024 (0.470)	0.003 (0.002)	−1.177 (0.217)	−0.139 (0.013)	.9742
36. Entertainment	−4.486 (7.016)	1.080 (1.198)	0.001 (0.003)	−1.147 (0.334)	−0.157 (0.041)	.9713
37. Other services	−10.12 (2.88)	2.269 (0.491)	0.000 (0.002)	−0.514 (0.268)	0.211 (0.028)	.9961

Figure 5.4: Income elasticities for linear expenditure system and unrestricted loglinear system (1963)

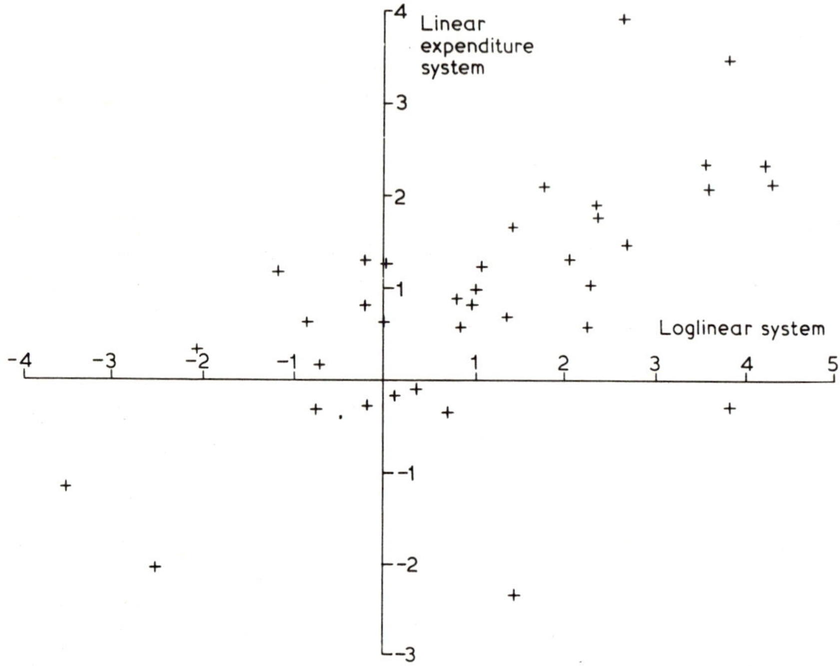

illustrates how the combination of the imposition of Pigou's Law and the choice of functional form affects the measurement of elasticities, will be referred to again later and for the present we shall consider the income–price elasticity relationship. Figure 5.3 is probably what would be expected by an observer who had never heard of Pigou's Law. And although, to the eye that is looking for it, there might appear to be some evidence of a negative relationship, the actual correlation is in fact positive, though barely so ($\rho = .0088$). The chart certainly contains no evidence which could be interpreted as positive confirmation of the universal applicability of a negative proportional relationship such as Pigou's Law demands.

The law may be assessed more directly within the log–linear model by applying the constraint and re-estimating. We write

$$\gamma_i = \phi\beta_i , \tag{5.7}$$

and the model becomes

$$\log q_i = \alpha_i + (\beta_i^0 + \beta_i'\theta)\left(\log\frac{\mu}{\pi} + \phi\log\frac{p_i}{\pi}\right) . \tag{5.8}$$

I have chosen to estimate these equations for a range of values of ϕ, computing the parameter estimates for each value and comparing the resulting equations with the estimates of the unrestricted forms (5.5). This seems to me preferable to attempting to maximize some global residual sum of squares or likelihood function with respect to β and ϕ since once again such a procedure would only derive its validity by assumption about the error structure. The alternative adopted here has the advantage of allowing an assessment of the law on a commodity basis. This is done by comparing the residual sum of squares for each good for the free and restricted estimates; it is convenient to use an F-ratio for this purpose, though since ϕ is being varied and is not known in advance, the statistics calculated for each value of ϕ, will only have an approximate F-distribution under the null-hypothesis. The test statistics are calculated from

$$F_{2,12} = \frac{(\text{RSS}^* - \text{RSS})/2}{\text{RSS}/12}, \tag{5.9}$$

where RSS stands for residual sum of squares and an asterisk indicates that the restriction has been imposed. A range for ϕ from 0 to -1 was tried and a value of -0.55 was found to give the maximum number of acceptances to the law. The values of the parameters, with R^2 and F-ratios, are given for this value of ϕ in Table 5.4; note that these differ both from the linear expenditure system and loglinear estimates. These should be regarded as formalising the information in Figure 5.3 since the F-ratios, plus the value of ϕ, define a 'best' line through these points and tell which points lie significantly off it. Though more complicated than the obvious alternative of running a weighted (or errors in variables) regression through the points in the chart, the technique uses all the information available in the original data and thus gives a clearer and more reliable picture. Even so, this formalization only confirms the overall picture in Figure 5.3; out of the 37 commodities, 16 conflict with the law at the 5% level, 12 still do so even at 1%. On the other hand, many of the commodities which have both significant price and income elasticities in the unconstrained version conform quite closely to the law. It is clear from this that for some commodities the law is acceptable not simply because there is little price information, but because it is genuinely a good description of behaviour.

While the differences in functional form, between linearity and

TABLE 5.4
Loglinear model restricted $\phi = -.55$

	α_i	β_i^0	β_i'	R^2	F
1. Bread and cereals	−0.291	0.469	−0.003	.9697	0.15
	(0.793)	(0.136)	(0.000)		
2. Meat and bacon	−1.993	0.878	−0.002	.8978	0.58
	(1.543)	(0.265)	(0.001)		
3. Fish	9.549	−1.445	0.005	.2317	4.47
	(4.971)	(0.850)	(0.003)		
4. Oils and fats	−1.792	0.561	−0.003	.5111	9.18
	(0.980)	(0.167)	(0.001)		
5. Sugar and sweets	−0.515	0.459	−0.003	.9065	3.80
	(1.070)	(0.183)	(0.001)		
6. Dairy produce	−3.953	1.114	−0.004	.9576	3.76
	(1.054)	(0.180)	(0.001)		
7. Fruit	−4.173	1.000	−0.003	.8506	2.77
	(1.729)	(0.296)	(0.001)		
8. Potatoes and vegetables	0.462	0.318	0.002	.9749	1.35
	(0.891)	(0.152)	(0.001)		
9. Beverages	3.237	−0.261	0.004	.9524	1.93
	(1.808)	(0.309)	(0.002)		
10. Other manufactured food	−16.90	3.057	−0.010	.8627	3.26
	(6.75)	(1.152)	(0.005)		
11. Footwear	−9.841	1.983	−0.005	.9002	5.67
	(6.314)	(1.077)	(0.005)		
12. Clothing	−10.22	2.319	−0.007	.9922	0.31
	(1.41)	(0.241)	(0.001)		
13. Rents, rates, etc.	2.894	0.104	0.003	.9917	8.69
	(0.829)	(0.141)	(0.000)		
14. Household repairs	−8.557	1.799	0.001	.9768	5.11
	(5.416)	(0.926)	(0.003)		
15. Coal	4.332	−0.450	−0.006	.8640	15.22
	(6.104)	(1.040)	(0.002)		
16. Electricity	−10.93	2.180	0.005	.9767	8.17
	(5.31)	(0.910)	(0.004)		
17. Gas	−19.73	3.572	−0.008	.9597	42.59
	(2.43)	(0.412)	(0.002)		
18. Other fuel	17.48	−2.857	0.010	.6204	3.59
	(6.95)	(1.182)	(0.003)		
19. Beer	2.736	−0.024	0.004	.9534	2.34
	(1.052)	(0.180)	(0.001)		

TABLE 5.4 continued

	α_i	β_i^0	β_i'	R^2	F
20. Wines and spirits	−6.301 (1.700)	1.460 (0.292)	0.002 (0.001)	.9819	12.75
21. Cigarettes and tobacco	−6.144 (2.556)	1.589 (0.437)	−0.004 (0.001)	.4854	2.68
22. Post, telephone	−0.872 (1.111)	0.352 (0.189)	0.005 (0.001)	.9868	5.91
23. R.c. of m.v.	−12.88 (1.70)	2.635 (0.291)	0.007 (0.001)	.9974	2.83
24. Rail travel	−8.56 (2.78)	1.647 (0.472)	−0.005 (0.001)	.9118	2.73
25. Other travel	−4.052 (3.269)	1.078 (0.559)	−0.002 (0.001)	.4927	18.38
26. Expenditure abroad	−15.28 (2.94)	2.912 (0.503)	−0.006 (0.002)	.8742	2.27
27. Textiles and hardware	−9.512 (1.247)	1.974 (0.213)	−0.003 (0.001)	.9934	0.00
28. Matches, soap, etc.	0.466 (1.098)	0.151 (0.187)	−0.000 (0.001)	.5591	0.66
29. Books and magazines	−3.516 (3.118)	0.739 (0.533)	−0.002 (0.001)	.3462	0.60
30. Newspapers	−1.617 (1.346)	0.466 (0.231)	−0.003 (0.000)	.9368	0.67
31. Recreational goods	−9.214 (2.009)	1.921 (0.344)	−0.001 (0.001)	.9889	1.85
32. Chemists' goods	−10.499 (1.778)	2.083 (0.304)	−0.003 (0.001)	.9821	8.30
33. Other goods n.e.s.	−9.764 (0.820)	1.940 (0.141)	−0.004 (0.001)	.9762	1.59
34. Domestic service	1.237 (4.432)	−0.082 (0.759)	−0.004 (0.001)	.9235	97.65
35. Catering	−10.15 (4.62)	2.243 (0.791)	−0.004 (0.002)	.6396	77.90
36. Entertainment	−4.352 (3.048)	1.062 (0.521)	0.000 (0.002)	.9283	9.01
37. Other services	−10.12 (5.01)	2.273 (0.856)	−0.000 (0.002)	.9623	51.62

loglinearity, do not allow us to assert that these results also apply to the linear expenditure system, it would be a remarkable phenomenon if the linear expenditure system were not to suffer some loss of explanatory power as well as some distortion in the measurement of the income responses as a result of the operation of the law. This might be expected to apply particularly strongly to those half-dozen or so commodities in Table 5.4 which have particularly large F-ratios. We shall see below that this expectation is borne out by the analysis of individual results. It might be added that, although it may seem obvious that the imposition of a strong relationship between price and income elasticities would tend to distort the measurement of both, this has not at all been emphasized in the literature. This failing seems primarily due to a less than full realization of the implications of the models used and of the extent

Figure 5.5: Income elasticities for linear expenditure system and restricted loglinear system, $\phi = -.20$ (1963)

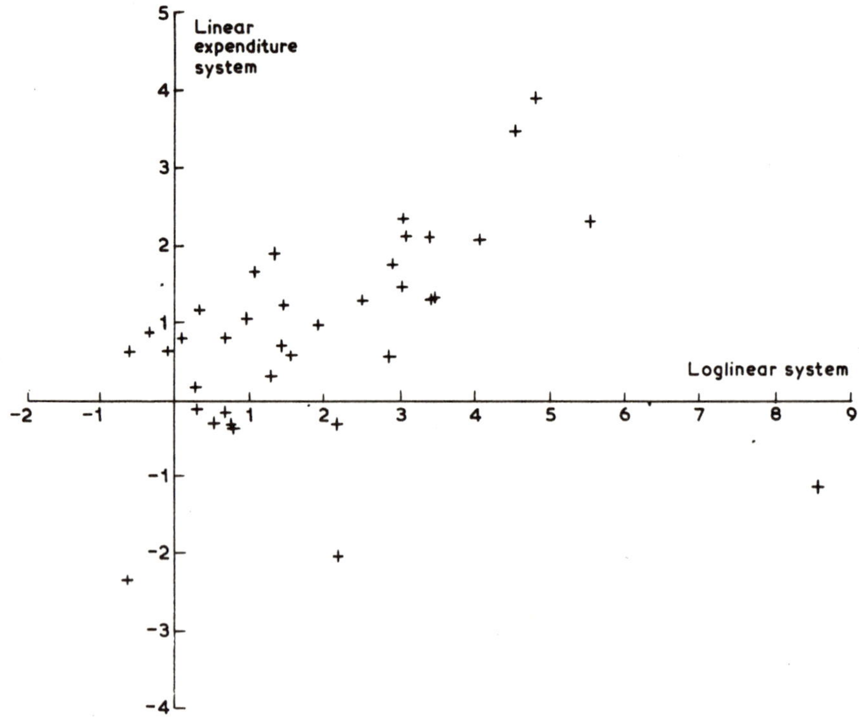

to which assumption was being allowed to dominate over the evidence under analysis. I think it is fair to say that while a great deal of attention has been paid to the theoretical development of demand models and, more recently, to the overcoming of the problems posed by their estimation, little energy has been devoted to the critical evaluation of the results.

Pigou's Law is not the only source of discrepancies between the income elasticities in the two models. The different functional forms of the systems also have an important influence on the measurement process. This may be seen by comparison of Figures 5.4 and 5.5. In the former, the income elasticities of the freely estimated loglinear model and those of the linear expenditure system are compared; in the latter the comparison involves again the linear expenditure system but this time with the constrained loglinear model. For this second comparison a value of ϕ of $-.20$ was selected and this, though not the best value for the loglinear model, is close to the value for 1963 generated by the linear expenditure system. With the exception of three inferior goods, the relationship is much closer in the second chart though the slope is much less than the ideal 45°. This is to be expected for a year such as 1963 in which most observations lie above their means, since if the true relationship lies somewhere in between, a linear model will tend to understate elasticities while a loglinear model will tend to do the opposite. And this tendency is much clearer in Figure 5.5 where both models stand on the same basis *vis-à-vis* Pigou's Law. Thus, while the removal of the restriction as a source of difference between the models tends to reduce the dispersion of measurement, a considerable amount of systematic variation is still left to be attributed to the selection of functional form. This is an excellent example and warning of the extent to which the act of model selection, even when there is no difference of principle, can affect the measurement of quite simple responses even in situations where data are plentiful.

5.6 Analysis of individual items

The commodity by commodity results are not intended as the justification of a final selection of equations; that state has not been reached. Rather it is an attempt to continue the methodological discussion in concrete terms by illustrating the way in which each of the systems responds when attempting to describe a wide range of behaviour. This is by far the clearest way of assessing the performance of the models, and of deciding how they might be expected to behave outside the sample period. We shall find that both models have advantages as well as disadvantages and that, while some commodities can be described equally well be either, some commodities are better described by one or the other, and some commodities cannot be described at all.

I have attempted to include additional information in these notes; in particular where it is essential to the understanding of the behaviour of the category in question, or where it is less than obvious which commodities are included in the group. A full description of the data is given in pages 147–201 of the C.S.O.'s, *National Income Sources and Methods*, Maurice (1968), and this has been used extensively in the compilation of what follows. Two small adjustments have been made to the basic data; income in kind has been allocated *pro rata* over footwear, clothing, and the food categories, i.e. groups 1 to 12, and the subcommodity 'coke' has been reallocated from 'coal' to 'other fuel'. In brackets after each commodity is given the percentage of the budget spent on it on average over the period; the ranking of the good by this criterion, from 1 to 37, and a letter, A, B or C, given in *Sources and Methods*, which indicates the relative reliability of the series. I shall also use the abbreviations LES for the Linear Expenditure System and LLS for the Log–Linear System.

The notes for each commodity are accompanied by two graphs. The upper graph of each pair illustrates the values of the price relative for the commodity from 1954 to 1970; this is the implicit price deflator of the good divided by the implicit price deflator of consumers' expenditure as a whole. The lower graph illustrates purchases per head in 1963 prices so that the y-axis is marked in £1963; the solid line gives actual purchases, the dotted line purchases predicted by the linear expenditure system. The points marked on the graphs after 1970 are projections of one sort or another. These are not relevant to this chapter and will be presented in Chapter VII below.

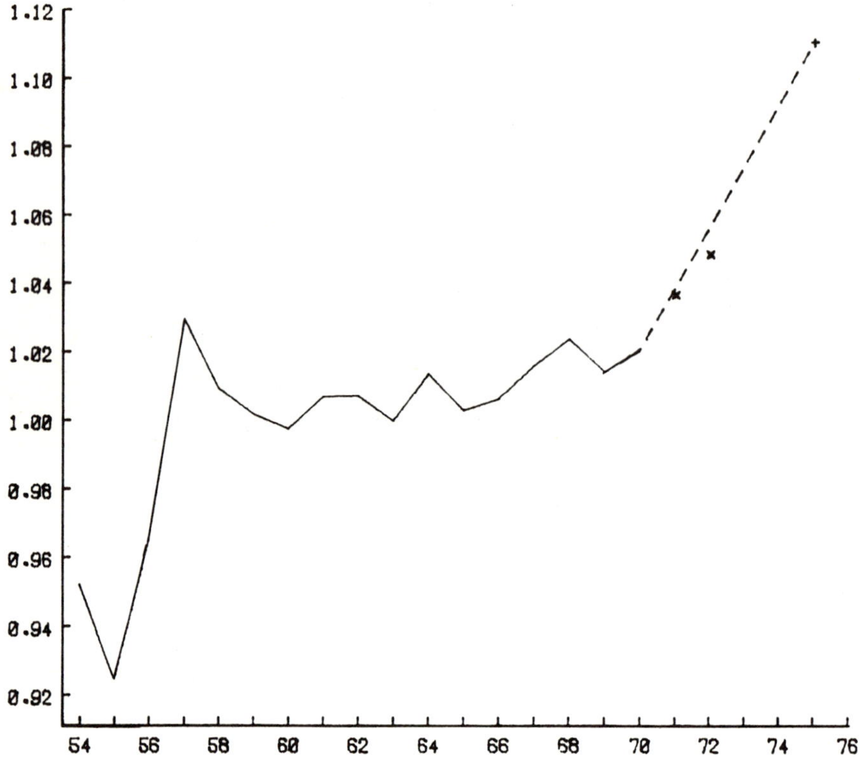
1.12
1.10
1.08
1.06
1.04
1.02
1.00
0.98
0.96
0.94
0.92
54
56
58
60
62
64
66
68
70
72
74
76

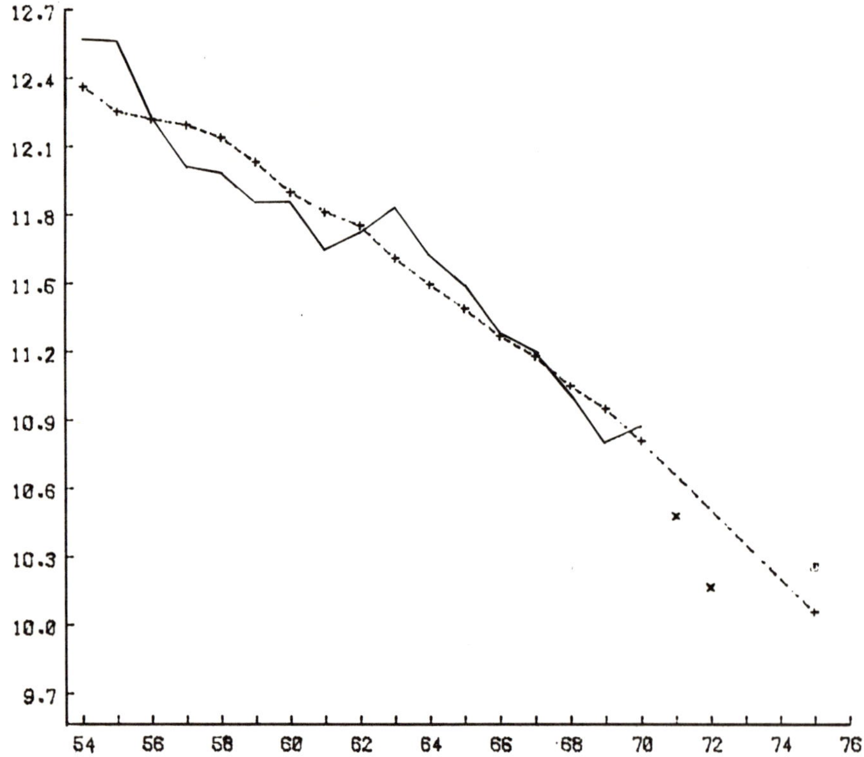
12.7
12.4
12.1
11.8
11.6
11.2
10.9
10.6
10.3
10.0
9.7
54
56
58
60
62
64
66
68
70
72
74
76

1. BREAD & CEREALS
(3.4%: 10th: B)

The quantity purchased fell from £(1963)12.50 *per capita* in 1954 to just over £10.80 in 1970. The price-relative rose very sharply by 10% or so between 1955 and 1957, but with minor fluctuations has moved little since. This price seems to have had little impact on the quantity purchased and price terms are not significant in the LLS. Both this model and the LES explain the fall in purchases within the income term, the LES registering the good as inferior while the LLS gives a normal response with a negative time trend. Both explanations give rise to much the same result since it does not seem possible to distinguish clearly the effects of income from those of time. The difference between inferiority and normality between the two models is thus more a matter of functional form than of reality: for the LLS income with a negative time trend in the coefficient does best; for the LES the negative of income does best. Which is chosen is largely a matter for *a priori* preference. Neither model fits particularly well but, in the absence of significant price information Pigou's Law cannot be blamed for this.

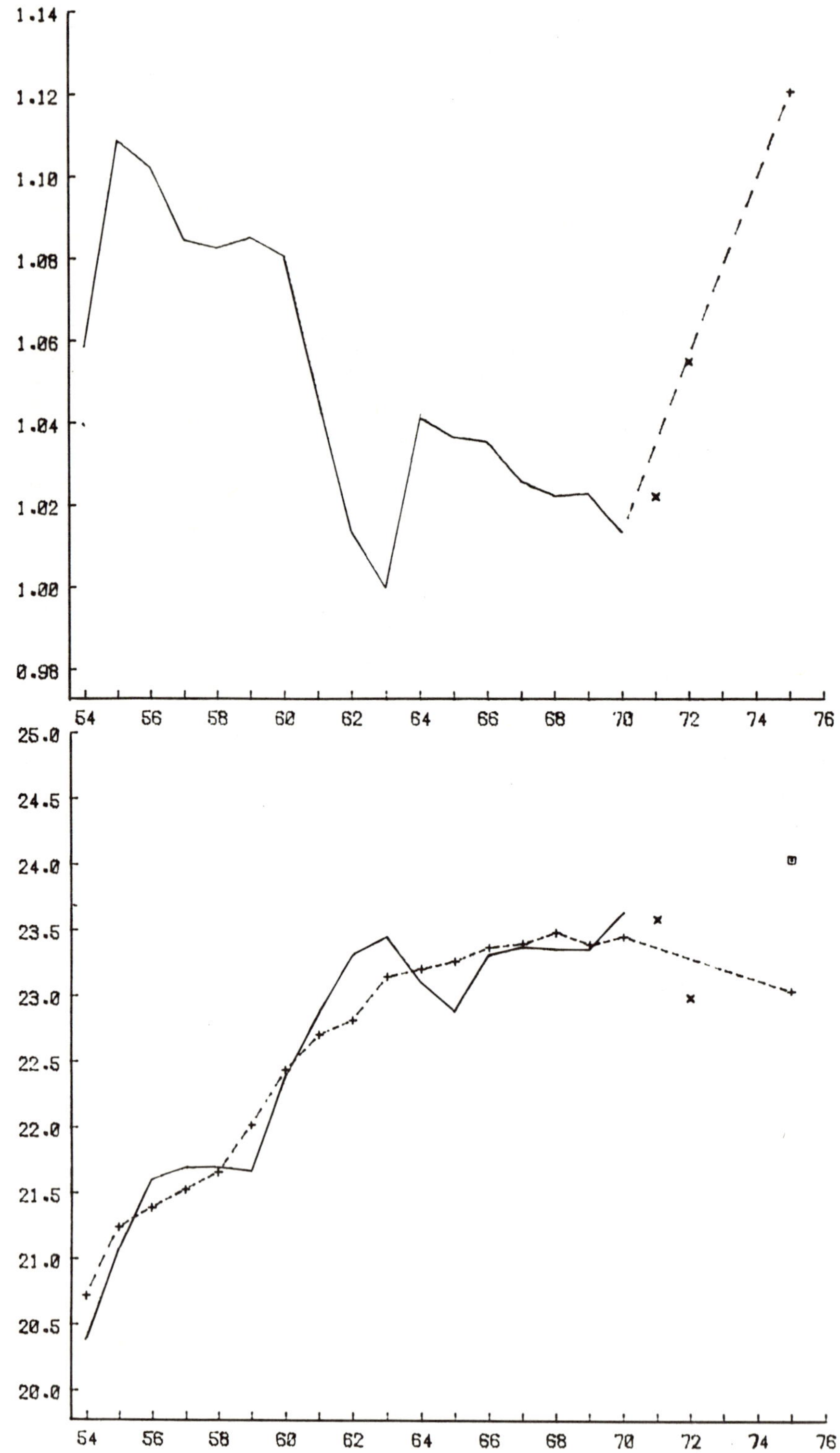
1.14
1.12
1.10
1.08
1.06
1.04
1.02
1.00
0.98
54 56 58 60 62 64 66 68 70 72 74 76
25.0
24.5
24.0
23.5
23.0
22.5
22.0
21.5
21.0
20.5
20.0
54 56 58 60 62 64 66 68 70 72 74 76

2. MEAT & BACON
(7.0%: 3rd: B)

Quantities purchased rose (in 1963 prices) from £20.4 *per capita* in 1954 to £23.5 *per capita* in 1962; there has been little change since. The price relative fell secularly – about 10% over the period – though there have been a number of interruptions, none of which seem to have had much impact on demand. Once again, both models rely on the income response; both give the good a positive elasticity and both use falling time trends to explain the slow-down in purchases from 1962–70. There is little to choose between the models for this category though both leave a good deal unexplained. The price of substitutes might possibly be an important variable here.

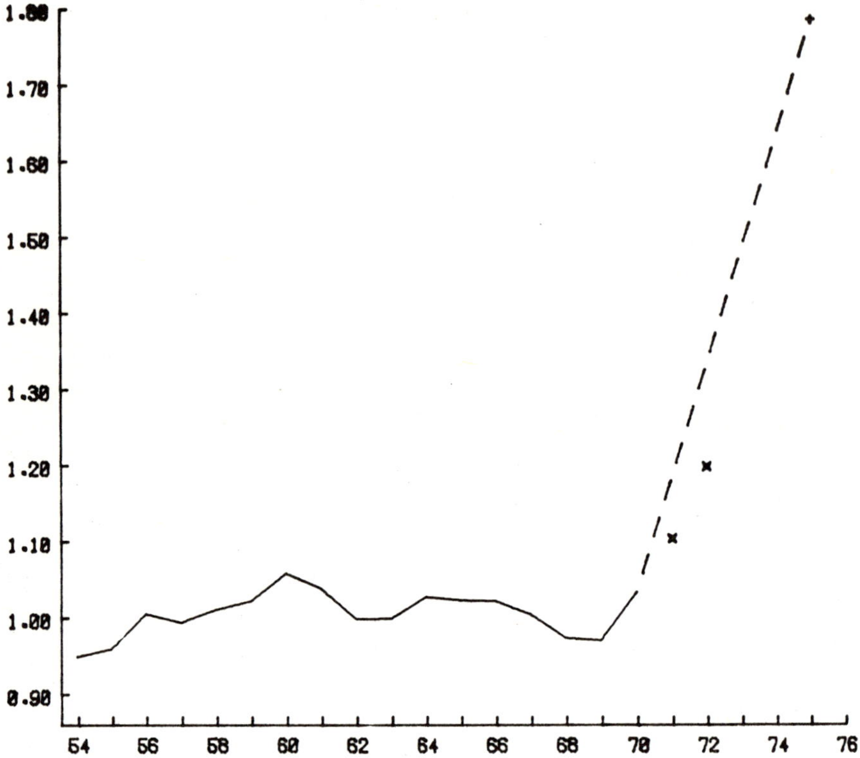
1.80
1.70
1.60
1.50
1.40
1.30
1.20
1.10
1.00
0.90
54
56
58
60
62
64
66
68
70
72
74
76
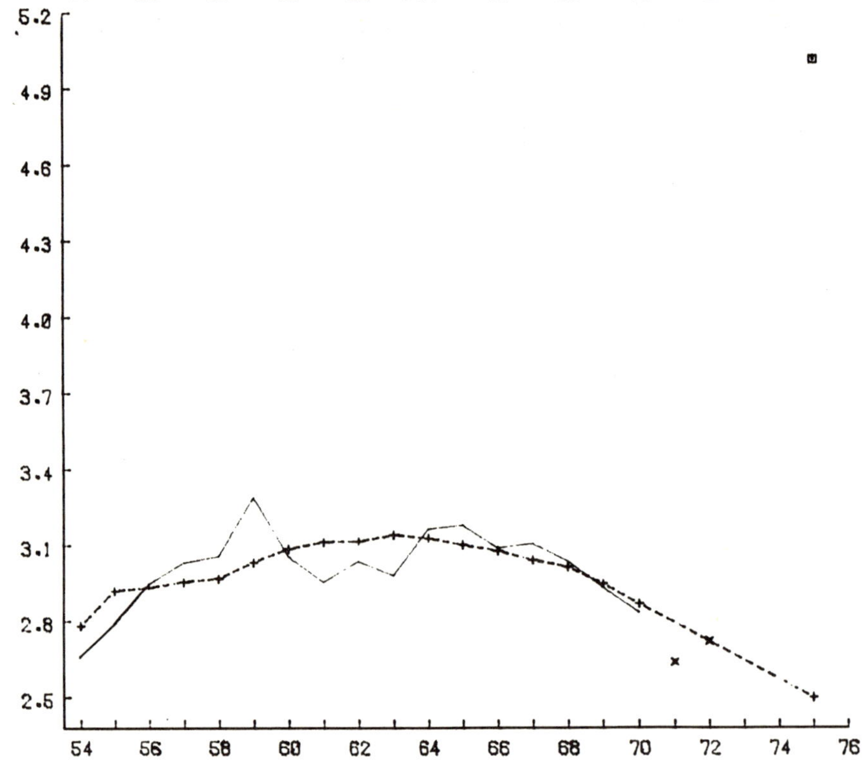
5.2
4.9
4.6
4.3
4.0
3.7
3.4
3.1
2.8
2.5
54
56
58
60
62
64
66
68
70
72
74
76

3. FISH
(0.9%: 31st: B)

This is a small but volatile category. The price relative, like the quantity purchased, has no discernible trend, though one of the peaks in the price coincides with a dip in expenditure. This is not true of all however and the LLS can pick up some explanatory power by allowing the price term to be perverse in the early part of the period and normal in the late part. Pigou's Law prevents the LES from attempting any such explanation and, in this context, this is probably an advantage. Even so, in the absence of any explanatory power of income, expenditure on fish remains largely unexplained.

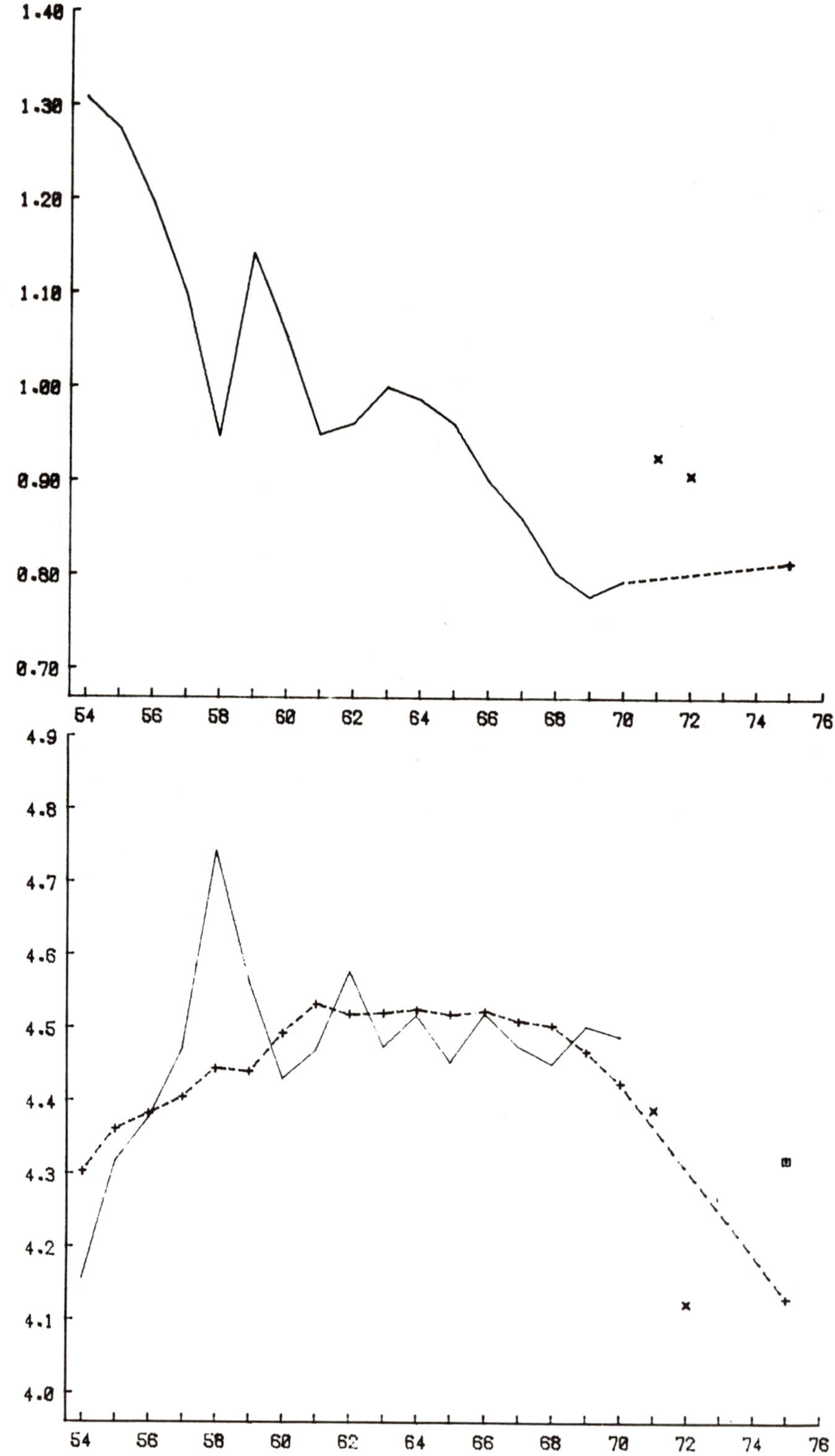

1.40
1.30
1.20
1.10
1.00
0.90
0.80
0.70
54
56
58
60
62
64
66
68
70
72
74
76
4.9
4.8
4.7
4.6
4.5
4.4
4.3
4.2
4.1
4.0
54
56
58
60
62
64
66
68
70
72
74
76

4. OILS & FATS
(1.3%: 27th: B)

Butter is included in this category rather than in dairy produce. After a rise in purchases of some 15% from 1954 to 1958, the series has zig-zagged without any apparent trend. The commodities in this group were rationed and price controlled before 1954 and the surge in demand in the four years after was almost certainly due to decontrol and to the simultaneous sharp drop in price. However, fluctuations in price after 1958 seem to have had little effect on demand; possibly this may indicate that the increase in the early years owed more to the increased availability of supplies than to the drop in price which accompanied this. In these circumstances it is not surprising that the more flexible LLS has considerable advantages though its explanation is open to doubt. Price is allowed a strong influence to start with but this is eradicated later by a large time trend; the combination of this with a negative income elasticity explains the relative stability after 1958. This is not an explanation one would be happy about using to predict the future and the LES, though fitting less well, may be preferred for its rather more honest confession of ignorance. Thus, Pigou's Law though rejected, seems to play a useful role in preventing a foolish explanation.

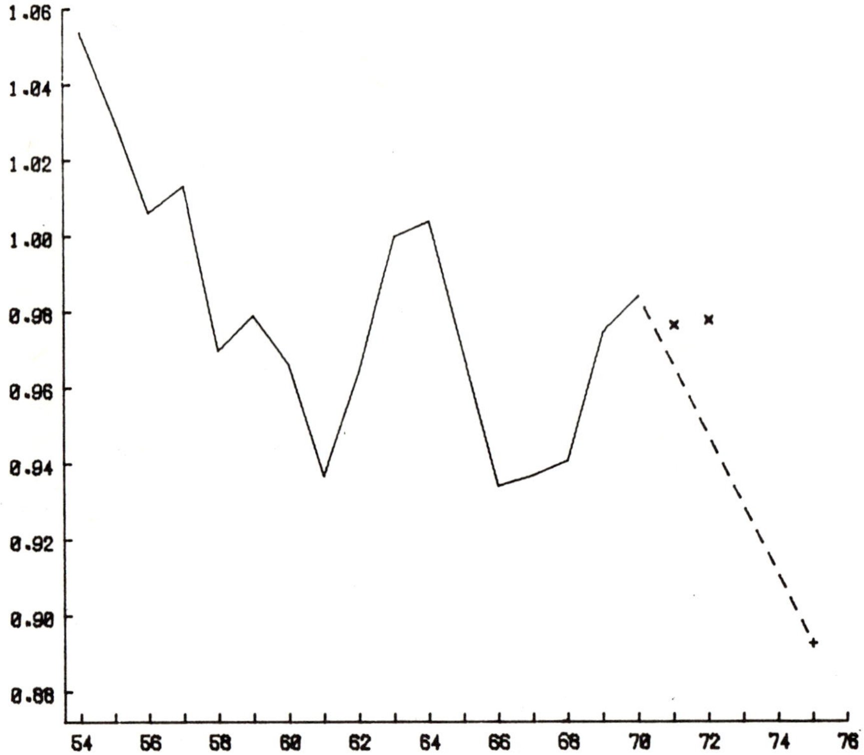
1.06
1.04
1.02
1.00
0.98
0.96
0.94
0.92
0.90
0.88
54 56 58 60 62 64 66 68 70 72 74 76

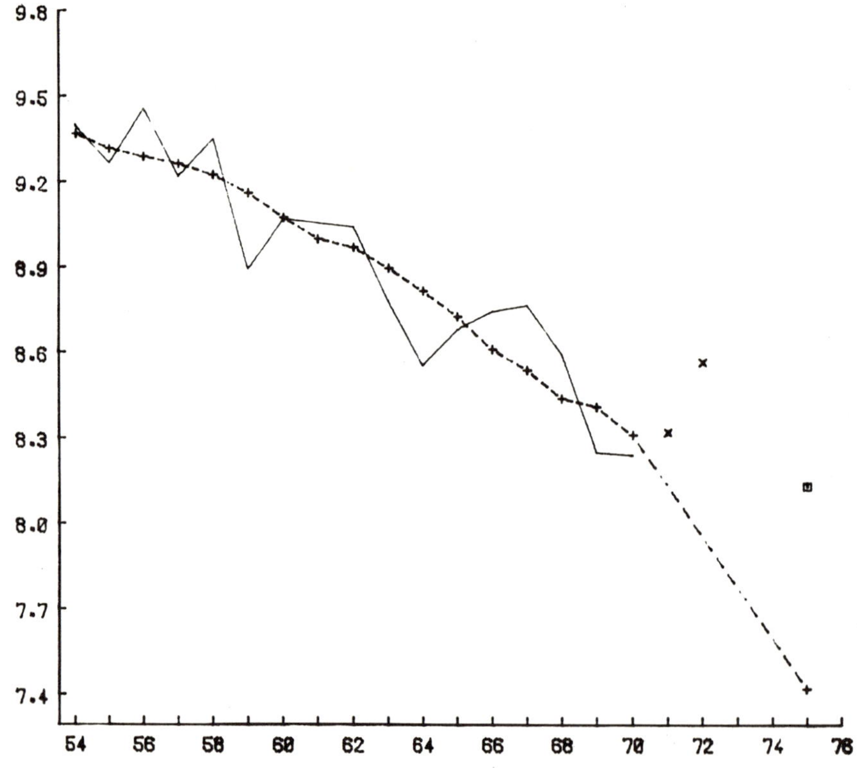
9.8
9.5
9.2
8.9
8.6
8.3
8.0
7.7
7.4
54 56 58 60 62 64 66 68 70 72 74 76

5. SUGAR, PRESERVES & CONFECTIONERY (2.6%: 14th: B)

Purchases have a falling trend, from £(1963)9.4 *per capita* in 1954 to £(1963)8.2 in 1970, with a strong cyclical element which seems explicable in terms of variations in relative prices. This is an excellent example of the combination of circumstances with which the LES is least equipped to deal and the LLS gives a much superior equation. Since the price of the good is rising much less rapidly than average, supernumerary income divided by price is rising quite rapidly; the LES then needs a negative income elasticity to explain the secular decline and thus imposes a *positive* (though small) price elasticity. Thus, the LES prediction, in order to get the trend right, actually moves slightly *contracyclically* while the LLS can explain the cycles as well as the trend by combining slight inferiority with a significant negative price elasticity.

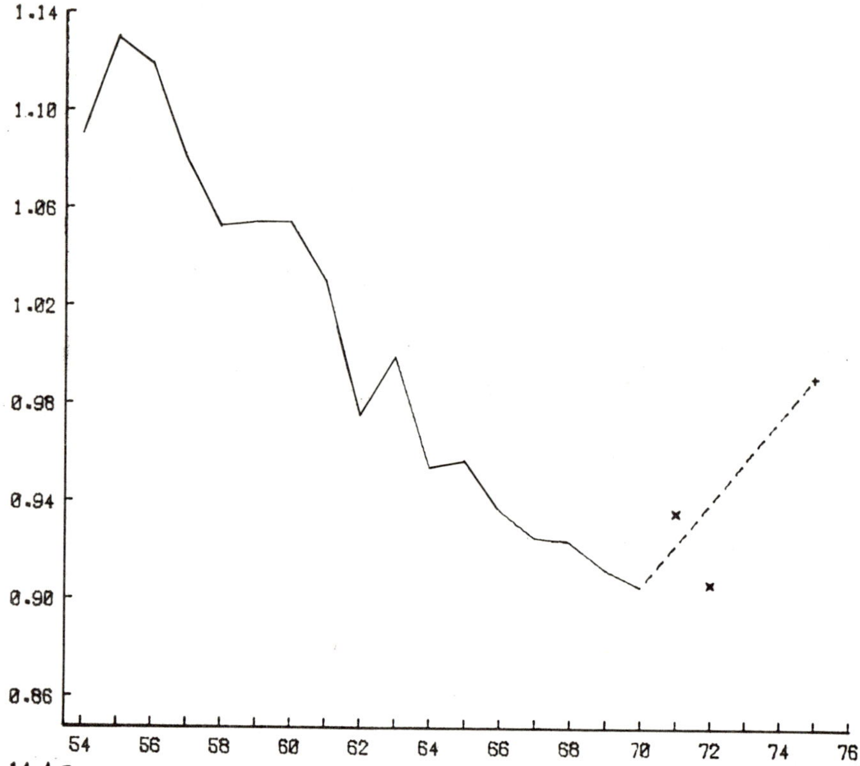
1.14
1.10
1.06
1.02
0.98
0.94
0.90
0.86
54
56
58
60
62
64
66
68
70
72
74
76

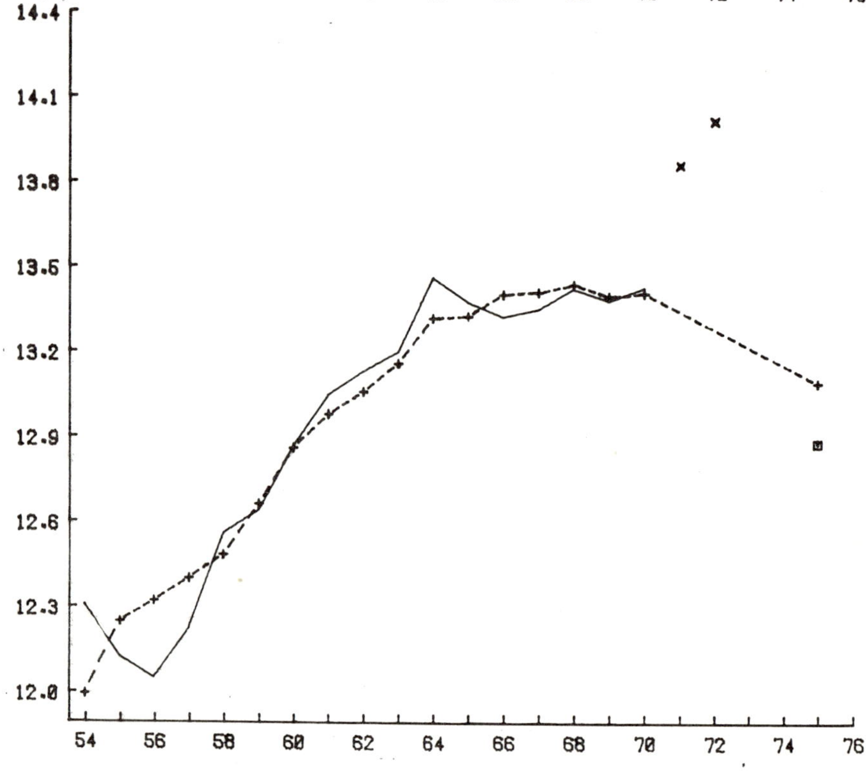
14.4
14.1
13.8
13.5
13.2
12.9
12.6
12.3
12.0
54
56
58
60
62
64
66
68
70
72
74
76

6. DAIRY PRODUCE
(3.8%: 8th: B)

This category includes milk, eggs and cheese but excludes butter. Behaviour is quite well explained by income and prices with a moderate income elasticity around 3/4 and a price elasticity around −1/3. This configuration is about right for the LES. Thus, in contrast to the previous group, there is a good deal of conformity between the systems, and the LES gives a satisfactory estimating equation dealing with the effects of price and income with economy.

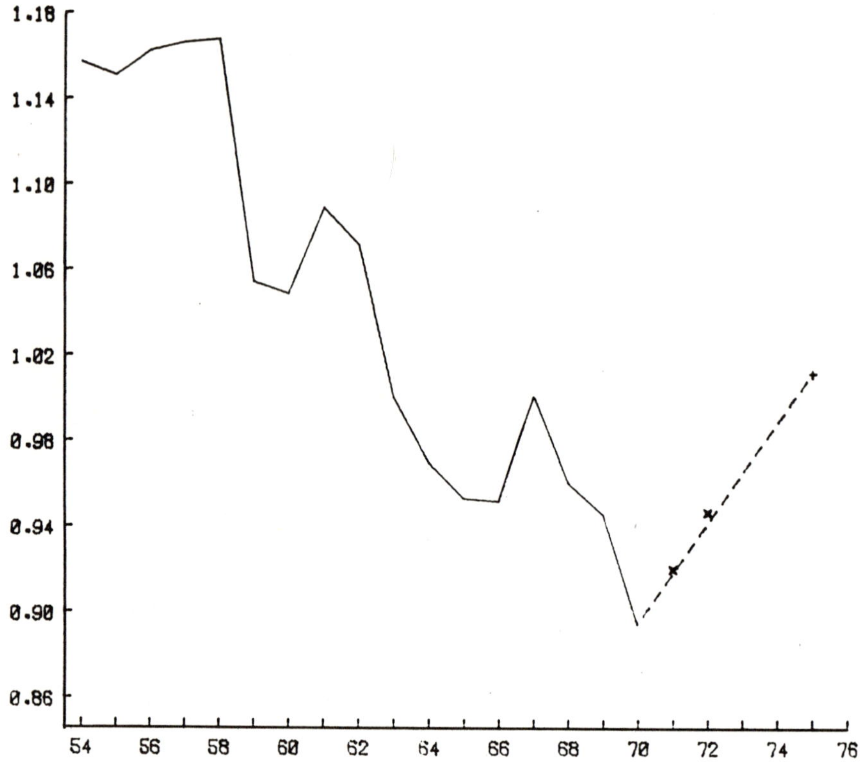

1.18
1.14
1.10
1.06
1.02
0.98
0.94
0.90
0.86
54
56
58
60
62
64
66
68
70
72
74
76

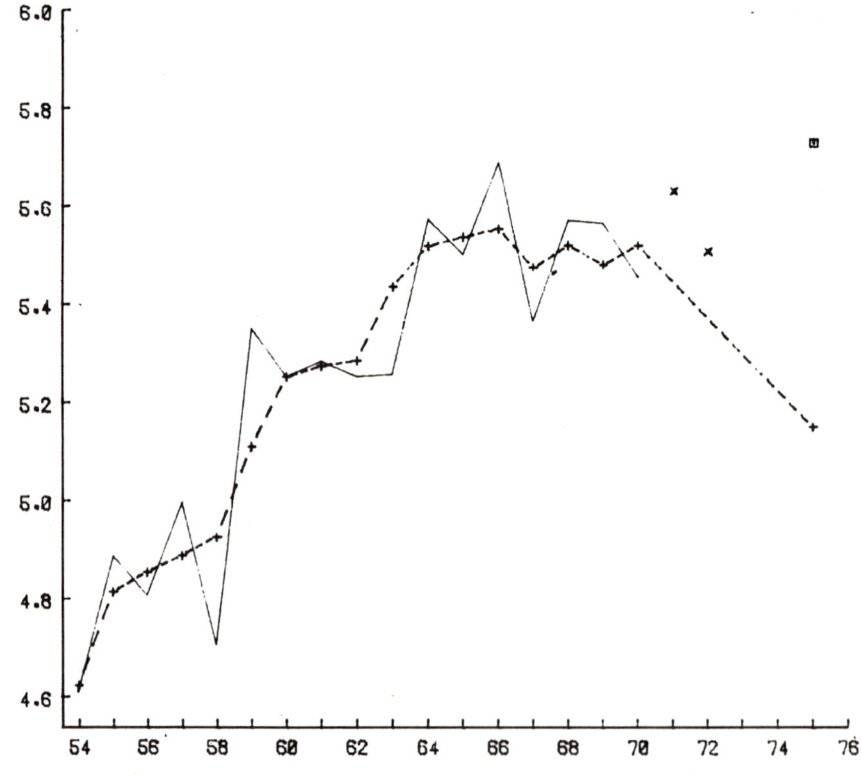

6.0
5.8
5.6
5.4
5.2
5.0
4.8
4.6
54
56
58
60
62
64
66
68
70
72
74
76

7. FRUIT
(1.6%: 23rd: B)

The trend of purchases is upwards, from £(1963)4.6 to 5.5, though a number of sharp dips and peaks appear which can only partially be explained by prices. Once again there is a fair measure of agreement between the systems, though the operation of Pigou's Law prevents the LES making more than a token attempt to fit the year to year cycle, though the longer 4–5 year cycle is much better approximated. Nevertheless though the LLS is better, the LES is not entirely unsatisfactory.

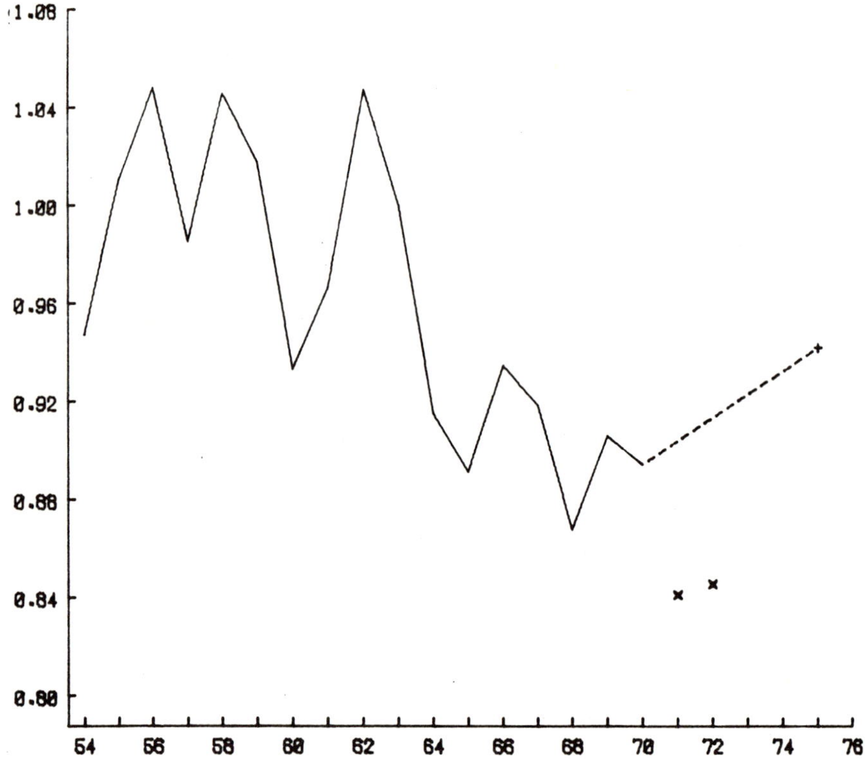

1.08
1.04
1.00
0.96
0.92
0.88
0.84
0.80
54
56
58
60
62
64
66
68
70
72
74
76

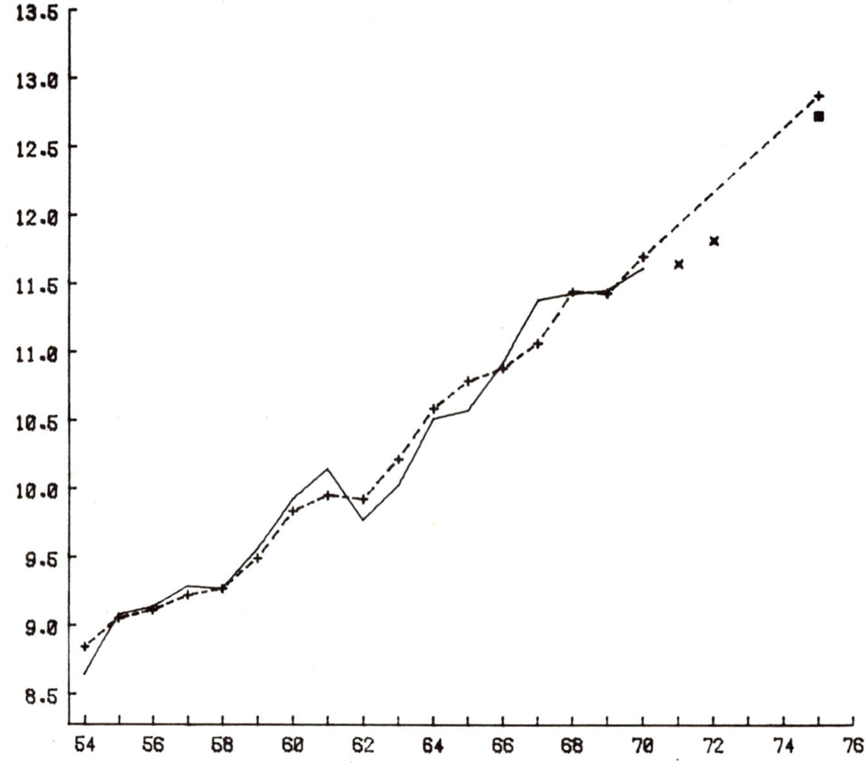

13.5
13.0
12.5
12.0
11.5
11.0
10.5
10.0
9.5
9.0
8.5
54
56
58
60
62
64
66
68
70
72
74
76

8. POTATOES & VEGETABLES
(2.9%: 11th: B)

In spite of quite violent year to year fluctuations in the price-relative, there are only minor fluctuations about a rising trend £(1963)8.6–11.6 in the purchases bought and the price term plays a minor though significant role in the explanation. Once again the configuration of elasticities is right for the LES and purchases are reasonably well characterized by both models. The relatively high income elasticity (nearly 1 in Table 2) is presumably a consequence of the presence of such items as frozen vegetables and does not suggest that potatoes are luxury goods!

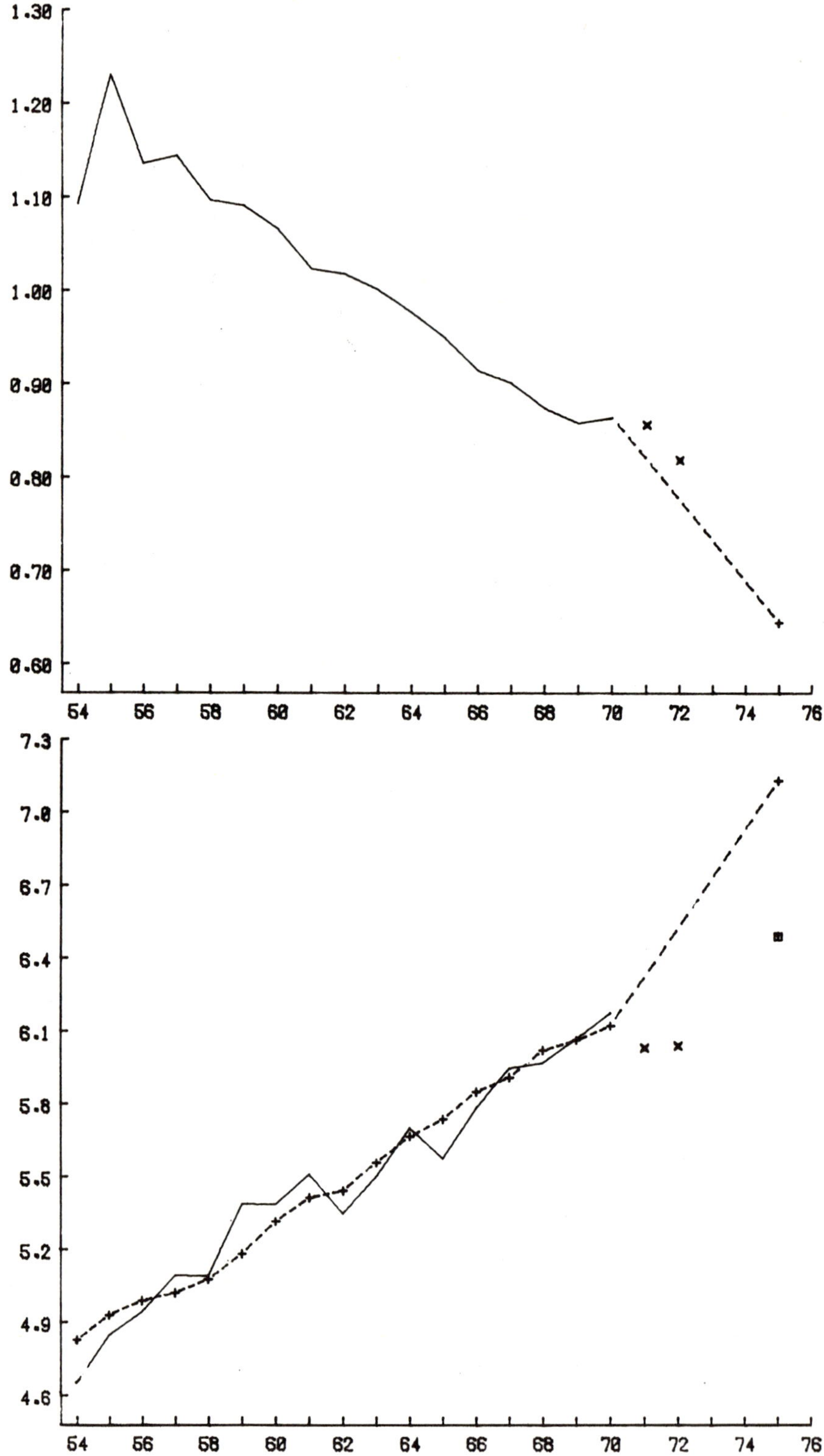
1.30
1.20
1.10
1.00
0.90
0.80
0.70
0.60
54
56
58
60
62
64
66
68
70
72
74
76
7.3
7.0
6.7
6.4
6.1
5.8
5.5
5.2
4.9
4.6
54
56
58
60
62
64
66
68
70
72
74
76

9. NON-ALCOHOLIC BEVERAGES
(1.6%: 22nd: B)

The yearly sawtooth pattern about a rising trend which is observable in the purchases series has no counterpart in the price-relative which, after 1955, is a smooth falling trend. Indeed this is so smooth that the LLS prefers it to income as an explanation of the upward trend; the LLS thus makes income insignificant while giving the price-relative a significant coefficient with a positive time trend. In these circumstances, the LES, with its more pedestrian explanation, is to be preferred.

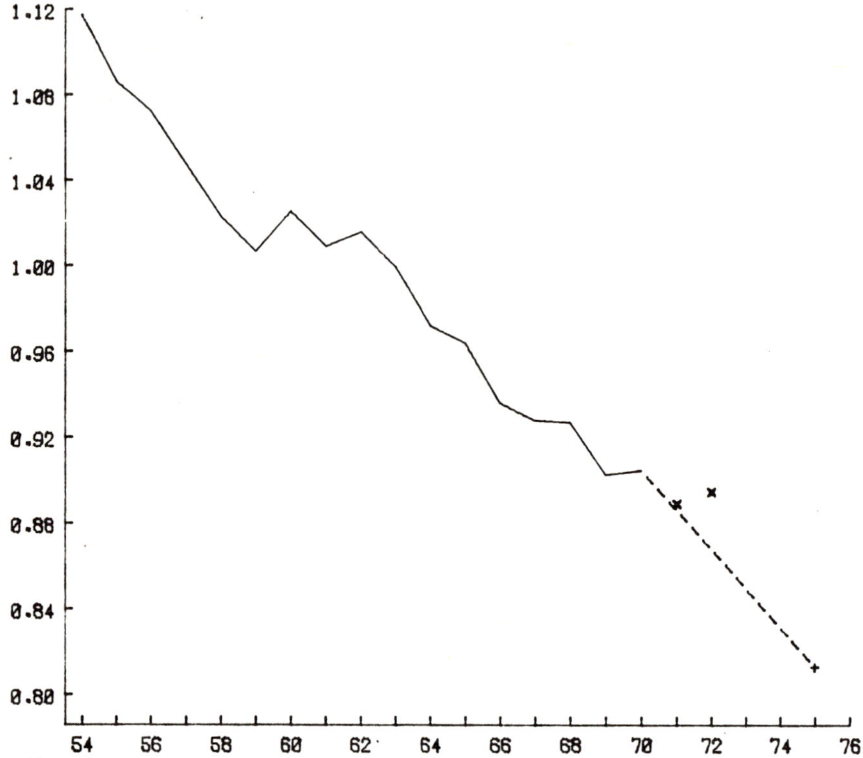
1.12
1.08
1.04
1.00
0.96
0.92
0.88
0.84
0.80
54
56
58
60
62
64
66
68
70
72
74
76

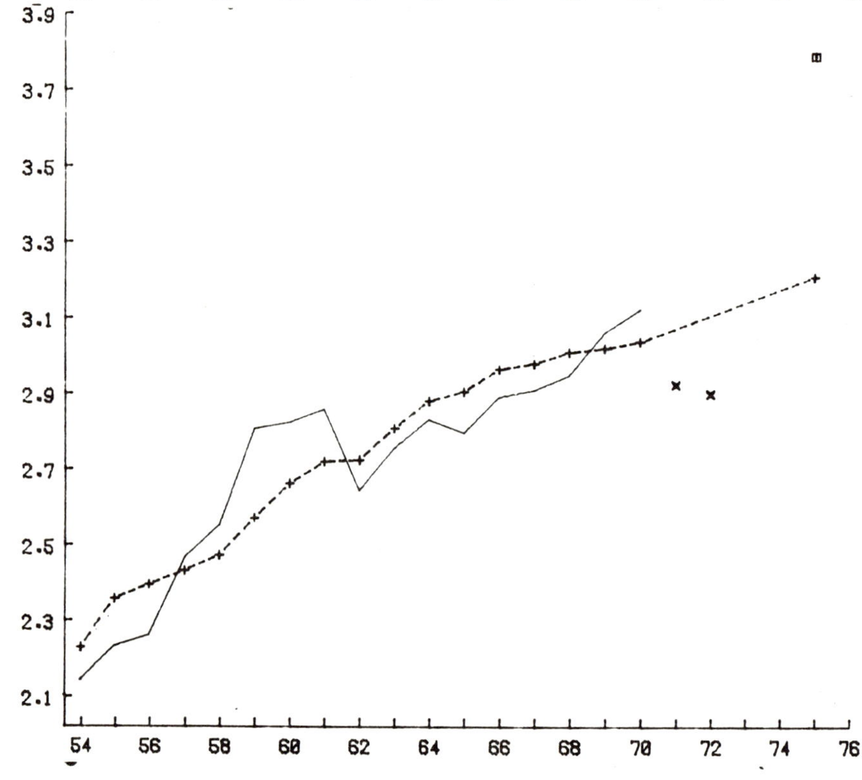
3.9
3.7
3.5
3.3
3.1
2.9
2.7
2.5
2.3
2.1
54
56
58
60
62
64
66
68
70
72
74
76

10. OTHER MANUFACTURED FOOD
(0.8%: 34th: B)

This small category includes "infant and invalid foods, welfare foods (for example, cod liver oil, orange juice) and miscellaneous manufactured foods, of which the most important are ice cream, canned soups, and condiments" Maurice (1968), p. 160. Neither of the models predicts these expenditures very well and there seems to be a wide range of configurations of price and income elasticities between which there is little to choose. There is probably rather more price elasticity than the LES can allow but on the other hand, the unrestricted LLS uses relative-price with a time trend to do all the work leaving income only an insignificant negative role. The imposition of Pigou's Law renders the good income elastic, both in the LES and the restricted LLS. Since this is intuitively plausible the LES is probably to be preferred. The important role of the time trend in the LLS is another reason for selecting the LES for forecasting purposes: by 1974 the price term in the LLS becomes perverse.

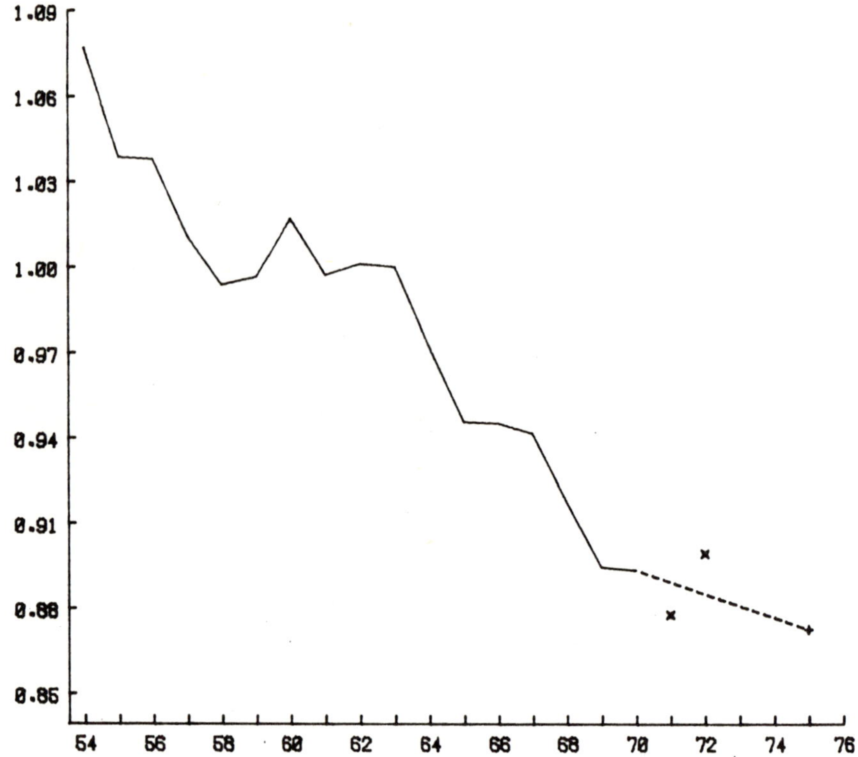
1.09
1.06
1.03
1.00
0.97
0.94
0.91
0.88
0.85
54
56
58
60
62
64
66
68
70
72
74
76

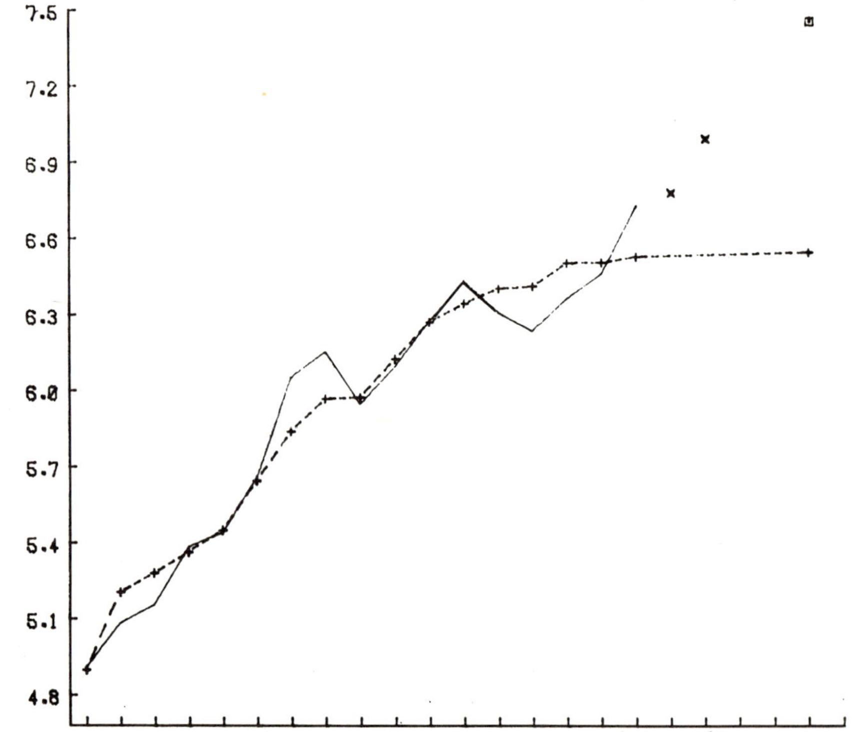
7.5
7.2
6.9
6.6
6.3
6.0
5.7
5.4
5.1
4.8
54
56
58
60
62
64
66
68
70
72
74
76

11. FOOTWEAR
(1.7%: 20th: B)

This is the first of the goods considered where some degree of durability may cause problems for a static interpretation. Certainly neither income nor price seem to be able to explain satisfactorily the 4–5 year cycle in purchases though that this should be due to stock effects in a good with such limited durability is implausible. In the LLS model, only the time trend on the price is significant, and once again this causes the elasticity to become perverse, this time within the sample period. Pigou's Law is not rejected for values of ϕ in the LES range and so the LES is once again to be preferred. The equation does not however fit very well and relies too much on a negative time trend; a more sophisticated model could almost certainly do better here.

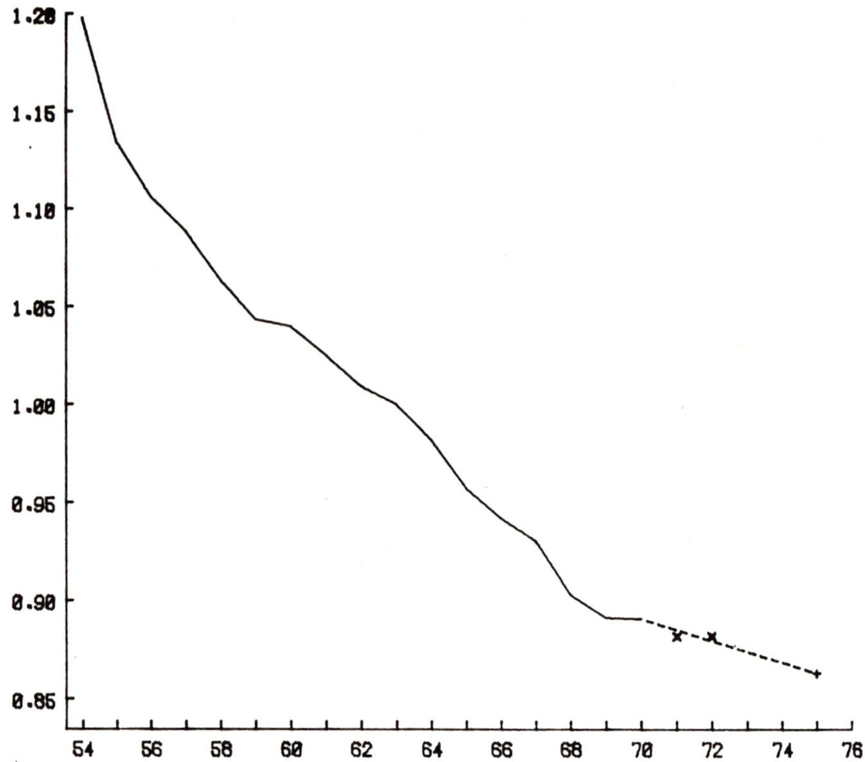
1.20
1.15
1.10
1.05
1.00
0.95
0.90
0.85
54
56
58
60
62
64
66
68
70
72
74
76

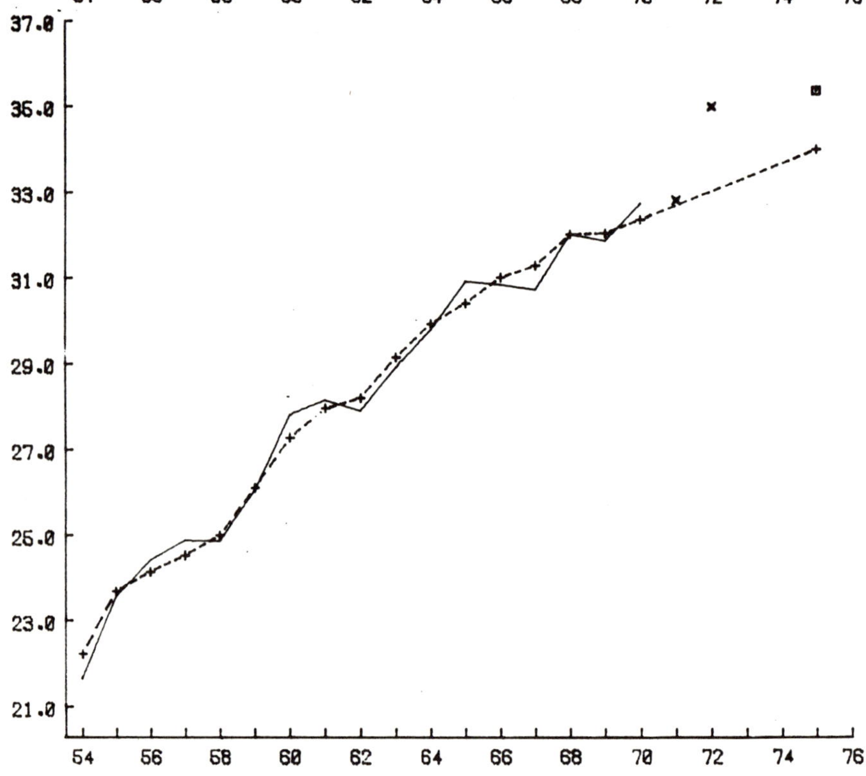
37.0
35.0
33.0
31.0
29.0
27.0
25.0
23.0
21.0
54
56
58
60
62
64
66
68
70
72
74
76

12. CLOTHING
(8.3%: 2nd: B)

Again this category has a 4–5 year cycle which can probably be explained by fluctuations in income though not by total expenditure. Neither is a static model appropriate since what seems to be needed is a higher short- than long-run elasticity. Apart from not predicting the full amplitude of the cycle, both models perform well and are consistent with one another.

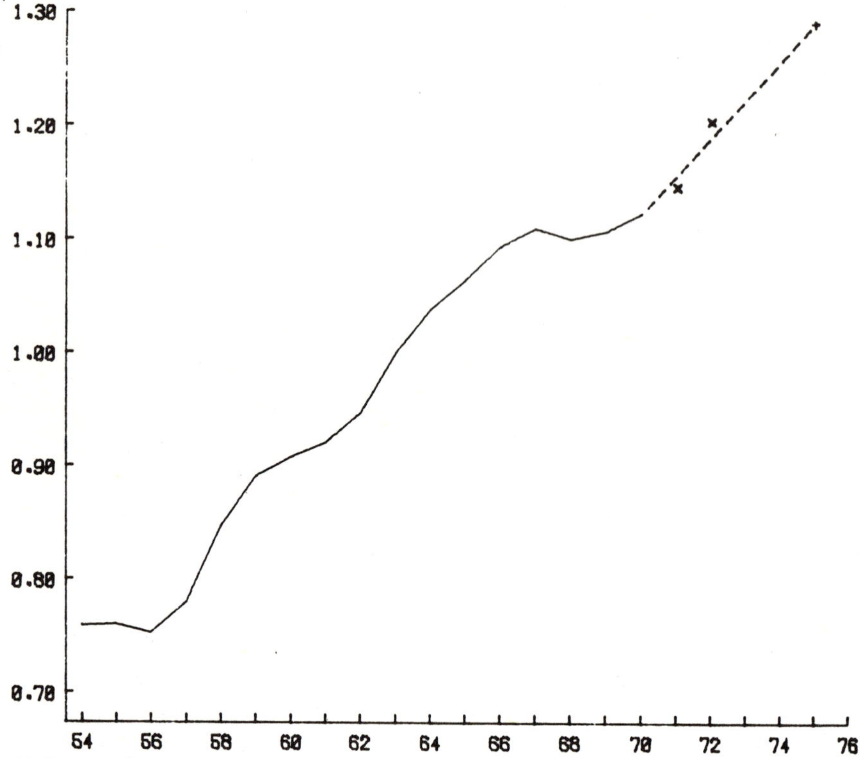

1.30
1.20
1.10
1.00
0.90
0.80
0.70
54
56
58
60
62
64
66
68
70
72
74
76

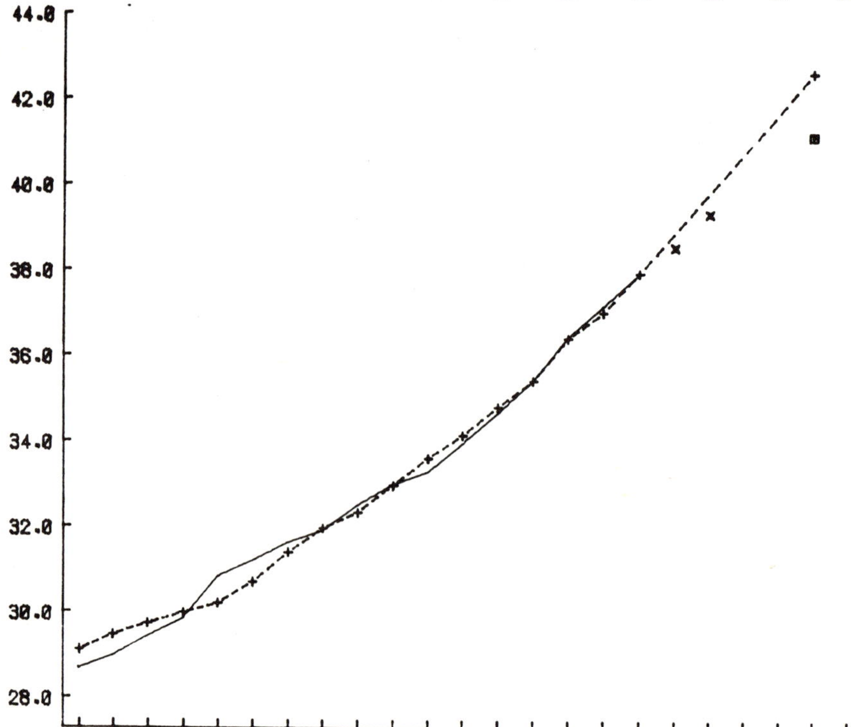

44.0
42.0
40.0
38.0
36.0
34.0
32.0
30.0
28.0
54
56
58
60
62
64
66
68
70
72
74
76

13. RENTS, RATES, & WATER CHARGES (9.1%: 1st: B)

This group includes a large imputed element, the rent of home-owners occupying their own houses and this part, like the others, can only be expected to be weakly sensitive to current prices and incomes. The LLS is rather unsatisfactory in that the time trend on income is doing most of the work; the inferiority is only technical since the positive time trend more than offsets the negative effect of the coefficient multiplying rising income. Pigou's Law is rejected in this case, mainly because the large increase in the price-relative over the period seems to have had little effect; thus any price elasticity under the law must be small and this adversely affects the income term. In the LES the deviations from actual are mainly due to the imposition of a *higher* price elasticity than actually exists; the system dutifully predicts a fall in expenditure when the relative price is high, this being necessitated by the need to get the trend right and thus to have a positive income elasticity. This is one of the relatively few examples where the LES *overstates* the price elasticity relative to the income elasticity; in more cases the opposite is true. Indeed, since this is the largest of the categories considered, it may be largely responsible for the low value of ϕ imposed for the system, and thus for the general underestimation of price elasticities within the LES. For the commodity itself, neither model is really satisfactory given its relative lack of variation about trend: perhaps the best way to predict it would be in the same way that it is constructed, i.e. by forecasting home occupation and then imputing rents.

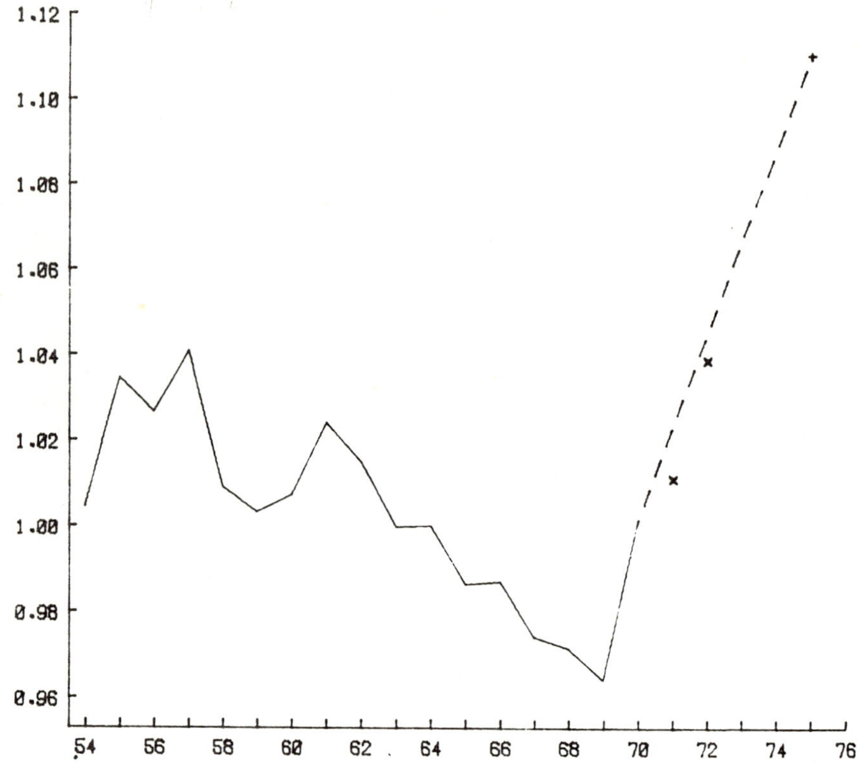
1.12
1.10
1.08
1.06
1.04
1.02
1.00
0.98
0.96
54
56
58
60
62
64
66
68
70
72
74
76

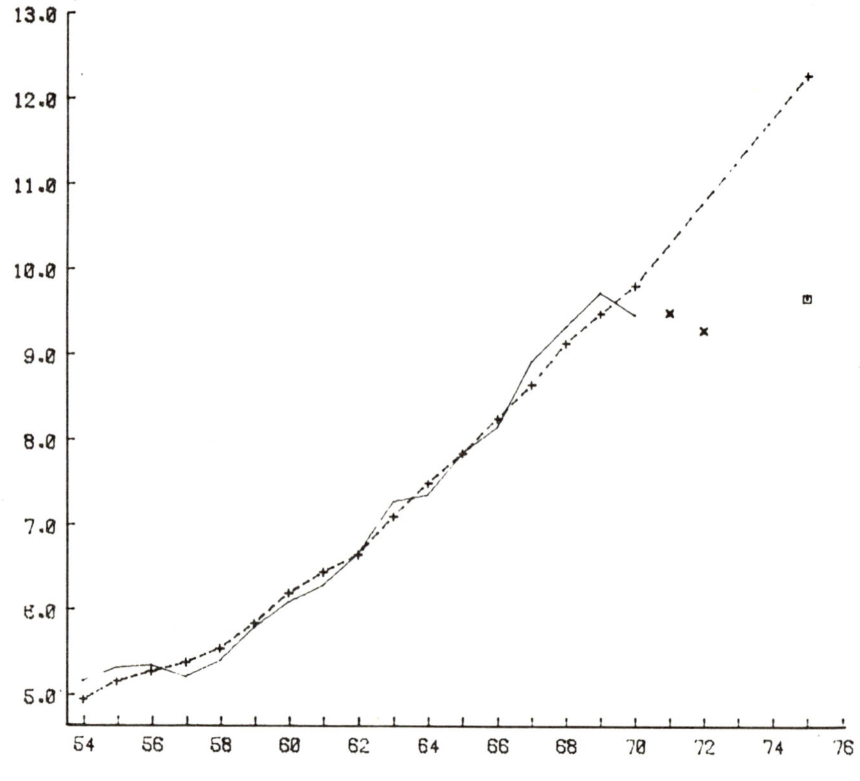
13.0
12.0
11.0
10.0
9.0
8.0
7.0
6.0
5.0
54
56
58
60
62
64
66
68
70
72
74
76

14. MAINTENANCE, REPAIRS & IMPROVEMENTS (2.0%: 17th: C)

There are particular difficulties about the measurement of this category; in particular, it is not clear that the price index relates directly to the goods purchased, Maurice (1968), p. 164. However, both models give the category a high income elasticity, as would seem appropriate for a category which has a high investment content and which is concentrated in the better-off part of the population. Though the price terms in the unrestricted LLS are strongly significant and although Pigou's Law is rejected largely because of this, it would not necessarily be wise to accept the LLS equation as the better one. The large time trend in the price elasticity allows the price effects to be perverse in the early years of the period and will eventually result in an implausibly large impact for relative prices in the future. These figures may well be anomalous due to difficulties over the price index and again it might be best to take the quite satisfactory alternative yielded by the LES.

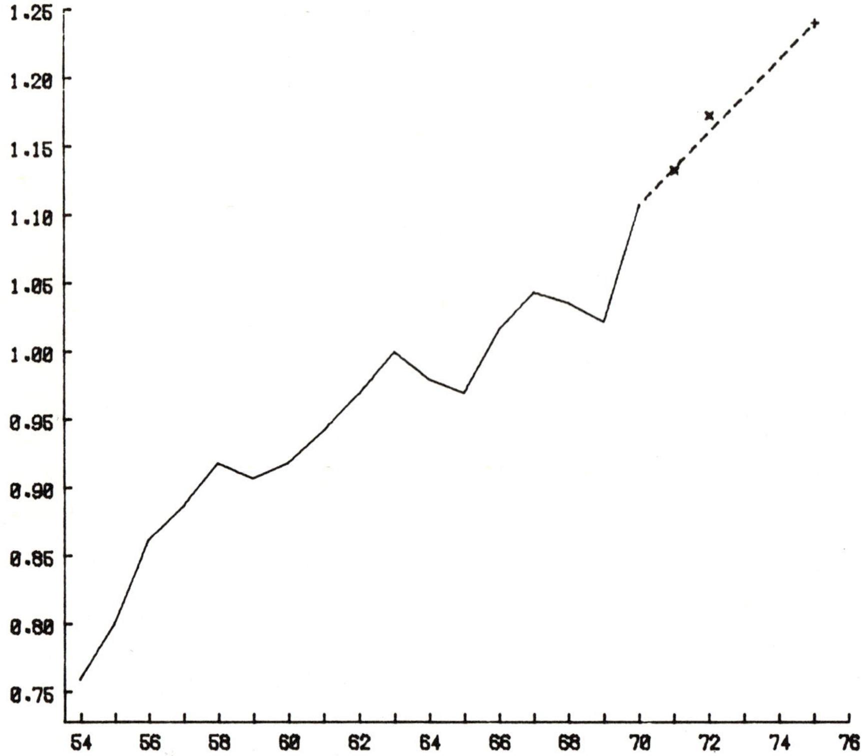
1.25
1.20
1.15
1.10
1.05
1.00
0.95
0.90
0.85
0.80
0.75
54
56
58
60
62
64
66
68
70
72
74
76

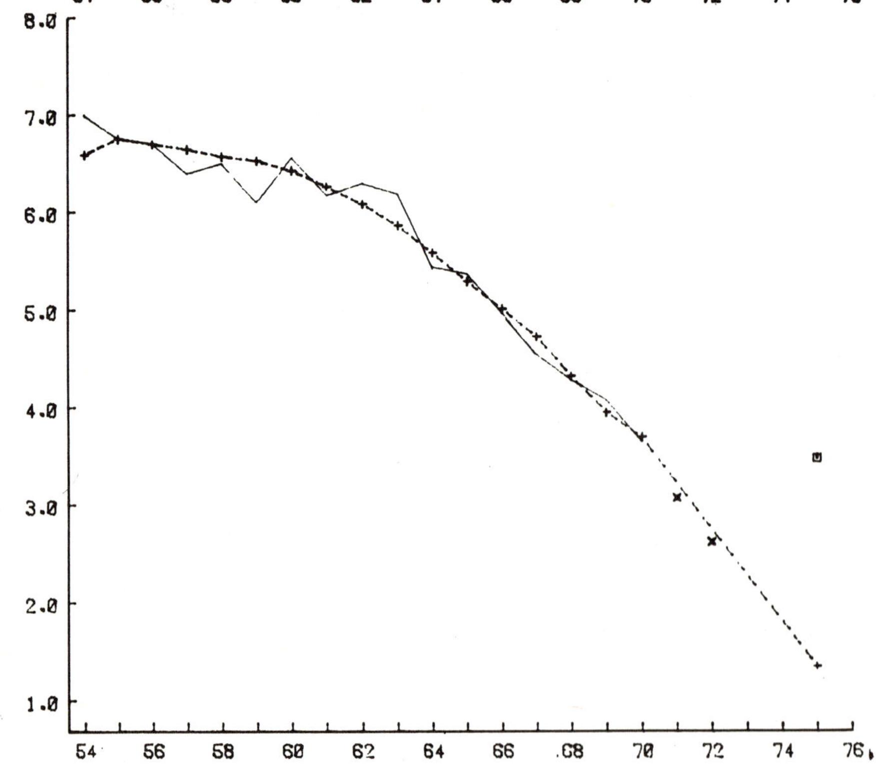
8.0
7.0
6.0
5.0
4.0
3.0
2.0
1.0
54
56
58
60
62
64
66
68
70
72
74
76

15. COAL (EXCLUDING COKE)
(1.6%: 24th: A)

Purchases of this fuel have declined by almost 50% between 1954 and 1970 and one might imagine this to be a classic example of an inferior good. The LES does in fact give this result though the LLS gives a positive income elasticity throughout. Once again however this is largely technical since this elasticity has a negative time trend allowing purchases to fall over time. The price response in the LLS is less than satisfactory since it is perverse for much of the period and is dominated by the time trend. The application of Pigou's Law to the LLS makes the good inferior but causes a significant deterioration in fit. The difficulty here may lie in the presence of lags caused by the presence of fuel consuming durable goods – heating systems etc. – which are specific to an individual fuel. Price and income would then have an important influence on purchases through their influence on the scrapping and purchase of these durables and this would tend to operate with sizeable lags. This difficulty applies to all of the fuels and unless it can be satisfactorily modelled these four equations are likely to be difficult. In this case, the LES is also unsatisfactory since, apart from the Pigou Law difficulties, the size of the negative *b*-coefficient leads to negative purchases in the foreseeable future.

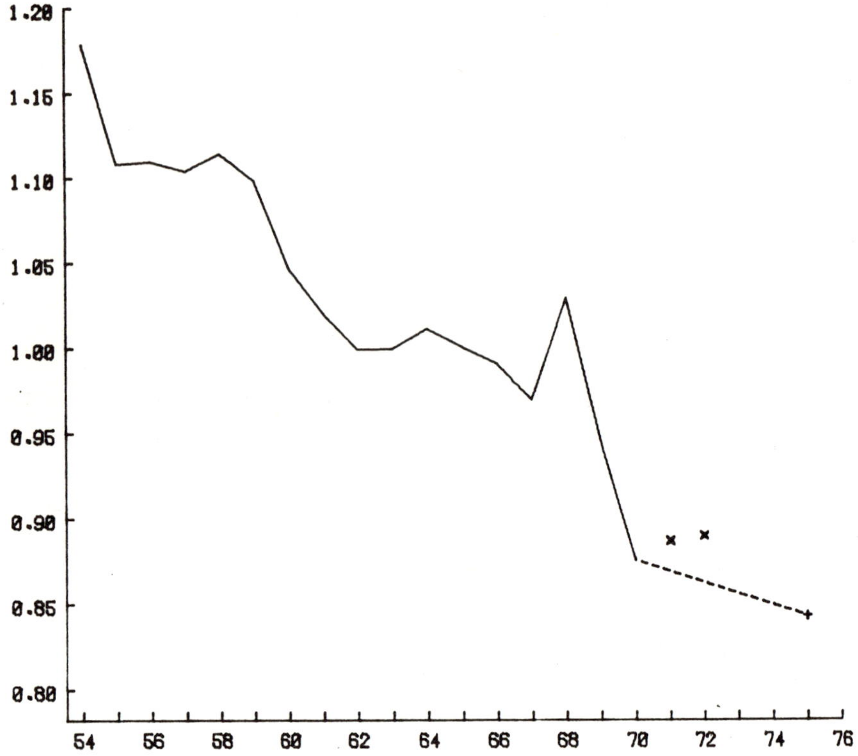

1.20
1.15
1.10
1.05
1.00
0.95
0.90
0.85
0.80
54 56 58 60 62 64 66 68 70 72 74 76

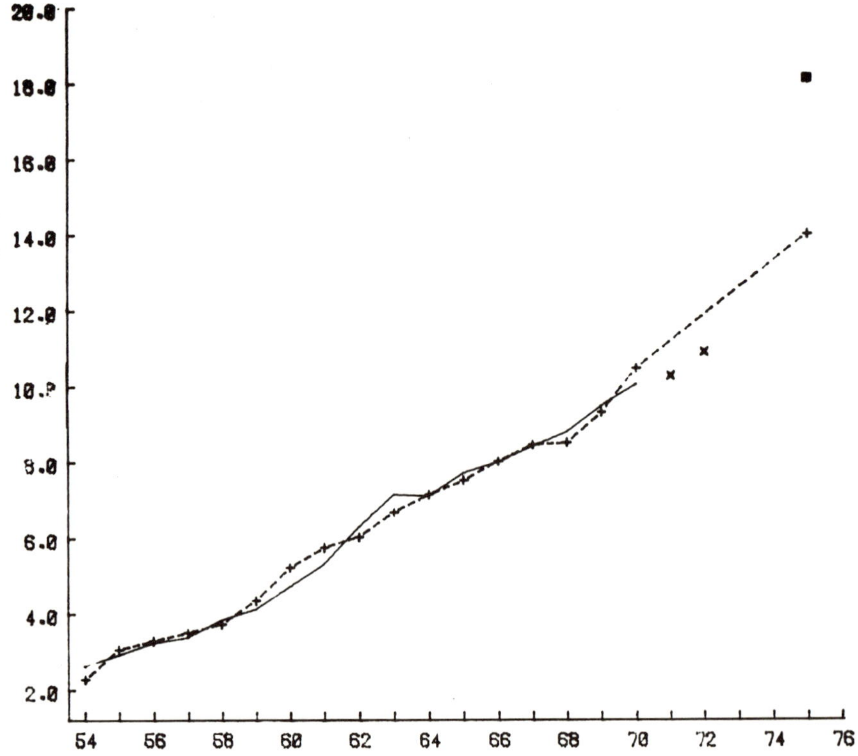

20.0
18.0
16.0
14.0
12.0
10.0
8.0
6.0
4.0
2.0
54 56 58 60 62 64 66 68 70 72 74 76

16. ELECTRICITY
(1.7%: 19th: A)

Once again there are the difficulties as outlined above although this time both models fit rather well. As in category 11, the LES, for some of the period at least, seems to be *overstating* the price elasticity. The LLS, which has a similar income elasticity, once again has a very large time trend in the price elasticity which would make one hesitant about using it to forecast too far. The LES is thus probably the safer of the two models.

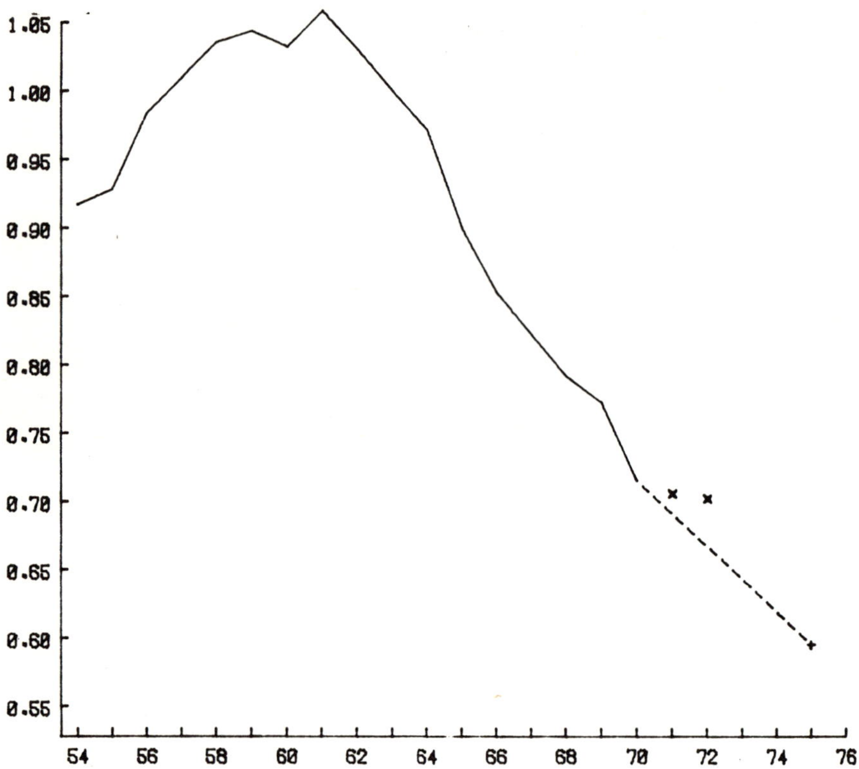
1.05
1.00
0.95
0.90
0.85
0.80
0.75
0.70
0.65
0.60
0.55
54
56
58
60
62
64
66
68
70
72
74
76

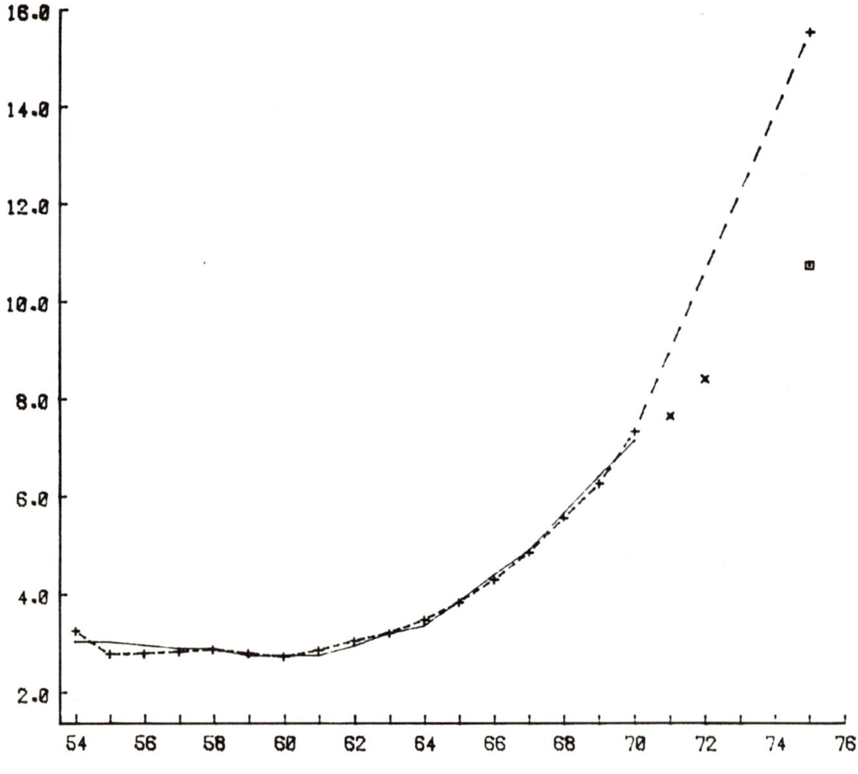
16.0
14.0
12.0
10.0
8.0
6.0
4.0
2.0
54
56
58
60
62
64
66
68
70
72
74
76

17. GAS
(1.0%: 29th: A)

This group is really two commodities rather than one since North Sea gas has been replacing town gas since the early 1960's. This new fuel is cheaper than the old so that the price relative rises from 1954 to 1961, falling steadily thereafter. Conversely, purchases, largely static till 1961, accelerate rapidly thereafter and while much of this acceleration must have been due to the decreasing price, some also must have been caused by the substitution of the cleaner and generally superior new fuel. In these circumstances it is not surprising that both models make heavy use of time trends, indeed, the LES gives an income elasticity rising from −5.1 in 1954 to 1.6 in 1970. The LLS is less extreme and makes heavy use of the relative price term which is extremely significant and contrary to Pigou's Law. So that while the LES certainly understates the role of relative prices, the LLS probably overstates it. As to forecasting, it cannot be expected that the factors operating in the sixties will continue in the seventies; the LES will overstate expenditure and the LLS will have too large a price elasticity. This can only be amended by some *a priori* correction since the information for predicting the future does not exist in the sample period.

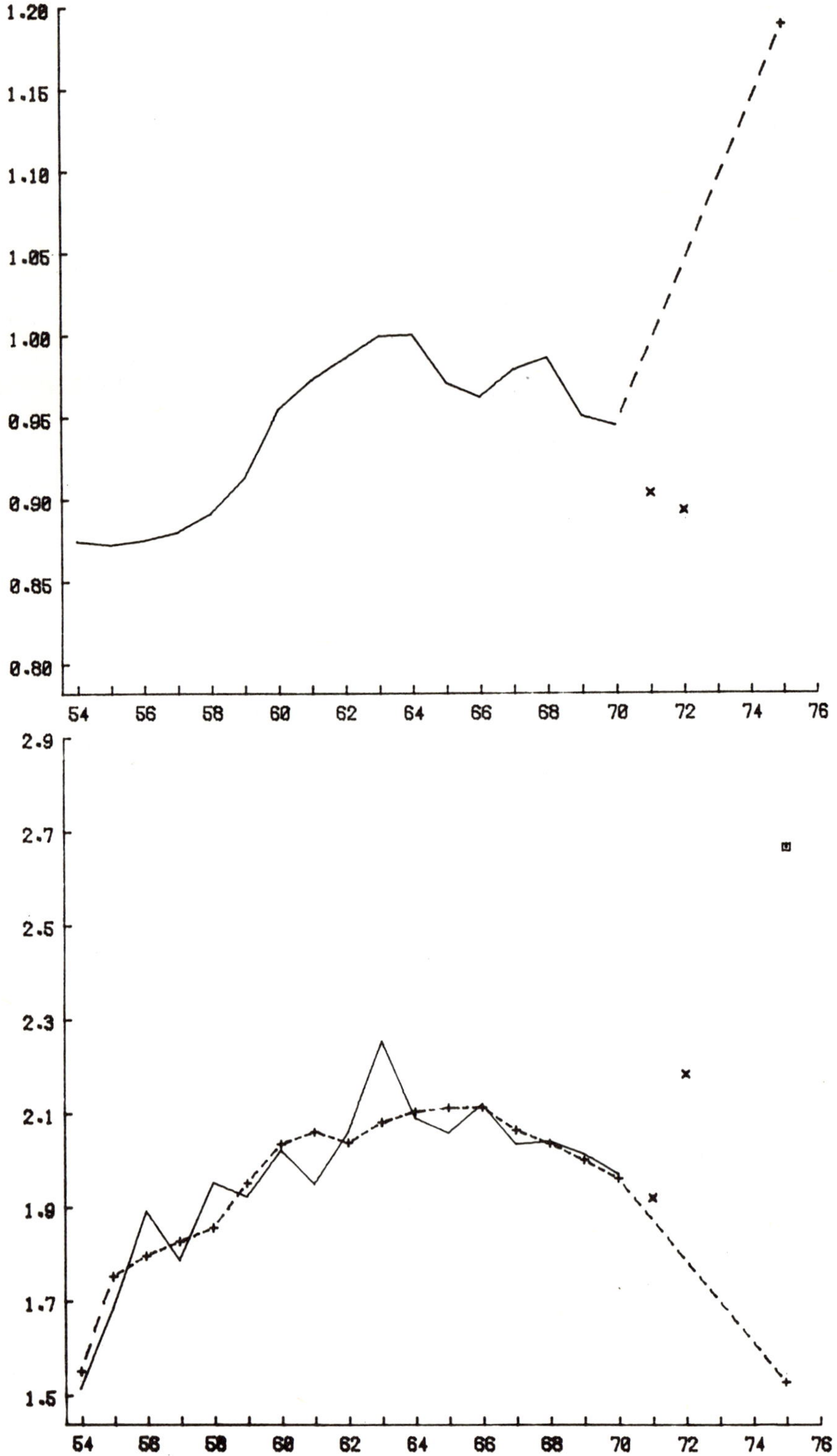

1.20
1.15
1.10
1.05
1.00
0.95
0.90
0.85
0.80
54
56
58
60
62
64
66
68
70
72
74
76
2.9
2.7
2.5
2.3
2.1
1.9
1.7
1.5
54
56
58
60
62
64
66
68
70
72
74
76

18. OTHER FUELS
(0.5%: 37th: B)

This is the smallest of the categories and includes expenditure on fuel oil, paraffin, liquid gases, coke, and wood. A rising trend till 1963 is reversed thereafter, in spite of a similar movement in the price-relative and this is presumably due to the inroads made by the expansion in the use of natural gas. Both models make the good normal but with a declining elasticity; both are plausible though neither fits very well. The prices of other fuels, especially of gas, may have an important influence here.

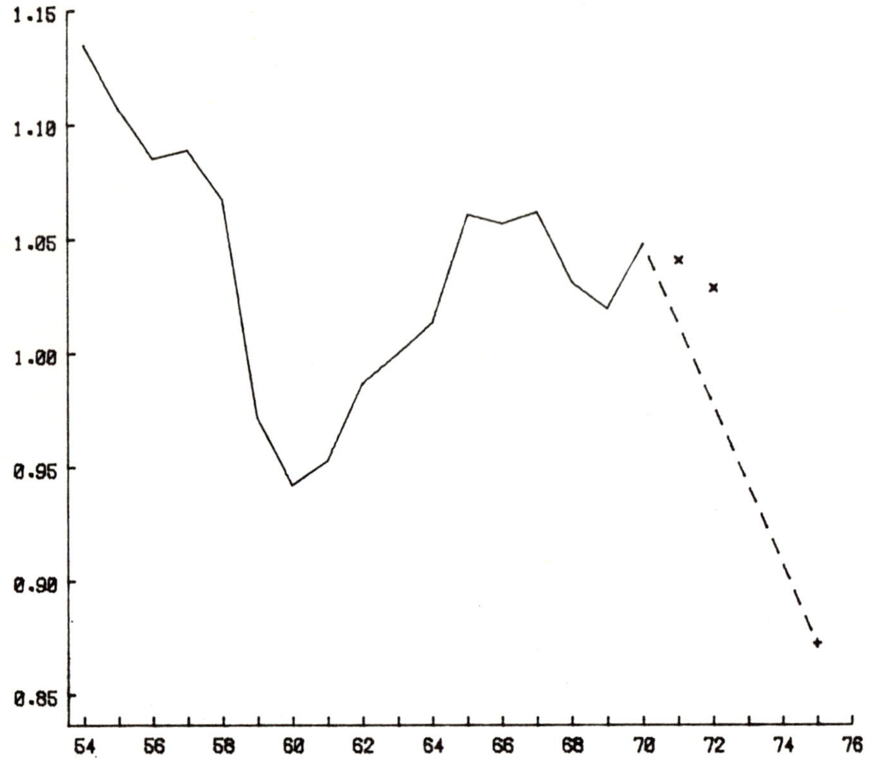
1.15
1.10
1.05
1.00
0.95
0.90
0.85
54
56
58
60
62
64
66
68
70
72
74
76

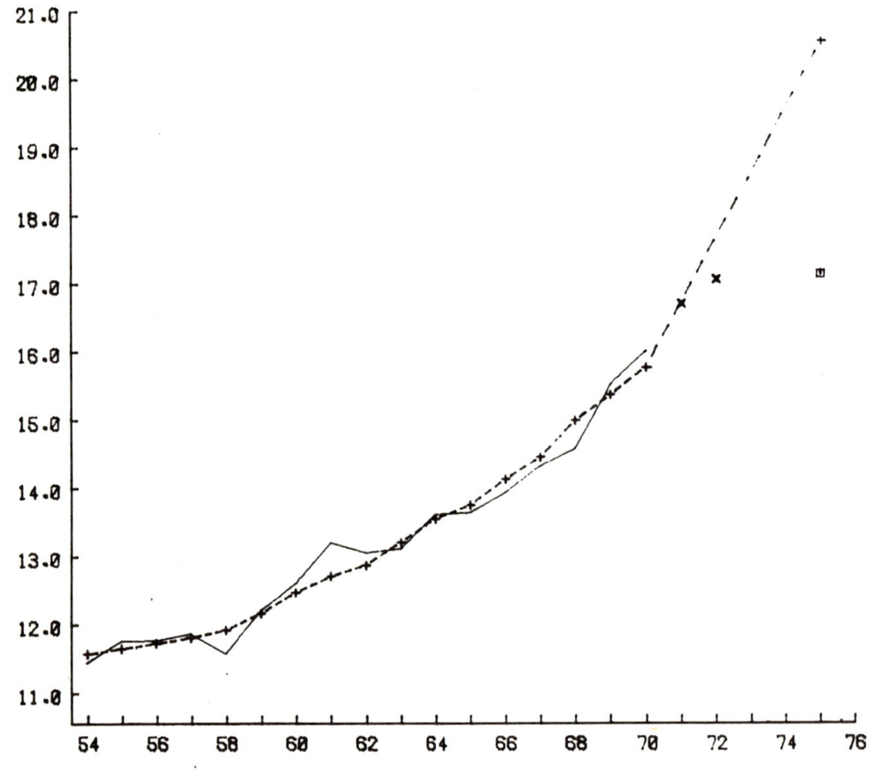
21.0
20.0
19.0
18.0
17.0
16.0
15.0
14.0
13.0
12.0
11.0
54
56
58
60
62
64
66
68
70
72
74
76

19. BEER
(4.0%: 7th: B)

This relatively large category is not very satisfactorily explained by either model; this is especially evident in the fact that the time trends are so large in all the coefficients that sign reversals within the data period take place in all cases. The LES uses the income term to track through the middle of the series while the LLS makes price do most of the explanation. Neither explanation is a very convincing one.

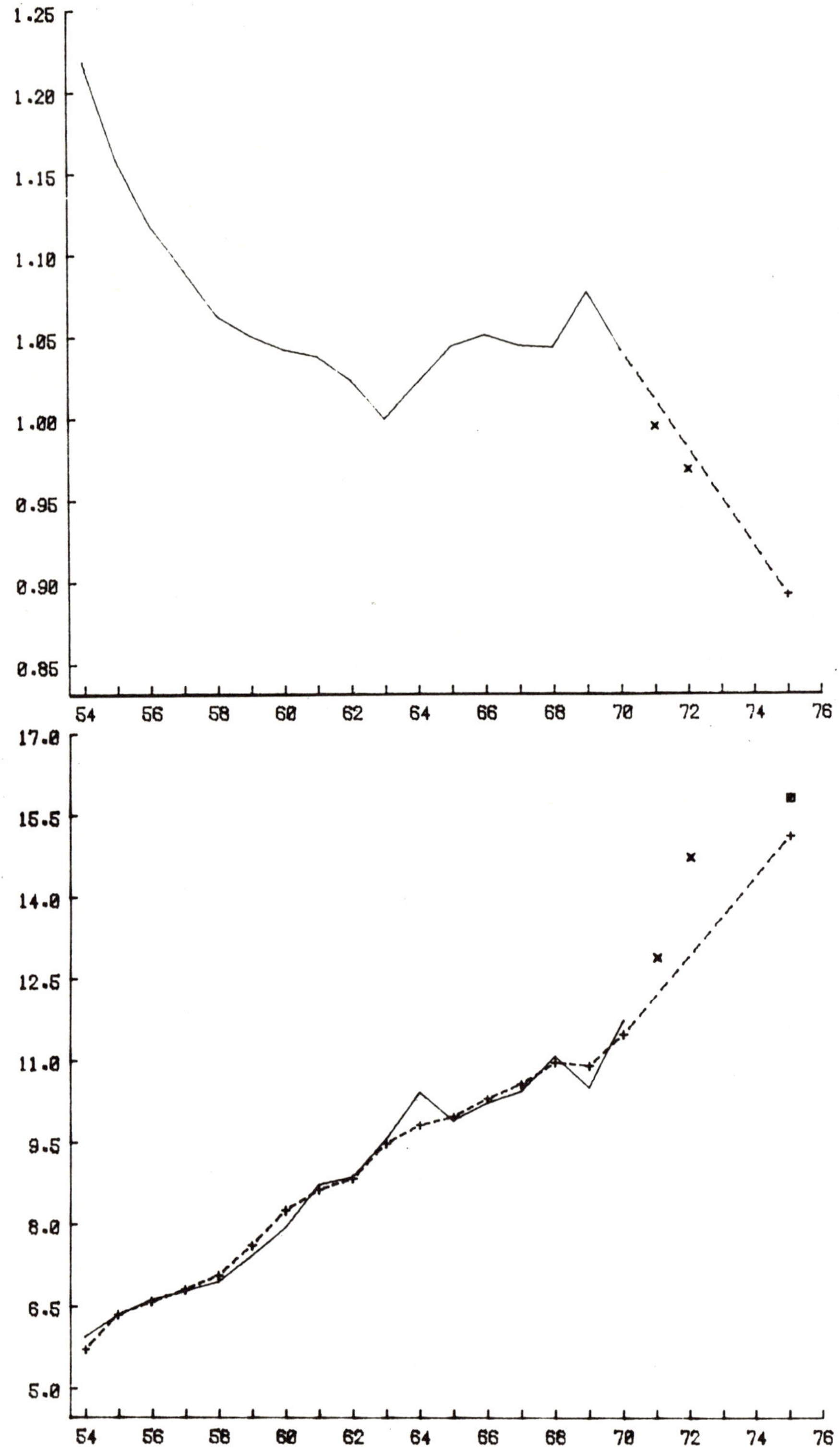

1.25
1.20
1.15
1.10
1.05
1.00
0.95
0.90
0.85
54 56 58 60 62 64 66 68 70 72 74 76
17.0
15.5
14.0
12.5
11.0
9.5
8.0
6.5
5.0
54 56 58 60 62 64 66 68 70 72 74 76

20. WINES & SPIRITS
(2.7%: 13th: B)

This commodity, as is to be expected, is characterized both by high income and price elasticities. In the LLS, these are very well determined and so even the relatively small changes required to accommodate Pigou's Law are unacceptable. Consequently the LLS equation is to be preferred for this category, although there is not a great deal of difference in the outcomes for the two models.

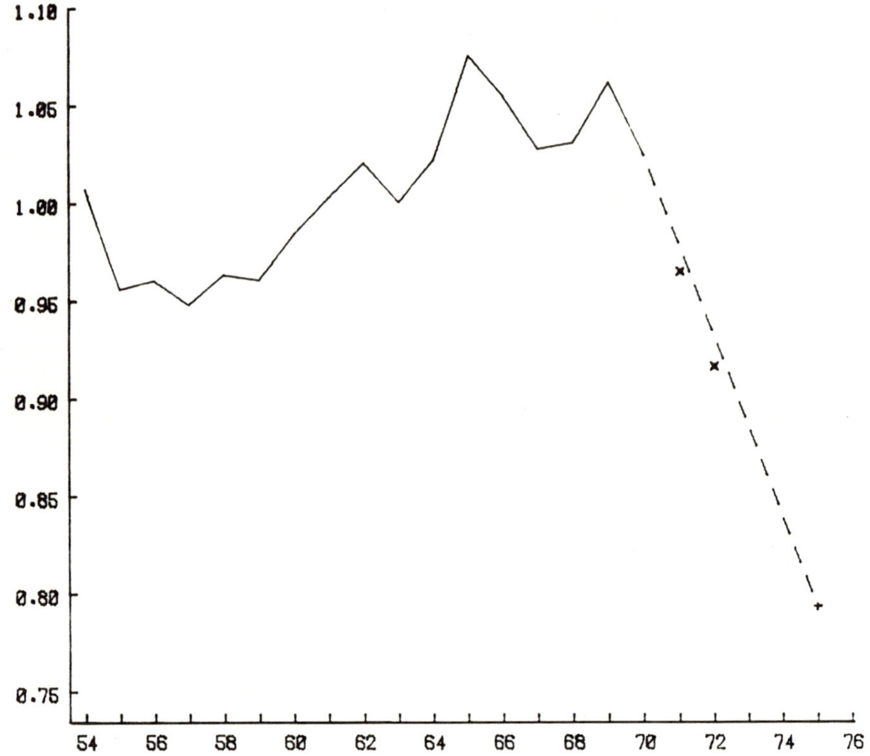

1.10
1.05
1.00
0.95
0.90
0.85
0.80
0.75
54
56
58
60
62
64
66
68
70
72
74
76

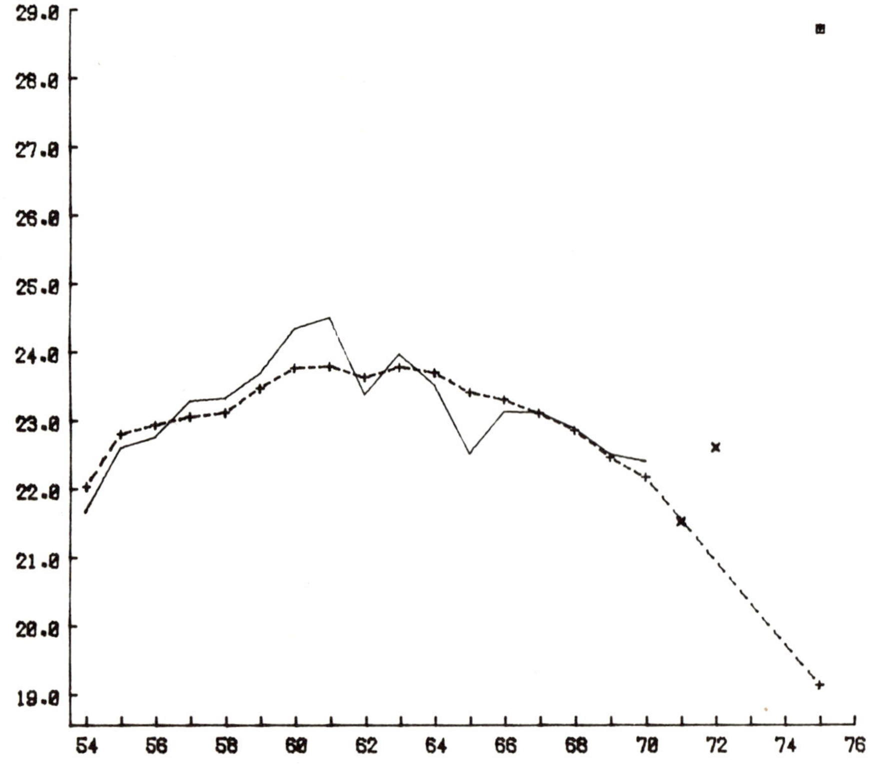

29.0
28.0
27.0
26.0
25.0
24.0
23.0
22.0
21.0
20.0
19.0
54
56
58
60
62
64
66
68
70
72
74
76

21. CIGARETTES & TOBACCO
(6.8%: 4th: A)

This is another category where other influences are of considerable importance; the considerable success of anti-smoking propaganda has induced an inverted U-shape in the series of purchases. The LES explains this by the time trend in the *b*-coefficient, i.e. a change in tastes away from the commodity. This seems reasonably appropriate in the circumstances although linearity almost certainly overstates the long-run effects of the propaganda. The LLS shows evidence of price elasticities not detected by the LES but Pigou's Law is not rejected, largely, it seems, because of the poor fit of the original equation. Considerable care would be needed in the forecasting of this item.

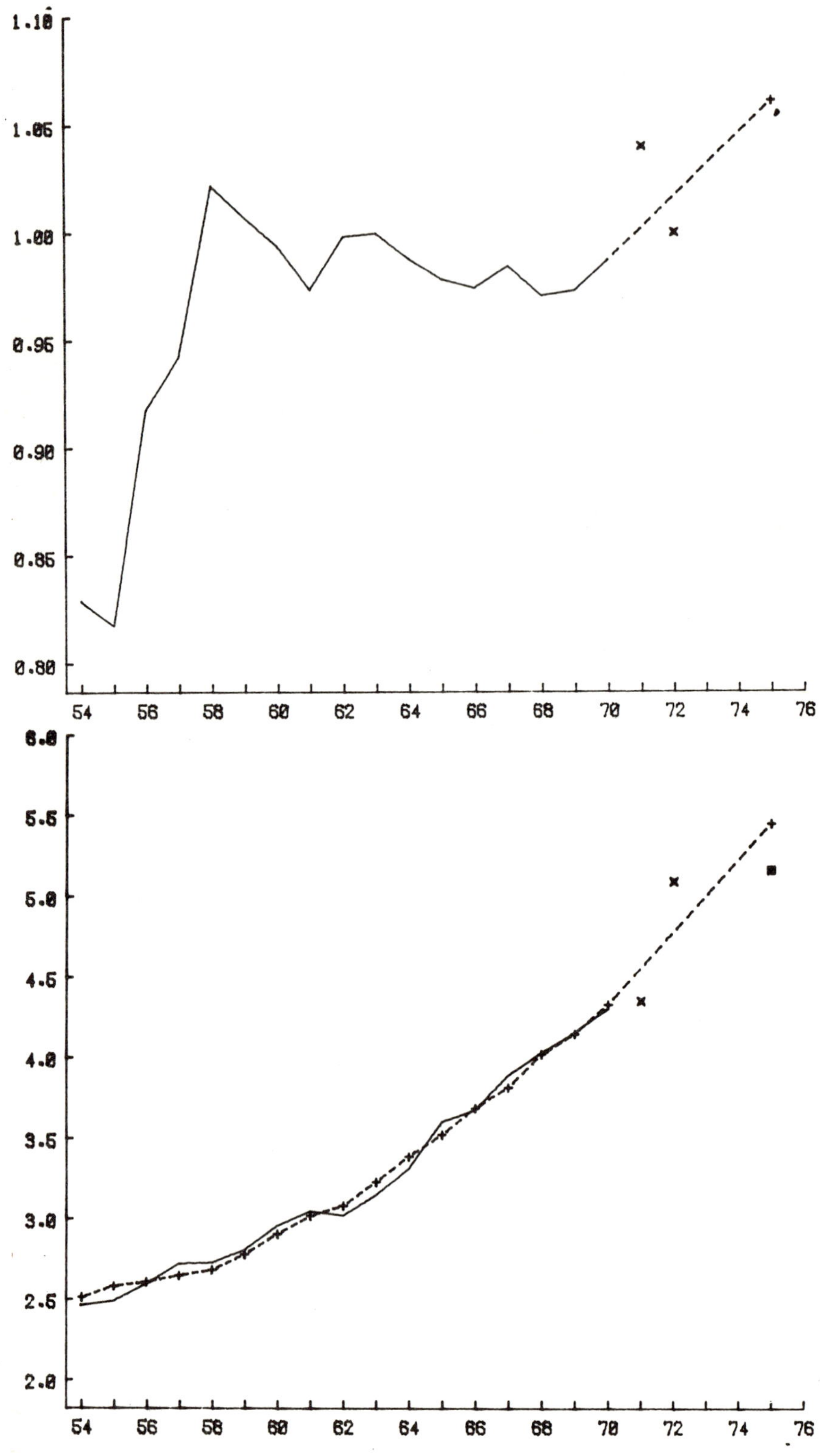

1.10
1.05
1.00
0.95
0.90
0.85
0.80
54
56
58
60
62
64
66
68
70
72
74
76
6.0
5.5
5.0
4.5
4.0
3.5
3.0
2.5
2.0
54
56
58
60
62
64
66
68
70
72
74
76

22. POST & TELEPHONE CHARGES
(0.9%: 30th: A)

Two quite different explanations are given for this category. The price-relative behaves rather oddly, rising by 25% between 1955 and 1958 and declining slowly since and although the large rise seems to have had no effect on purchases, the smaller changes after 1958 can explain some of the subsequent variations. The LLS handles this by using a high and rising price elasticity, the trend effects of this being offset by a negative income elasticity. The LES offers a more conventional, and probably more sensible, explanation. It is hard to see, if the LLS is to be believed, why the price sensitivity should change so dramatically.

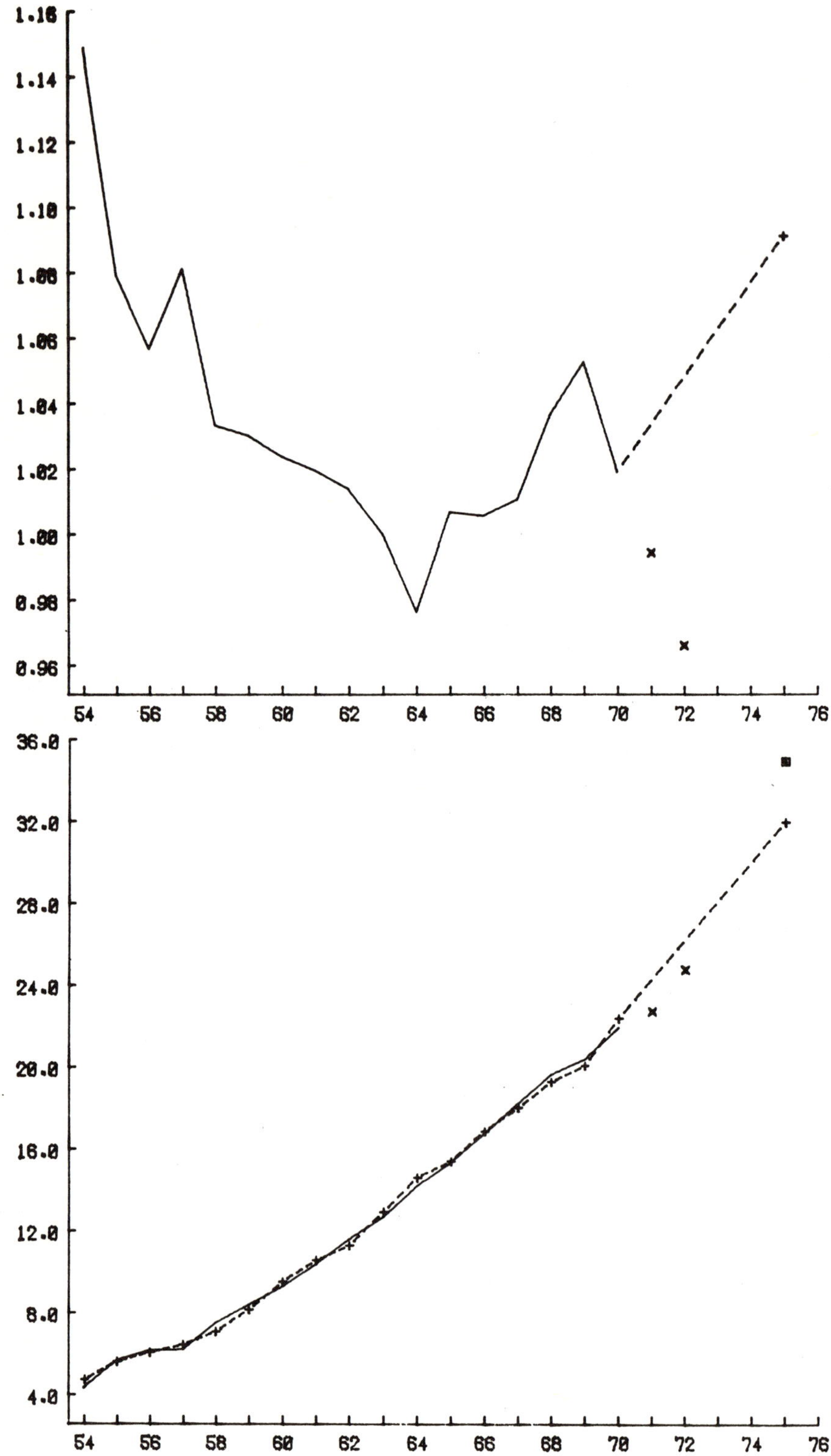
1.16
1.14
1.12
1.10
1.08
1.06
1.04
1.02
1.00
0.98
0.96
54
56
58
60
62
64
66
68
70
72
74
76
36.0
32.0
28.0
24.0
20.0
16.0
12.0
8.0
4.0
54
56
58
60
62
64
66
68
70
72
74
76

23. RUNNING COSTS OF MOTOR VEHICLES (3.6%: 9th: C)

This is rather a hybrid category including as well as petrol and oil, maintenance and accessories, garage rents, motor vehicle insurance, driving licences, and costs of driving tests and tests of road worthiness. Like the rents category, expenditure is closely associated with the use of a durable good and should perhaps not be explained in isolation from it. Nevertheless the LLS gives a reasonable explanation with a high income elasticity and a low, and falling, price elasticity. The LES is in agreement with the income elasticity though as seen from the graph, overstates the price response. Even so, the correspondence to the actuals is close.

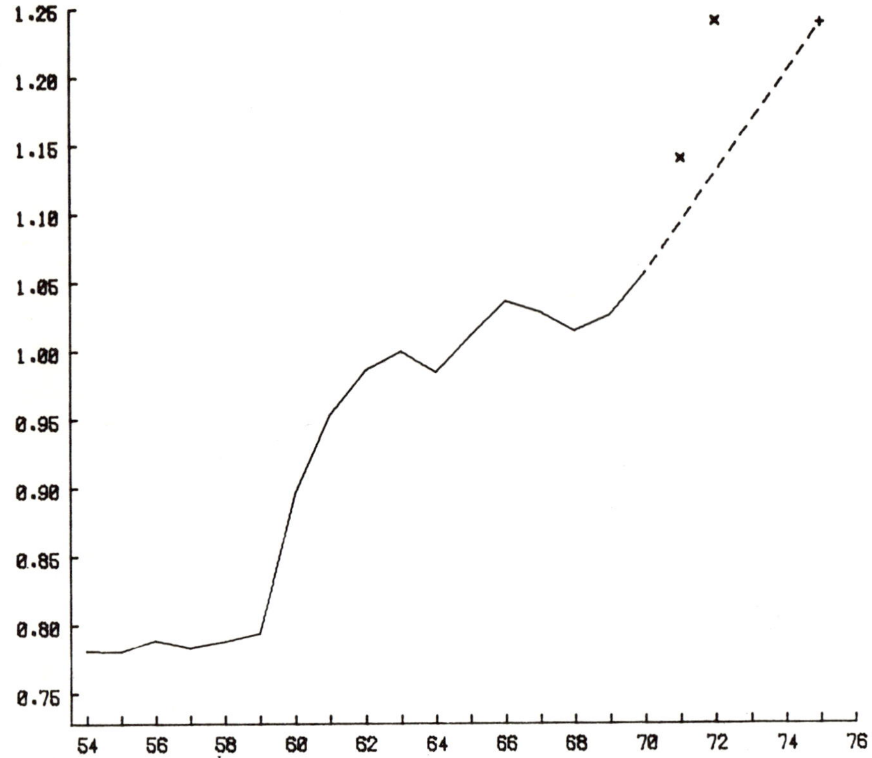

1.25
1.20
1.15
1.10
1.05
1.00
0.95
0.90
0.85
0.80
0.75
54
56
58
60
62
64
66
68
70
72
74
76

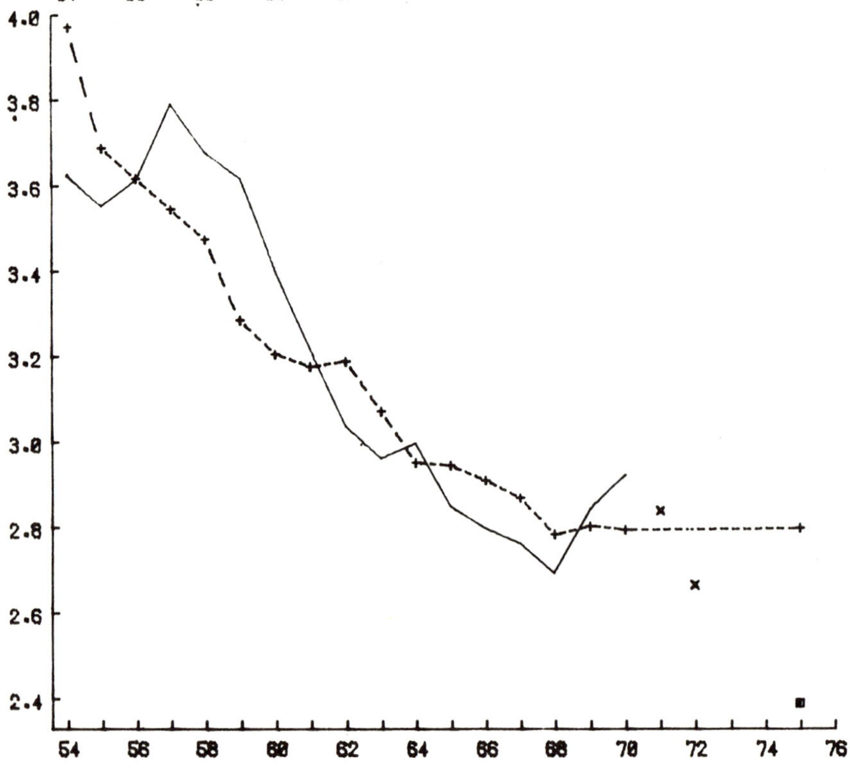

4.0
3.8
3.6
3.4
3.2
3.0
2.8
2.6
2.4
54
56
58
60
62
64
66
68
70
72
74
76

24. RAIL TRAVEL
(0.9%: 33rd: A)

This is the best example since category 5 of a situation which the LES cannot handle at all. The good appears to be genuinely inferior with both systems giving an income elasticity near -2. It is also clear from the LLS and from inspection of the series that the good is normally price responsive. But the LES with a negative income response is forced to yield perverse price effects and the LLS equation is much more satisfactory.

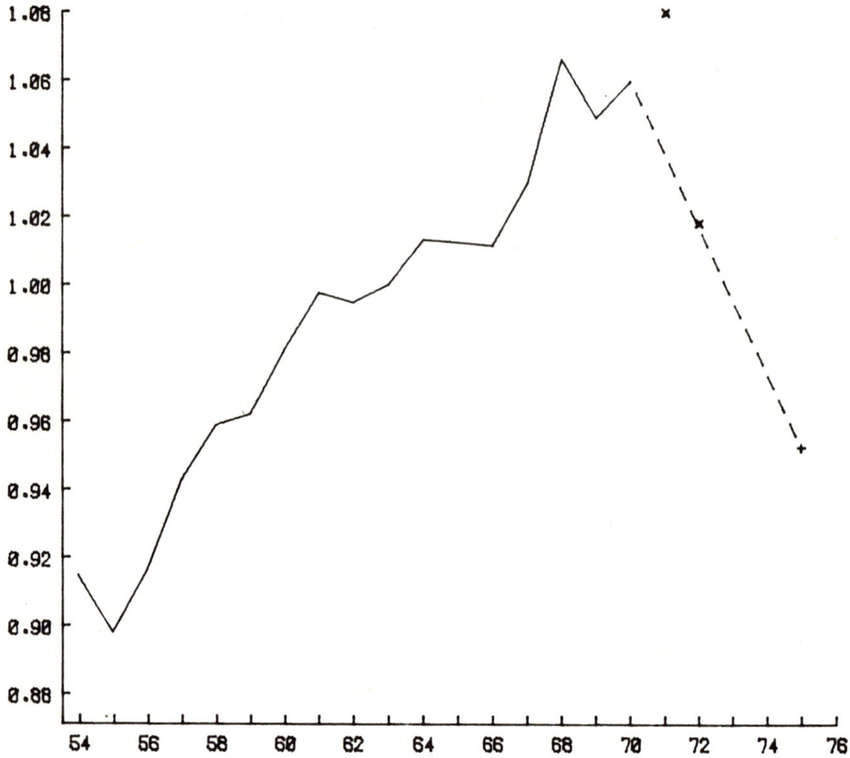
1.08
1.06
1.04
1.02
1.00
0.98
0.96
0.94
0.92
0.90
0.88
54
56
58
60
62
64
66
68
70
72
74
76

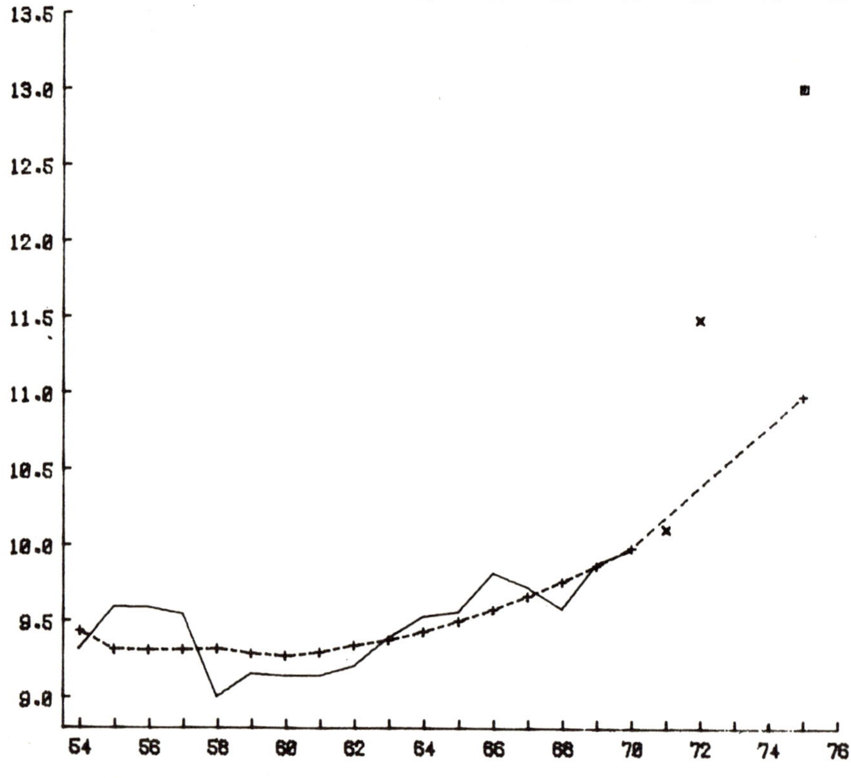
13.5
13.0
12.5
12.0
11.5
11.0
10.5
10.0
9.5
9.0
54
56
58
60
62
64
66
68
70
72
74
76

25. OTHER TRAVEL
(2.7%: 12th: A)

This is a heterogeneous category consisting of travel by bus, coach, tram, taxi, private hire car, air, sea and car ferries. These might be expected to have widely varying income and price elasticities and this diversity with weights changing over time may have something to do with the odd behaviour of expenditure on the group. Income has apparently little effect on purchases though there seems to be a fair amount of price sensitivity; to allow this would destroy the trend in the LES and so that model offers virtually no explanation at all for the category. The LLS is better and gives probably as good an explanation as can be given for this group.

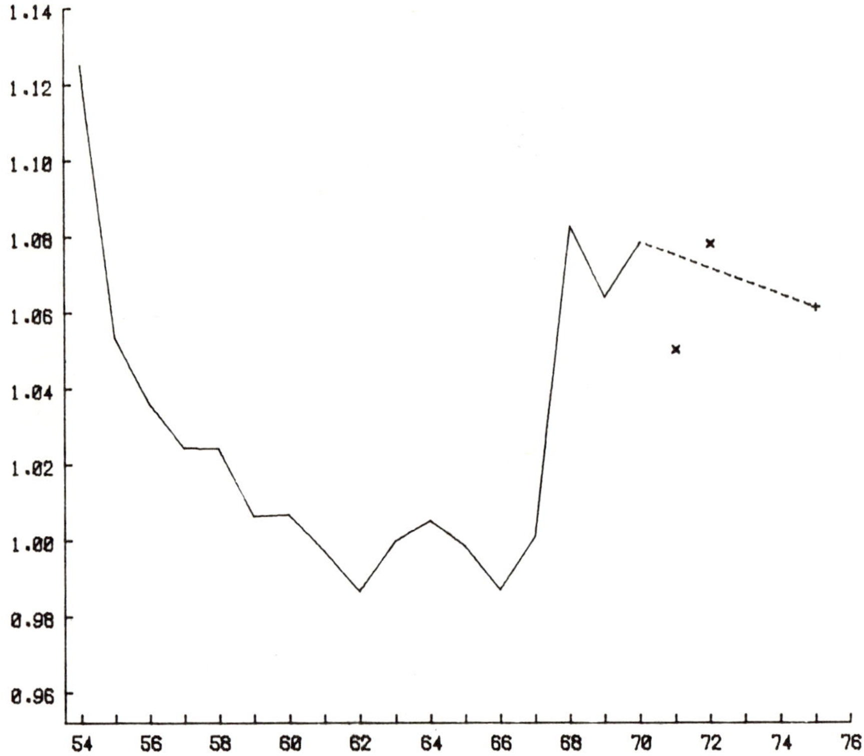

1.14
1.12
1.10
1.08
1.06
1.04
1.02
1.00
0.98
0.96
54
56
58
60
62
64
66
68
70
72
74
76

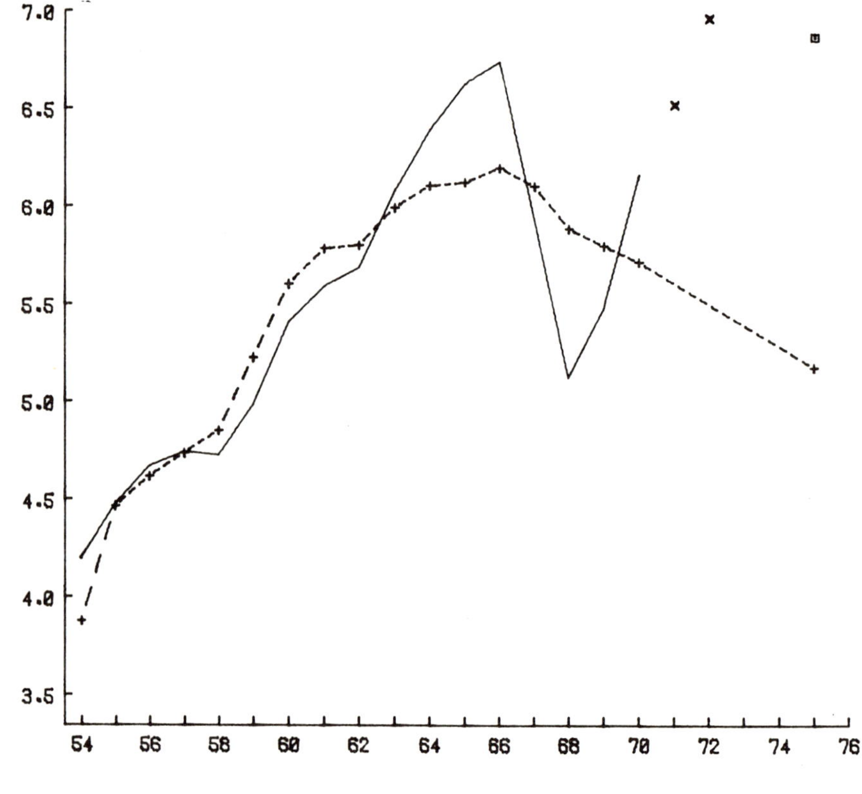

7.0
6.5
6.0
5.5
5.0
4.5
4.0
3.5
54
56
58
60
62
64
66
68
70
72
74
76

ORDER NUMBER

PO NYAATP08

BOOK NUMBER

8498082

BAY NUMBER

2810-3

AUTHOR	Deaton, A.
TITLE	Models and Projections of Demand in Post-War Britain

This is an ex-library book and may have the usual library/used-book markings inside.This book has hardback covers. In good all round condition. No dust jacket.

26. EXPENDITURE ABROAD
(1.6%: 21st: B)

This category *excludes* costs of travel to and from the U.K. which are included in category 25 (Other travel). Expenditure rose steadily until 1966 after which direct exchange controls, which limited the amount of money which could be taken out of the country, and devaluation caused a sharp two year fall which was partially made up in the two years which followed. The LLS uses the price rise which followed devaluation to explain some of the 67–68 drop but can only do so by use of a large time trend on the price elasticity since earlier falls in the price-relative had much less impact, presumably since they were not accompanied by direct controls. The LES has to fall back on changes in taste in order to average out the last few years and this is equally unsatisfactory. A proper explanation of the category would require some modelling of the impact of direct controls.

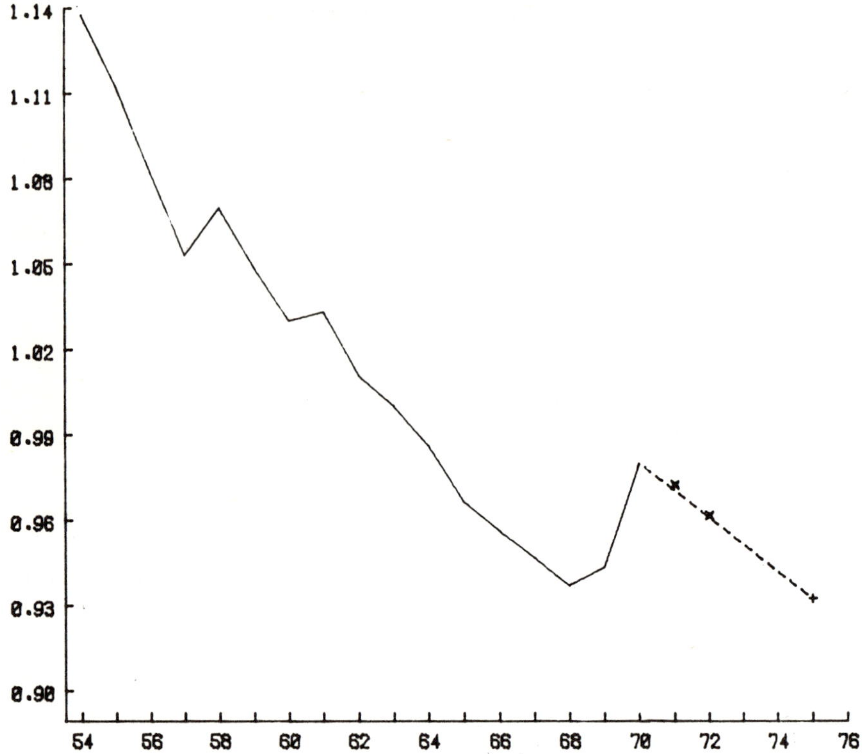
1.14
1.11
1.08
1.05
1.02
0.99
0.96
0.93
0.90
54
56
58
60
62
64
66
68
70
72
74
76
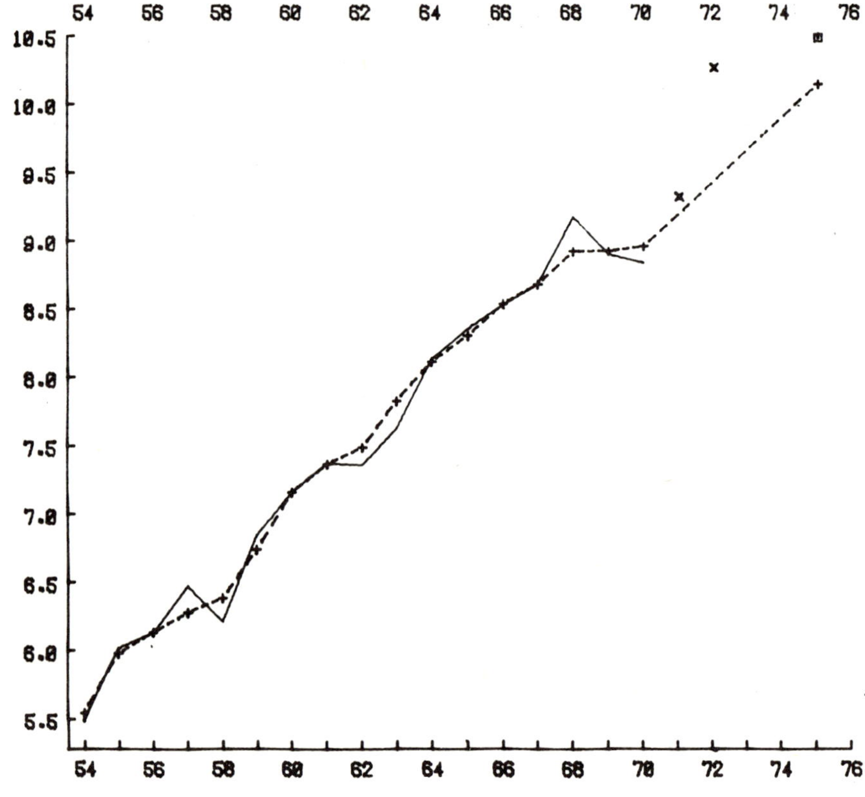
10.5
10.0
9.5
9.0
8.5
8.0
7.5
7.0
6.5
6.0
5.5
54
56
58
60
62
64
66
68
70
72
74
76

27. HOUSEHOLD TEXTILES & HARDWARE
(2.2%: 15th: C)

Both LES and LLS give similar pictures and Pigou's Law fits in well with the estimates of price and income elasticities. There appears to be a slight cycle which is presumably due to the durable element in these commodities; neither of these static models predicts it very well.

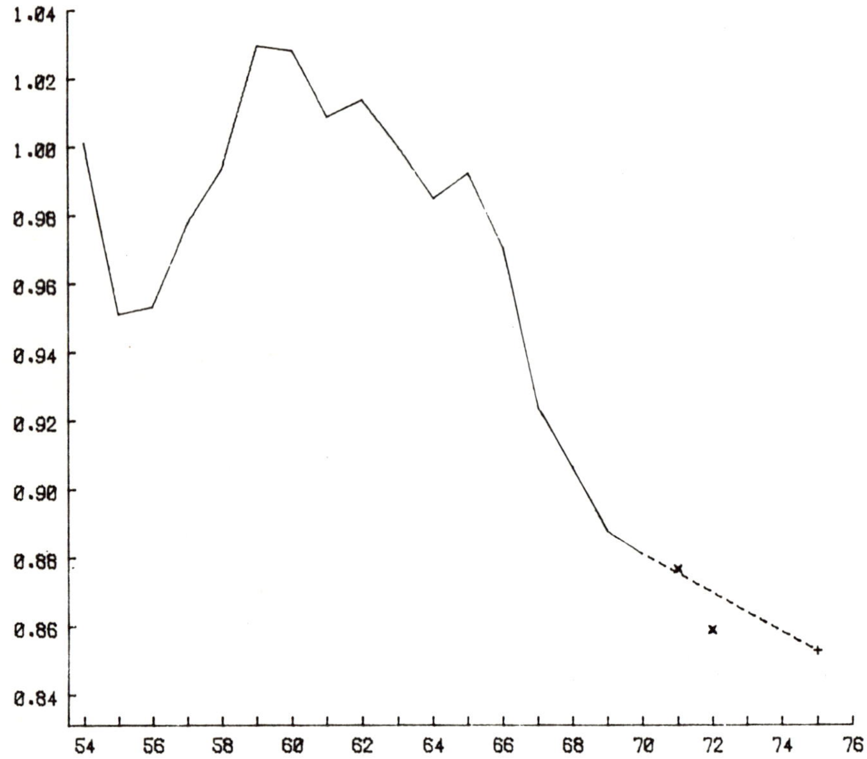

1.04
1.02
1.00
0.98
0.96
0.94
0.92
0.90
0.88
0.86
0.84
54
56
58
60
62
64
66
68
70
72
74
76

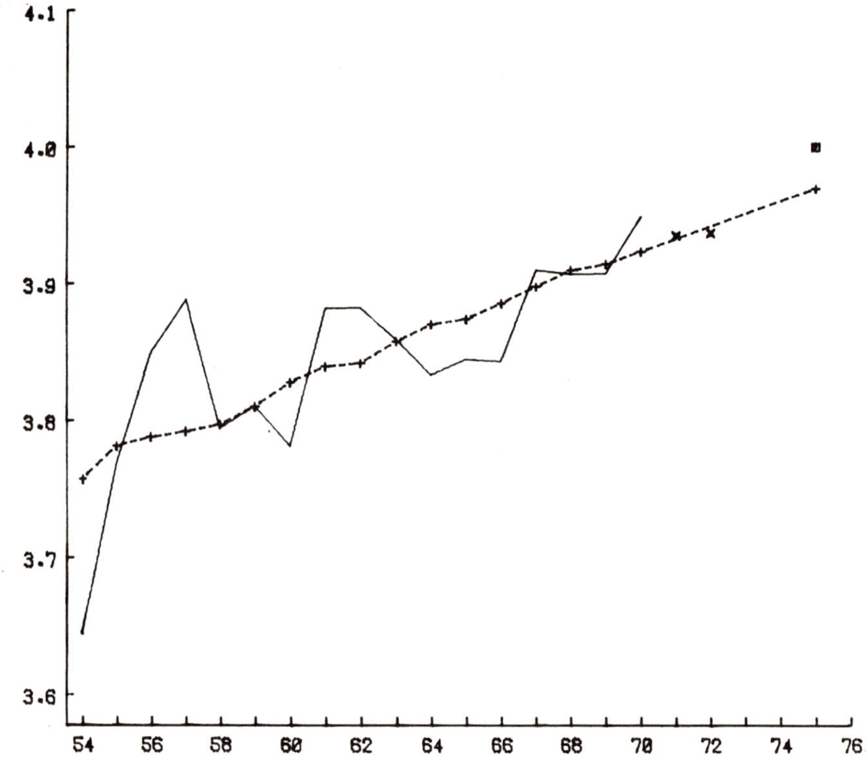

4.1
4.0
3.9
3.8
3.7
3.6
54
56
58
60
62
64
66
68
70
72
74
76

28. MATCHES, SOAP & CLEANING MATERIALS (1.1%: 28th: B)

Neither price nor income play much part in the explanation of this category and neither model has any predictive power.

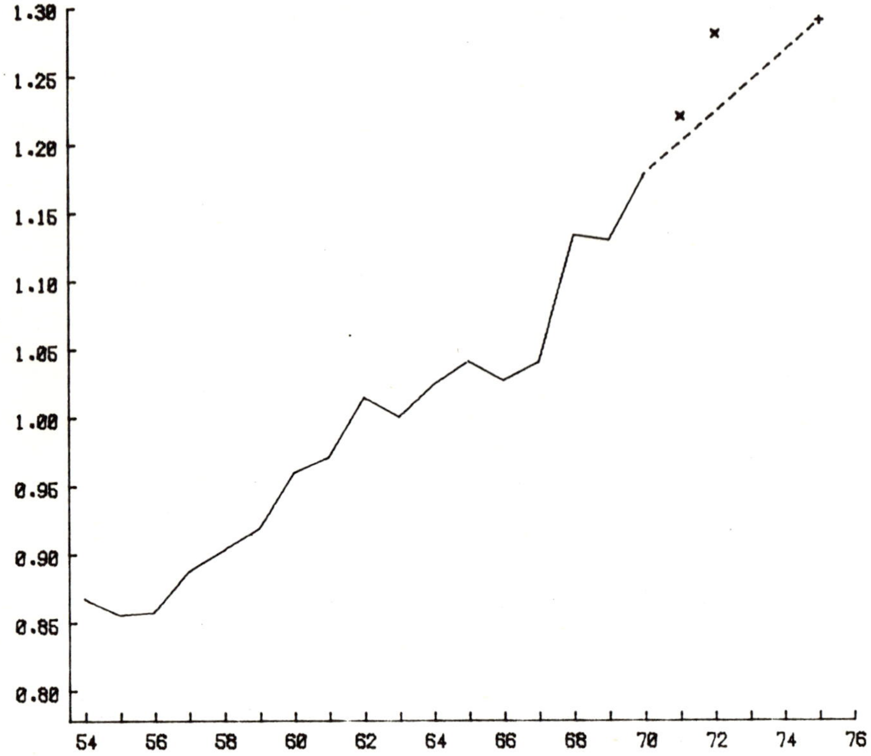

1.30
1.25
1.20
1.15
1.10
1.05
1.00
0.95
0.90
0.85
0.80
54
56
58
60
62
64
66
68
70
72
74
76

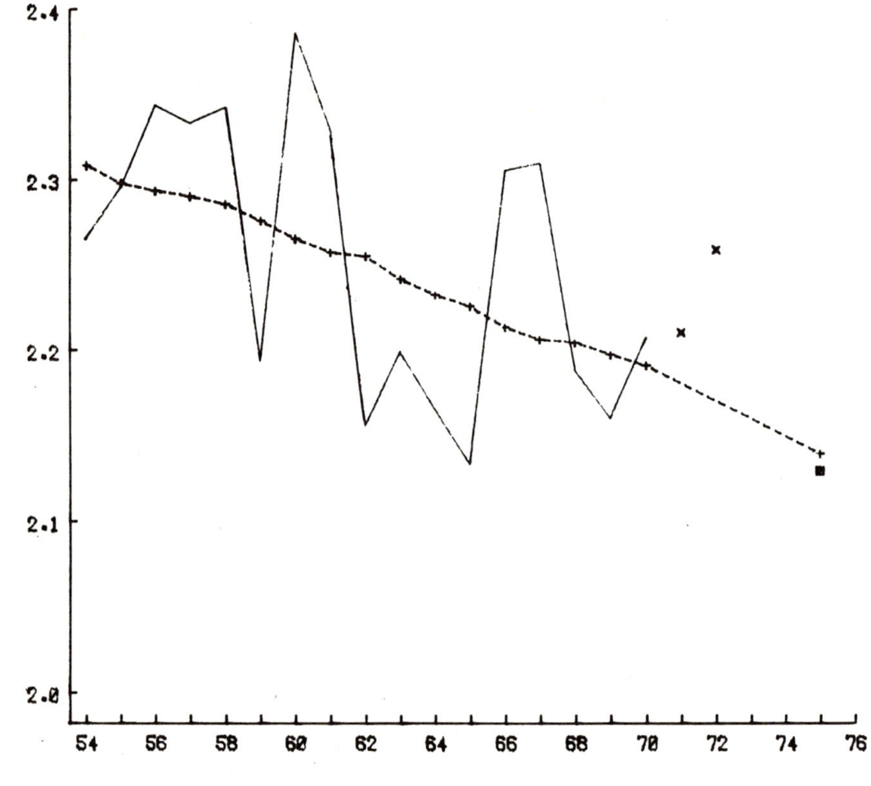

2.4
2.3
2.2
2.1
2.0
54
56
58
60
62
64
66
68
70
72
74
76

29. BOOKS & MAGAZINES
(0.7%: 35th: B)

This category is small and has quite sharp fluctuations about a declining trend. The LES makes the good slightly inferior while the LLS gives some weight to the increasing relative price. This latter is more plausible but neither model explains more than a small proportion of the variation in book purchases.

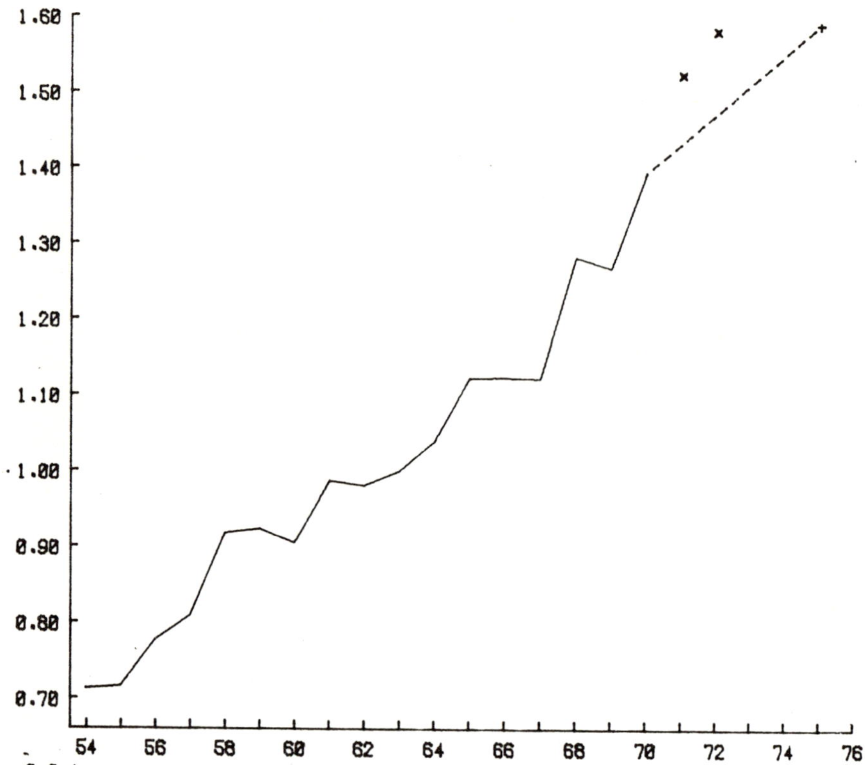

1.60
1.50
1.40
1.30
1.20
1.10
1.00
0.90
0.80
0.70
54
56
58
60
62
64
66
68
70
72
74
76

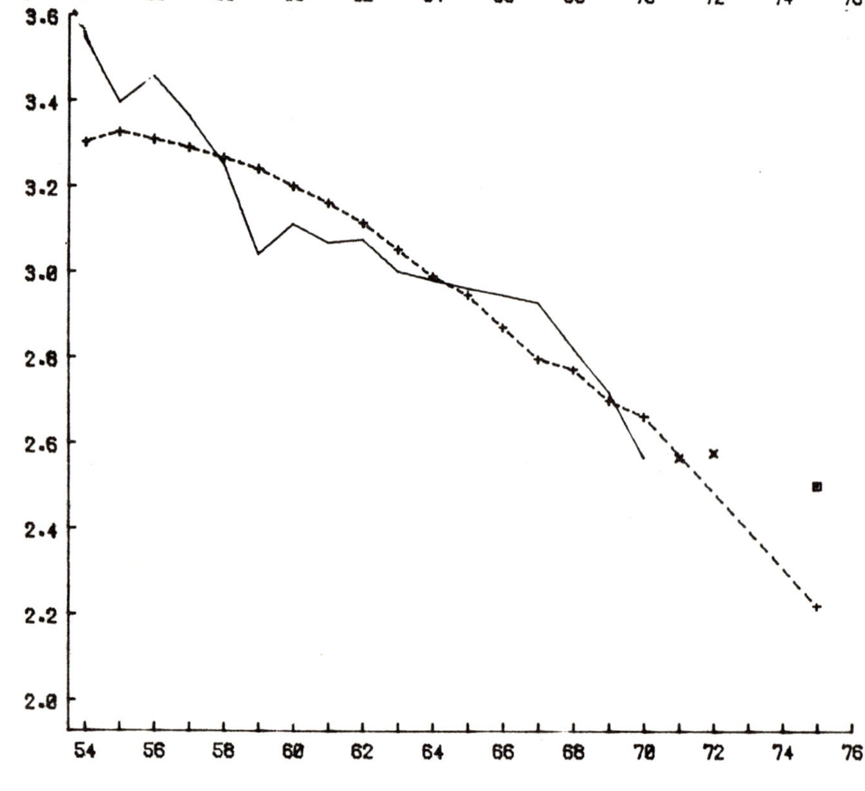

3.6
3.4
3.2
3.0
2.8
2.6
2.4
2.2
2.0
54
56
58
60
62
64
66
68
70
72
74
76

30. NEWSPAPERS
(0.9%: 32nd: A)

The LLS explains the fall in purchases by the rise in the price-relative, the LES is unable to do this and thus makes the good inferior. This results in a perverse price effect for a good which is clearly normally price sensitive and the poor fit for the LES is largely a consequence of this. In spite of the insignificance of the income effect in the LLS, this equation is much to be preferred.

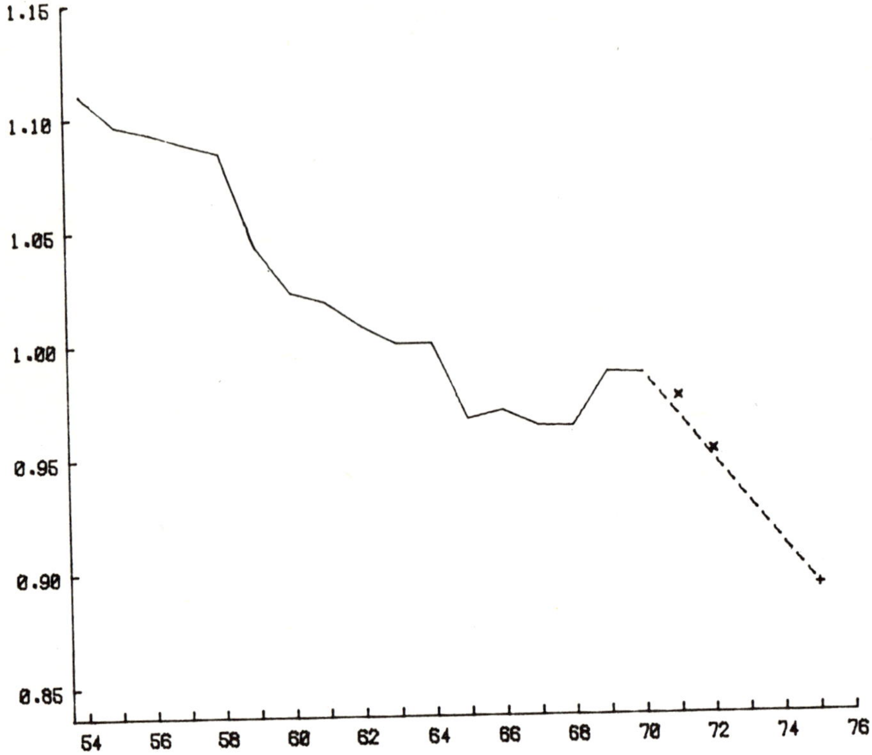

1.15
1.10
1.05
1.00
0.95
0.90
0.85
54 56 58 60 62 64 66 68 70 72 74 76

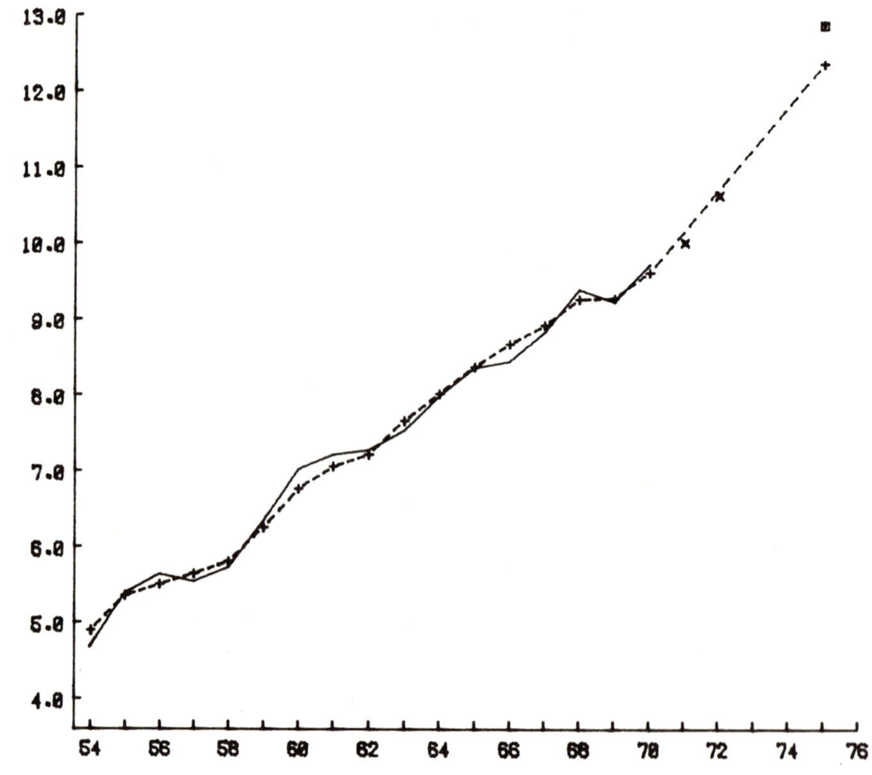

13.0
12.0
11.0
10.0
9.0
8.0
7.0
6.0
5.0
4.0
54 56 58 60 62 64 66 68 70 72 74 76

31. MISCELLANEOUS RECREATIONAL GOODS (2.1%: 16th: C)

Again a hybrid category; contains caravans, yachts, boats, gramophone records, toys and sports goods, photographic and hobby goods, as well as garden equipment (including plants) and purchases of domestic pets and their foods. Clearly, there is a distinct durable element in this and the series is marked by a distinct cycle. Even so, a good deal of this can be explained by variations in relative prices and a high income elasticity; the configuration necessary to do so fits well with Pigou's Law so that the LES and LLS each give satisfactory estimating equations.

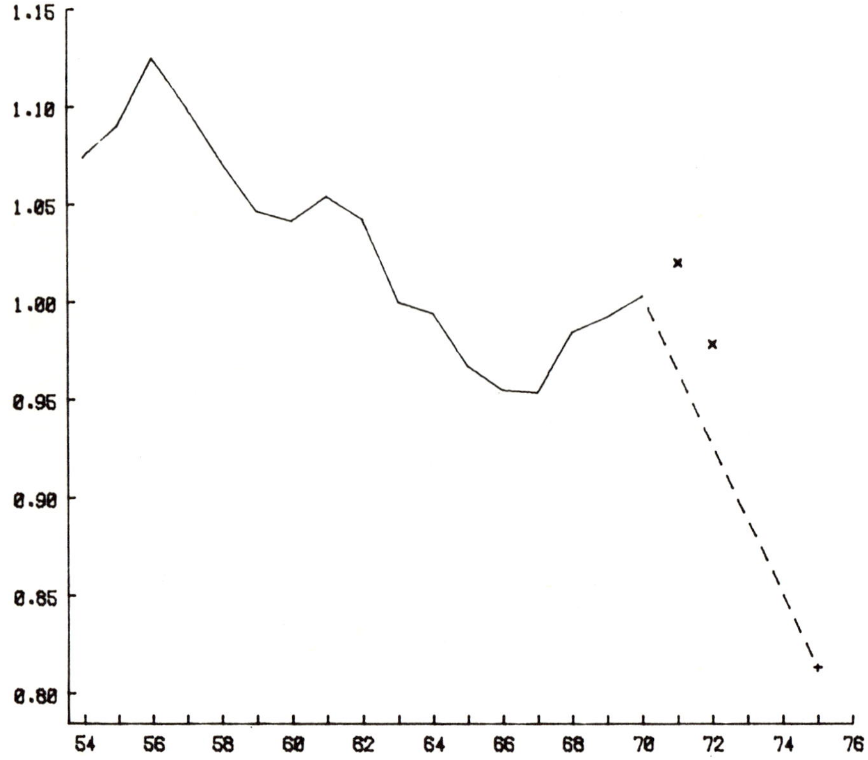
1.15
1.10
1.05
1.00
0.95
0.90
0.85
0.80
54
56
58
60
62
64
66
68
70
72
74
76

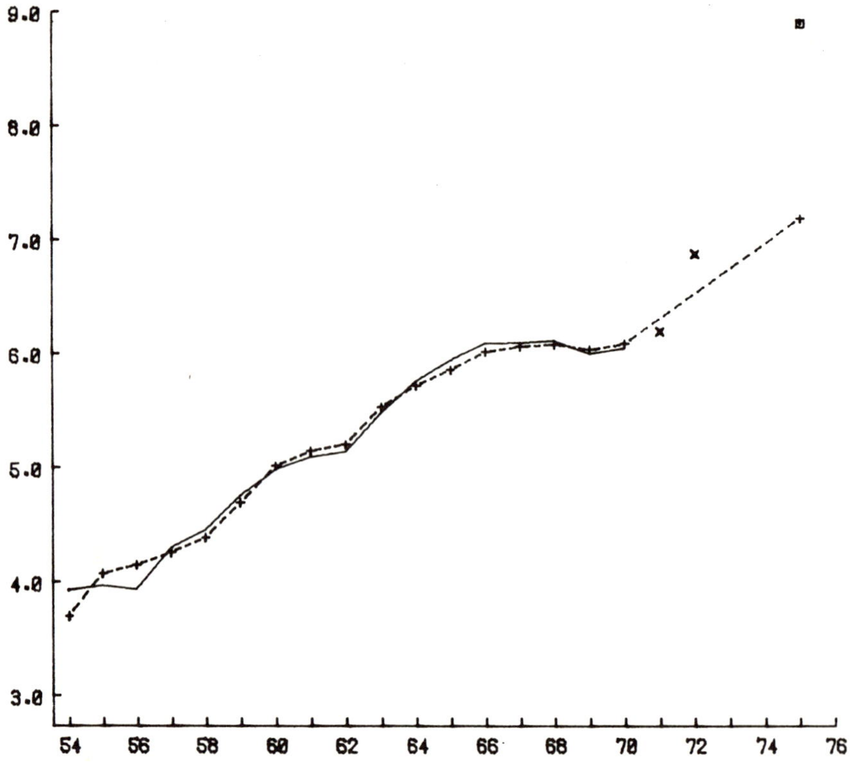
9.0
8.0
7.0
6.0
5.0
4.0
3.0
54
56
58
60
62
64
66
68
70
72
74
76

32. CHEMISTS' GOODS
(1.5%: 25th: C)

This group includes only drugs and medicines bought outside of the National Health Service; prescription charges are included in category 37. Cosmetics and toilet preparations are included though soap is excluded. The two explanations differ slightly and neither is entirely satisfactory. The LLS finds the relative price term significant enough to contradict Pigou's Law even though the relative magnitudes seem about right. The disadvantage is the size of the time trend in the price elasticity which will give perverse effects after 1972. The LES, though having 1963 price and income elasticities similar to the LLS, relies on a negative trend in the income response to explain the flattening out of purchases after 1966. Thus, though both models fit well over the sample period, both are liable to give trouble beyond it.

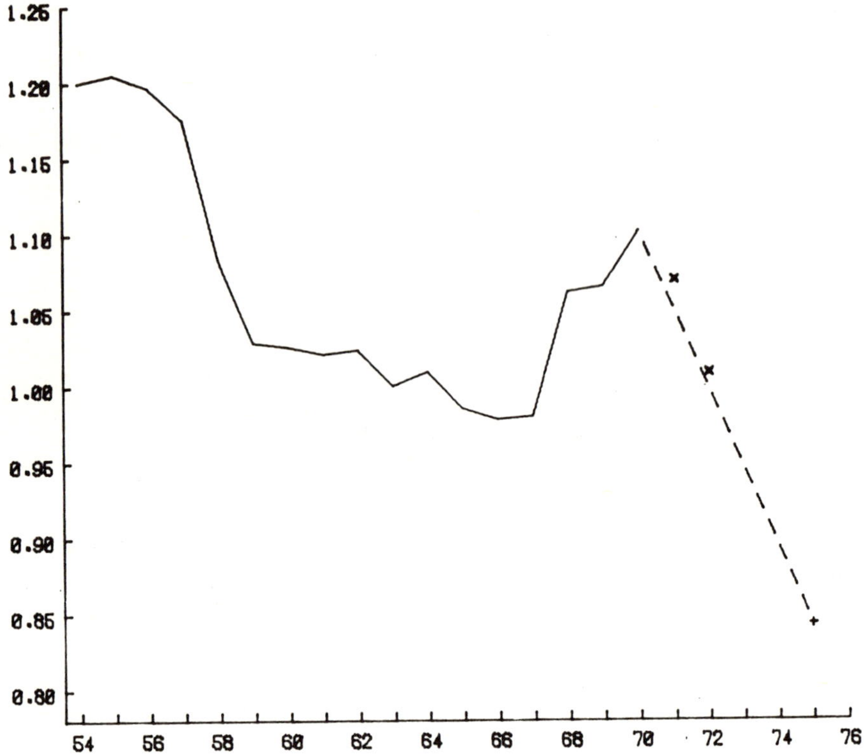
1.25
1.20
1.15
1.10
1.05
1.00
0.95
0.90
0.85
0.80
54
56
58
60
62
64
66
68
70
72
74
76

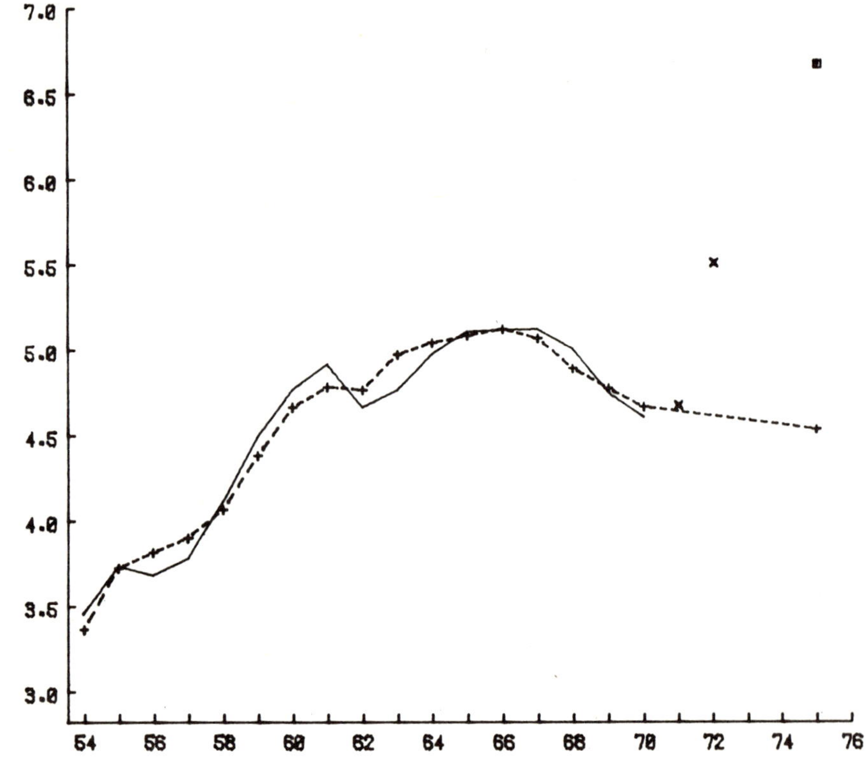
7.0
6.5
6.0
5.5
5.0
4.5
4.0
3.5
3.0
54
56
58
60
62
64
66
68
70
72
74
76

33. OTHER MISCELLANEOUS GOODS (1.4%: 26th: C)

The contents of this group are listed as "stationery and writing equipment, paper goods, umbrellas and walking sticks, handbags and purses, etc., travel goods, clocks and watches, jewellery, penknives, smokers' requisites, pictures, frames, vases and miscellaneous fancy or ornamental articles for personal or domestic use", Maurice (1968), p. 172. In spite of this diversity, the group is explained well by both systems, in terms of a high income elasticity and strongly significant price elasticity. The drop in purchases from 1966 to 1970 is explained well by the rise in the price relative within the loglinear model. The LES relies rather more on the time trend and this may give some difficulty beyond the sample period.

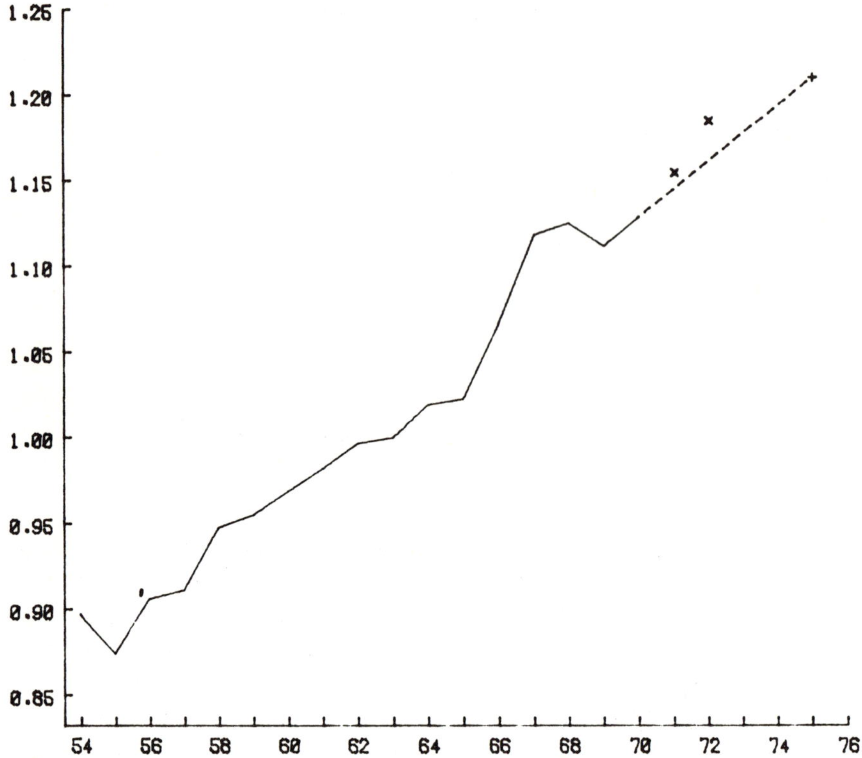
1.25
1.20
1.15
1.10
1.05
1.00
0.95
0.90
0.85
54
56
58
60
62
64
66
68
70
72
74
76

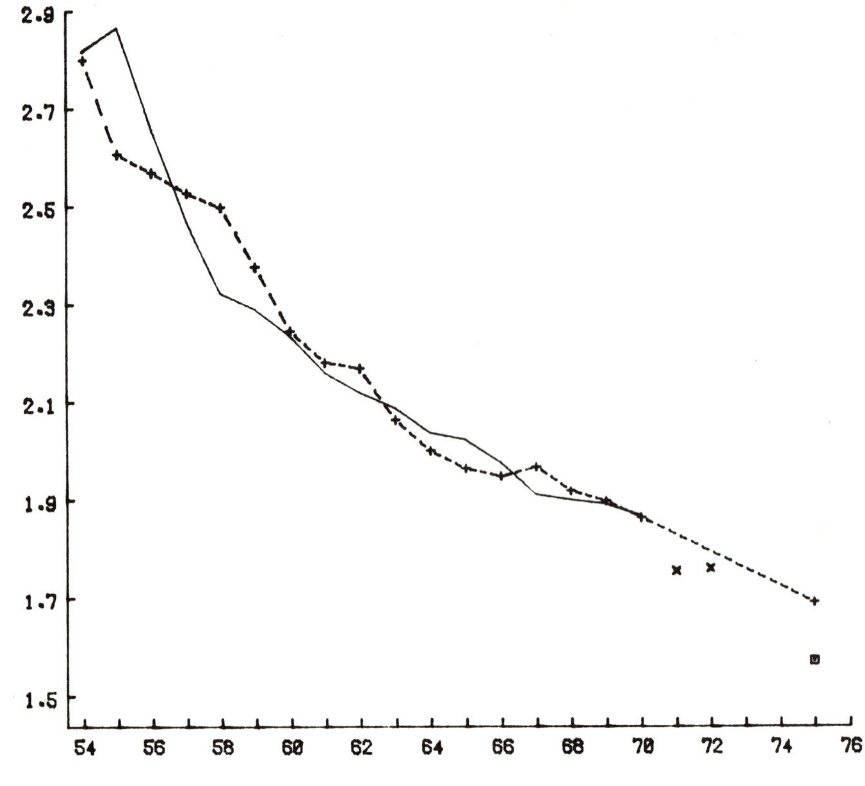
2.9
2.7
2.5
2.3
2.1
1.9
1.7
1.5
54
56
58
60
62
64
66
68
70
72
74
76

34. DOMESTIC SERVICE
(0.6%: 36th: C)

The LES has considerable difficulty with this category though perhaps not quite so much as comparison with the LLS would indicate. The difference between the income elasticities is again largely 'technical'; the LLS uses a negative time trend to convert rising real income into a falling series while the LES attributes inferiority directly. The real problems lie with the price elasticity. The good is quite obviously normal and in the LLS the price elasticity and its time trend are both highly significant. Pigou's Law requires the good to be a Giffen good and the exaggerated contra-cyclical LES predictions are the result. Note however that although the LLS remains superior both over the sample period and for forecasting, the time trend in the price elasticity renders this perverse after 1968.

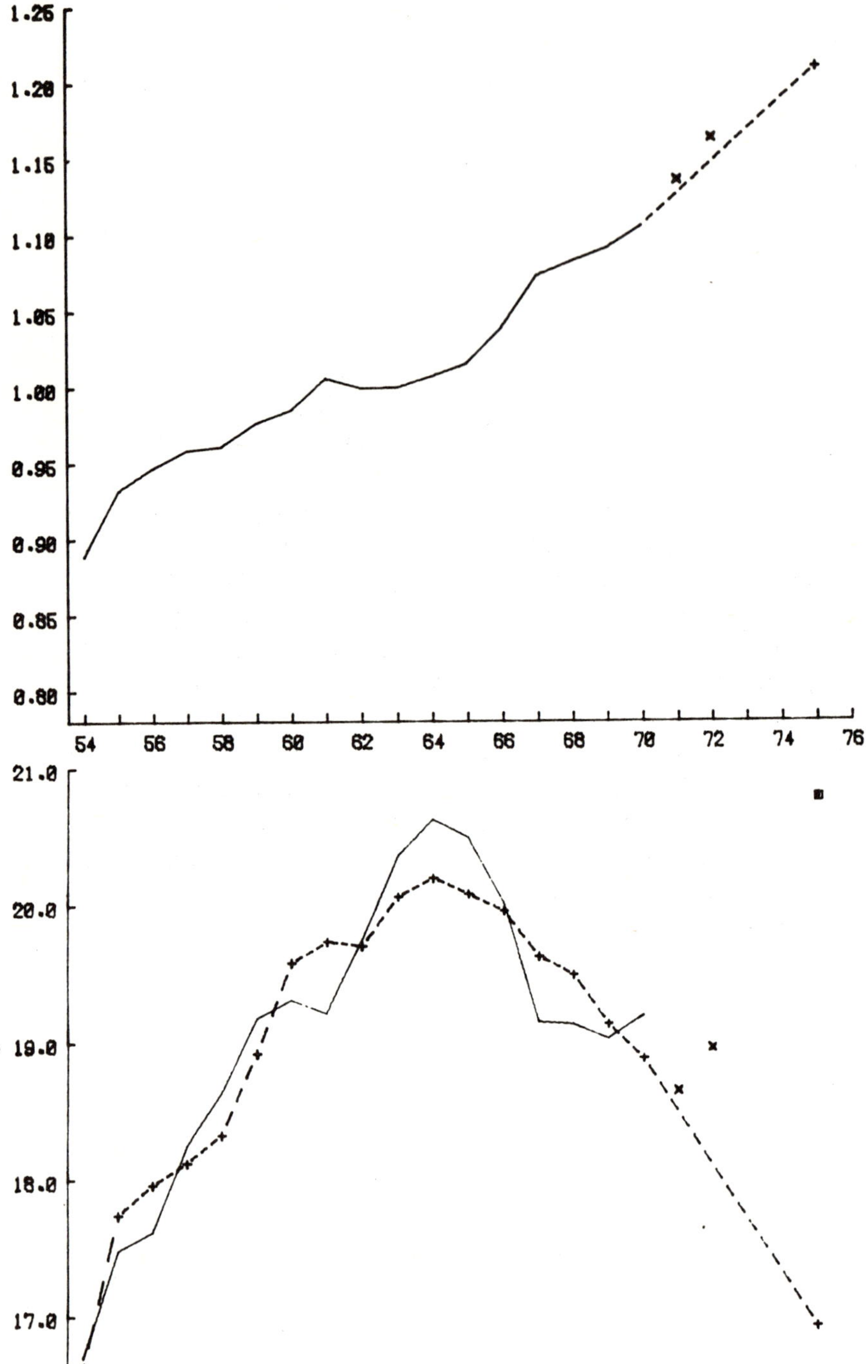

1.25
1.20
1.15
1.10
1.05
1.00
0.95
0.90
0.85
0.80
54
56
58
60
62
64
66
68
70
72
74
76
21.0
20.0
19.0
18.0
17.0
16.0
54
56
58
60
62
64
66
68
70
72
74
76

35. CATERING (MEALS & ACCOMMODATION) (5.6%: 6th: B)

The rising price relative can explain quite a high proportion of the variance in this category especially if a considerable upward trend in the price elasticity is permitted. However if Pigou's Law is enforced this can no longer occur without the overall trend becoming quite out of line and so the law is rejected very strongly within the LLS. The LES seems to do better than this but relies heavily on the time trend in the income coefficient and does not fit particularly well. Once again, on balance, the LLS is to be preferred, although neither model fits well enough to give much confidence in their forecasting properties.

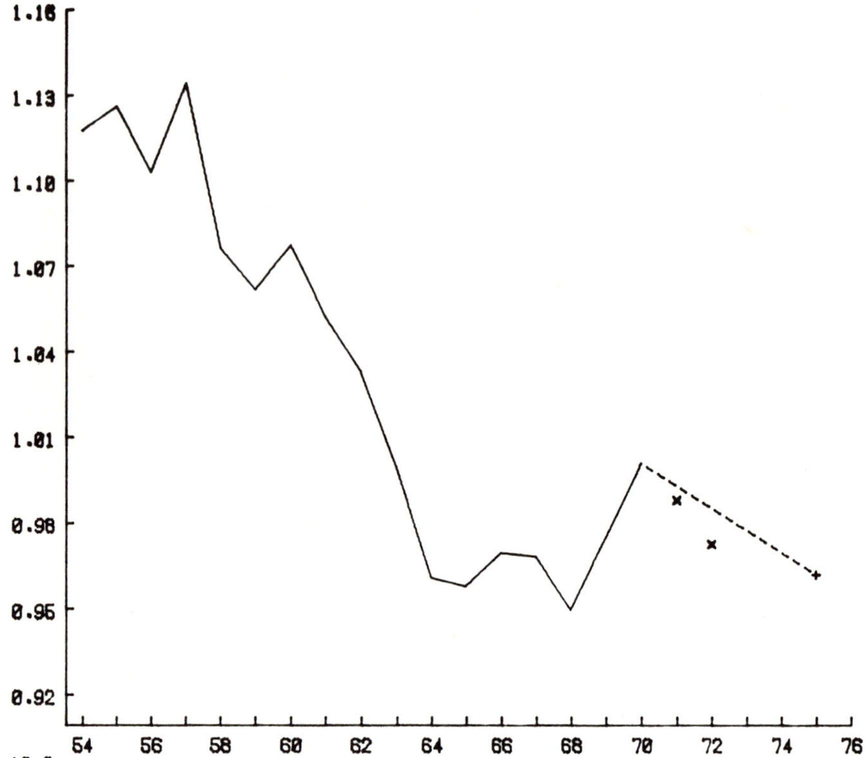
1.16
1.13
1.10
1.07
1.04
1.01
0.98
0.95
0.92
54
56
58
60
62
64
66
68
70
72
74
76

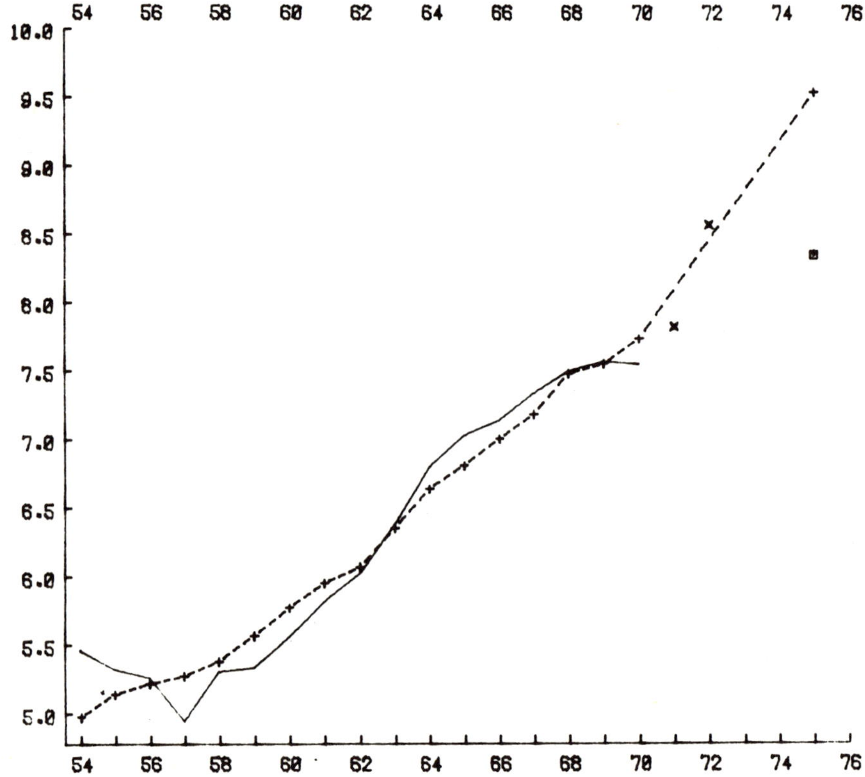
10.0
9.5
9.0
8.5
8.0
7.5
7.0
6.5
6.0
5.5
5.0
54
56
58
60
62
64
66
68
70
72
74
76

36. ENTERTAINMENT & RECREATIONAL SERVICES (1.9%: 18th: B)

This includes as well as cinemas, theatre, and concerts, admissions to sporting events and other entertainments, the renting of television and radio sets and payments for radio and television licences. Once again the LLS relies heavily on the relative price series with income relatively insignificant. The LES is forced to understate the price elasticity in order to get the trend right and so does not fit as well as is possible. In both models a considerable amount is left unexplained.

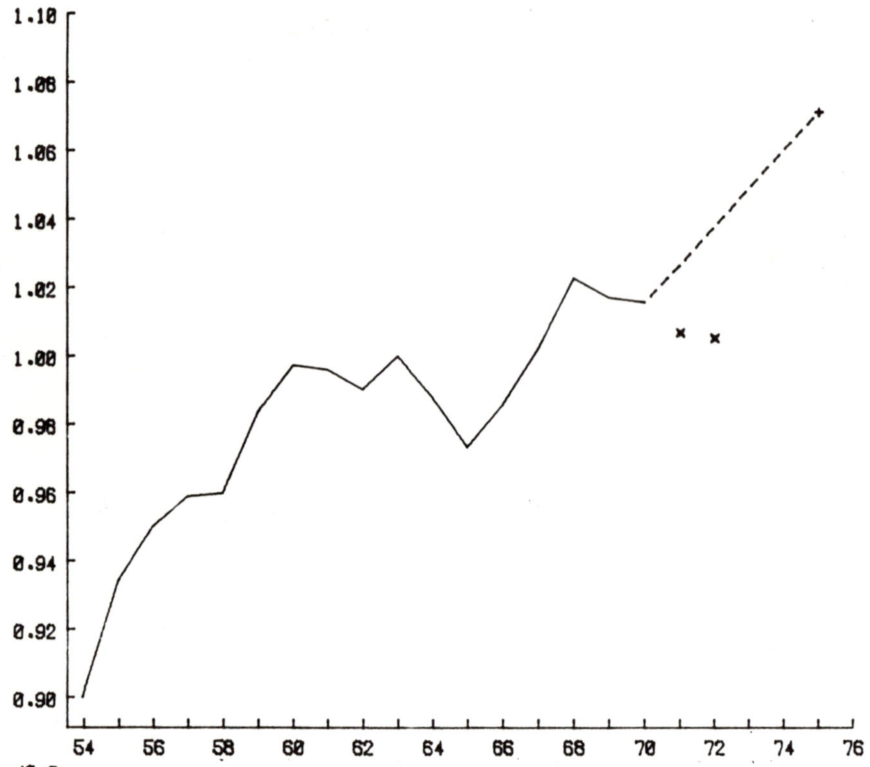
1.10
1.08
1.06
1.04
1.02
1.00
0.98
0.96
0.94
0.92
0.90
54
56
58
60
62
64
66
68
70
72
74
76

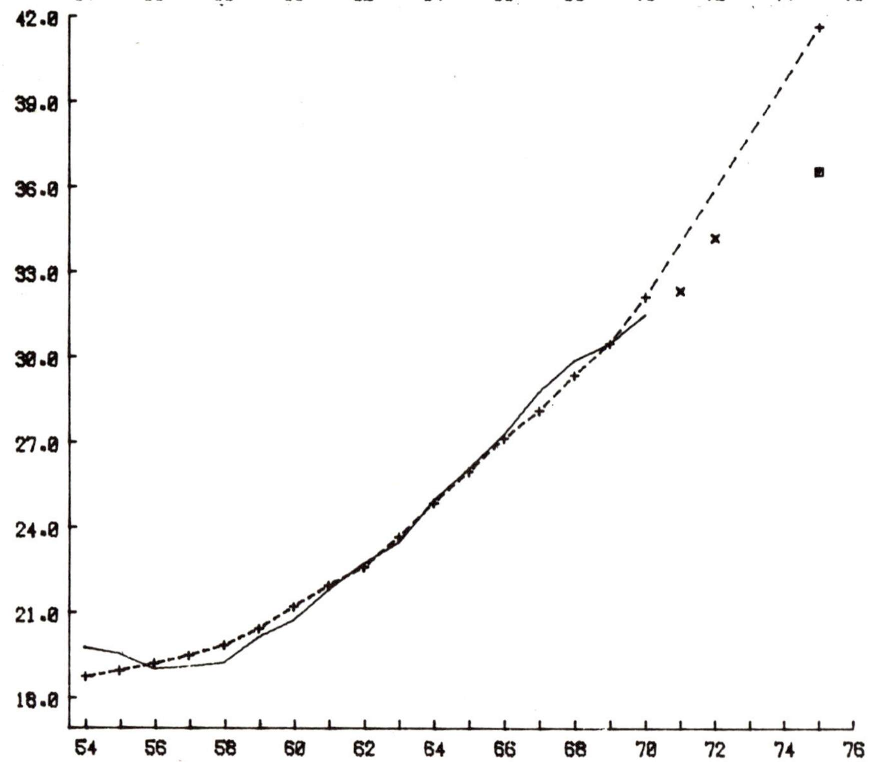
42.0
39.0
36.0
33.0
30.0
27.0
24.0
21.0
18.0
54
56
58
60
62
64
66
68
70
72
74
76

37. OTHER SERVICES
(6.8%: 6th: B/C)

This is an untidy category containing everything that cannot go elsewhere. It includes, for example, the wages and salaries paid by private non-profit making bodies (a double-entry item since these institutions are accounted as within the personal sector), insurance, private and National Health Service medical services, private education and training, laundry and dry-cleaning, miscellaneous repairs, dealers' margins on second-hand goods, hire of domestic appliances, hairdressing, undertaking, removals, window cleaning, chimney-sweeping, betting and gaming, fees to local authorities, professional charges and so on. The full list occupies 5 pages in Maurice (1968). The sum of all these turns out to be a relatively smooth rising trend which the LLS explains in terms of a high income elasticity and an originally normal but finally perverse price elasticity. This last contravenes Pigou's Law strongly and we have the choice of believing the implausible price behaviour or of accepting the worse fit and the LES. Once again the latter would appear to be safer.

5.7 Conclusions

Final judgement between the models discussed above must be postponed until a later chapter, for these will depend on the forecasting performance of each model, discussed in Chapter VII, and on the discussion of an alternative form of the linear expenditure system in the next chapter. In any case, it is not clear that universally acceptable judgements of this sort can be made since it must be recognized that many of the preferences for individual equations indicated in 5.6 above rest on subjective criteria. Even so, a number of common threads have appeared in the foregoing analysis, and, at the risk of appearing to be repetitive, it is worth drawing these together before continuing.

The linear expenditure system does well when the relationship between price and income elasticities is near the average for all the commodities. Since a relatively large number of goods are quite price inelastic, there may be relatively few commodities which closely approximate this ideal. Thus, for most commodities, the linear expenditure system either overstates price-sensitivity, creating fluctuations where none exist, or understates it, resulting in predictions which by and large merely follow trends. This explains the high serial-correlation of residuals which is often found in applications of the model. Nevertheless, for most commodities this difficulty is hardly serious since either the income elasticity is low and/or the price-relative does not move very much. There are of course exceptions where the model goes very wrong indeed and the most important of these should be noted again. The worst are those situations where purchases are falling due to rising relative price, i.e. where a low income elasticity is accompanied by a high price elasticity, and extending this, where a good is inferior but normally price responsive. In the first case the model enforces inferiority and in both it will give perverse price elasticities contrary to even the most obvious evidence to the contrary. It is probably the number of these cases, rather than the more commonly emphasized factors such as the absence of cross-price effects, which in the last analysis limits the applicability of the linear expenditure system or of additive models in general.

There is however another important point working in favour of the linear expenditure system and this is that the imposition of Pigou's Law, even when invalid, will sometimes result in a more convincing or credible result. The general rejection of the law thus understates its usefulness. The data are subject to error and this will occasionally cause chance correlations without economic significance and these are especially likely to occur when the basic independent variables are collinear. Absurdities are much less likely to arise when a strong relationship, such as the law, is imposed. Equally, the presence of a small number of anomalous or especially affected observations is less likely to distort parameter estimates if the law must hold. Although it is certainly preferable to use dummy variables or to allow directly for the distorting factors, it is not always known in advance that they exist or exactly what they are. It is for these reasons that for quite a number of the commodities analysed, where the unrestricted loglinear equations gave nonsensical answers, especially in the time trends or in the price effects, it was found that the linear expenditure system or Pigou's Law form made more intuitive sense even at the expense of some loss of fit.

There are of course other important grounds for distinguishing between the models. As was frequently emphasized for the individual commodities the linear expenditure system would often be 'safer' as a predictor than the loglinear form. This is a basic characteristic of any model which gives greater weight to *a priori* beliefs and less to the sample, always supposing that the *a priori* beliefs embodied are acceptable, either consciously or unconsciously, to the investigator. It is not only at the level of the individual commodity that this holds; another important advantage of the linear expenditure system is its adding-up property whereby predicted expenditures add to the total. This is not shared by the loglinear model and could, like the large number of dubious parameter estimates, undermine the credibility of the model's forecasts. In fairness, it must also be emphasized that an important advantage of the loglinear system, its ability to incorporate easily other prices or other factors, has not been exploited here and this further flexibility might tip the balance towards the model. Yet the linear expenditure system can also be modified in this direction, albeit with more difficulty, and such models may well be able to hold their own in comparison.

Unfortunately, the effects of the selection of functional form, even when there is no issue of principle involved, is such as to make the choice of considerable importance. Even when Pigou's Law is invoked, there are wide divergences between responses as estimated by the alternative models, see again Figure 5.5. In the discussion above many of these could be explained in terms of the difficulty of distinguishing between alternative but similar explanations; for example, between income and a time trend. In these cases, change of functional form will make a great deal of apparent difference since the change will often cause switches between competing but collinear explanatory variables. Although over the sample period, these can be reduced to a common explanation or at least it can be explained why the different explanations give the same answers, in forecasting and projection these models can give quite different answers. It is thus necessary to bring all possible resources to bear on the problem of choosing alternative forms; economic theory must be used where possible, not only to suggest variables for inclusion in modelling, but also to inform exactly how they ought to appear. At the other end of the scale, considerable attention must be paid to the detailed results of the application of the alternative models.

Chapter 6

A HIERARCHIC MODEL OF DEMAND

The concept of multi-stage or 'tree' budgeting is a simple one. Consumers allocate their expenditures to broad categories of goods at the first level, to more detailed commodities at the second, and so on until each of the commodities is reached along one of the branches of the tree. The broad categories may perhaps be identified with basic wants such as food, clothing, and housing while the sub-branches can be thought of as leading to the particular goods which satisfy these wants. Such trees are characterised by the economy with which they process information since allocation at each stage can be carried out using information relevant to that stage only. Thus, the division of expenditure among the broad groups which satisfy the basic wants can be done on the basis of total income and price indices for these groups only, while the allocation to the sub-branches is done using total branch expenditure and within-branch prices only; the prices of other goods become irrelevant at this second stage. Information need be passed on only along the branches; communication *between* branches is not necessary.

Whether or not a hierarchic system of this nature describes actual behaviour, it is certainly a very useful abstraction for the econometrician. By means of it, the large model with which we began can be broken up into a number of smaller subsystems each of which is much easier to handle than the original. This leads to a net saving of resources overall since the difficulties of estimation and of analysis increase more than proportionately with the increase in the number of commodities analysed. Specialist knowledge can also be brought to bear on sub-model construction in a way that is very clumsy or even impossible for large models. Furthermore, the structure of the hierarchic model can also be used to derive plausible restrictions on the variance–covariance matrix of the errors of the system. This is done by assuming that the errors made in the budgeting of goods on the same branch should be more closely related than the errors for goods which are only very loosely associated. On this basis it is possible to avoid the singularity problems discussed in chapter V, while still allowing the data considerable influence in the selection of the matrix.

The results of estimating a hierarchic version of the linear expenditure system are discussed in Sections 5, 6 and 7 of this chapter; in the first four sections a number of prior issues are discussed. In Section 1, I shall present the hierarchic form of the model; there are a number of difficulties here which, while not insuperable, affect the interpretation of the estimates. Section 2 deals with the hierarchic stochastic formulation while Section 3 discusses problems of bias inherent in hierarchic estimation. In Section 4, some consideration is given to the problem of selecting which goods go in which groups.

6.1 Reformulation of the linear expenditure system

Not all demand systems can be recast into the hierarchic form and utility functions which give rise to systems which can be so formulated must satisfy a number of stringent conditions; these conditions have been discussed in the literature in important contributions by Strotz (1957), (1959) and Gorman (1959). As was shown in Chapter III, the linear expenditure system derives from an *additive* utility function and it is this which allows the derivation of a multi-stage version. Indeed additivity is a much stronger condition than we really need; the independence of the wants satisfied by each good allows the construction of branches one to each good and does not prohibit the combination of any arbitrary pair of goods. The model itself gives us no structure for the tree and this must be derived from other considerations.

In what follows, I shall denote group indices by capital letter subscripts or superscripts, i.e. μ_G is the expenditure allocated to the Gth group; small letter subscripts continue to refer to individual goods. For the time being, we may assume that the n goods are partitioned into N groups and that this partitioning is known; the broad groups may be thought of as, say, food, clothing, housing, fuel and so on.

Then if, for an individual commodity i, belonging to the Gth group, we may write

$$p_i q_i = p_i c_i + b_i(\mu - p'c) + \epsilon_i \tag{6.1}$$

then, summing over all goods belonging to the group and writing group expenditure μ_G, then

$$\mu_G = \sum_{k \in G} p_k c_k + b_G(\mu - p'c) + \epsilon_G, \tag{6.2}$$

where b_G and ϵ_G are the corresponding quantities summed over G. Clearly then, if a group price index is defined with the constants c as weights, the equation (6.2) satisfies the prerequisites for the first stage of budgeting. For according to this, only knowledge of these group price indices and of total expenditure μ is necessary in order to calculate the expenditures μ_G. Note too that from (6.1) we could have derived an equation identical to (6.2) for any arbitrary collection of commodities; as was stated in the first paragraph of this section, the linear expenditure system, while allowing this aggregation, gives no information as to which commodities go into which group.

It is also possible, by approximation, to write (6.2) in a form identical to the usual model and this is useful for estimation purposes. Since the c's are measured in base year prices, we may define the group price indices p_G, as

$$p_G = \sum_{k \in G} p_k c_k \Big/ \sum_{k \in G} c_k \tag{6.3}$$

and corresponding quantity indices q_G, by the relation

$$p_G q_G = \mu_G. \tag{6.4}$$

These may be substituted in (6.2) to give (exactly),

$$p_G q_G = c_G p_G + b_G(\mu - \sum_H p_H c_H) + \epsilon_G, \tag{6.5}$$

which is the group equivalent of (6.1). The approximation occurs in practice because it is often inconvenient to have to know the individual c's before being able to measure the independent variables in the equation. The usual Paasche implicit price deflators, i.e.

$$p_G^* = \Sigma p_k q_k / \Sigma p_k^0 q_k, \tag{6.6}$$

are thus used instead of the exact indices p_G; these p^* can be calculated in advance from national income data *without* knowing the elements of c. I shall return to further discussion of this approximation below but it should be emphasised here that it will nearly always be a very close approximation. The individual prices are quite collinear and the indices are thus not very sensitive to the choice of weights. And, given the assortment of methodologies used in the construction of the data, great attention devoted to the precise form of indices used is likely to be misplaced.

So far we have presented only the upper level of the hierarchy; we turn now to the construction of the second stage. From equation (6.2), we may write

$$b_G(\mu - p'c) = (\mu_G - \sum_{k \in G} p_k c_k) - \epsilon_G, \qquad (6.7)$$

which if substituted into (6.1) gives,

$$p_i q_i = p_i c_i + \frac{b_i}{b_G}(\mu_G - \sum_{k \in G} p_k c_k) + \epsilon_i - \frac{b_i}{b_G}\epsilon_G \qquad (6.8)$$

Or writing $b_{iG} = b_i/b_G$,

$$p_i q_i = p_i c_i + b_{iG}(\mu_G - \sum_G p_k c_k) + \epsilon_i - b_{iG}\epsilon_G. \qquad (6.9)$$

This equation, which describes the second level of the hierarchic budgeting procedure, adds up in the usual way; the within-group marginal expenditure shares add to one and the equation errors to zero. The errors themselves, though different in form, still have zero expectation and constant variance if the original errors do. In the next sections I shall show that even though these errors may be a source of minor bias, it is possible to suggest a plausible error structure for the original equations such that the error structures for both levels of the hierarchy are precisely comparable.

Before discussing this it is necessary to deal with a rather more serious source of difficulty. Throughout equations (6.1) to (6.9) I have written the marginal budget shares without making the time trend explicit and though this makes no mathematical difference to the structure (6.1), (6.5) and (6.9), non-linearities arise which make estimation difficult and necessitate some further approximation. If we now write explicitly

$$b_i = b_i^0 + b_i^1 \theta, \qquad (6.10)$$

the aggregation to (6.5) goes through without difficulty, i.e.

$$b_G = b_G^0 + b_G^1 \theta, \qquad (6.11)$$

where $$b_G^0 = \sum_{k \in G} b_k^0 \quad \text{and} \quad b_G^1 = \sum_{k \in G} b_k^1. \tag{6.12}$$

However, at the second stage the b_{iG}'s of (6.9) are no longer linear functions of θ since

$$b_{iG} = \frac{b_i}{b_G} = \frac{b_i^0 + b_i^1\theta}{b_G^0 + b_G^1\theta}. \tag{6.13}$$

Now while is might be possible to estimate marginal budget shares of this form, there are already enough econometric problems without attempting to do so. Instead we must assume that b_G^1 is small enough relative to b_G^0 to allow the approximation of (6.13) by a linear expression. In any case, if b_G^1 is *not* small relative to b_G^0 there will be difficulties from another source; for in this case, either within the data period, or not far outside of it, the denominator of (6.13) will become zero at which point the multistage process breaks down. For, if the group marginal budget share is zero, expenditure on that group is equal to committed expenditure, group supernumerary expenditure is zero and so the first level of the process gives no information relevant in the second. Clearly then, the model must be confined to groups where this does not happen and so a linear approximation of (6.13) is unlikely to add any further restriction to the applicability of the model.

From (6.13) then, we may write

$$b_{iG} \doteq \frac{b_i^0}{b_G^0}\left(1 + \frac{b_i^1}{b_i^0}\theta\right)\left(1 - \frac{b_G^1}{b_G^0}\theta\right) \doteq \frac{b_i^0}{b_G^0}\left\{1 + \left(\frac{b_i^1}{b_i^0} - \frac{b_G^1}{b_G^0}\right)\theta\right\}, \tag{6.14}$$

or more conveniently

$$b_{iG}^0 = b_i^0/b_G^0, \tag{6.15}$$

$$b_{iG}^1 = b_i^0/b_G^0 \,.\, (b_i^1/b_i^0 - b_G^1/b_G^0). \tag{6.16}$$

It is worth pointing out that the hierarchic process can be carried on indefinitely leading to an ever finer classification of commodities. I shall not discuss this further here; there is no new issue of principle, the mathematics are identical, and for practical purposes two stages is quite sufficient to deal with all the detail that is available.

6.2 A stochastic specification

The idea of linking the stochastic specification to the theory of choice extends back at least to Allen and Bowley (1935). In their study of Engel curves, they calculated the correlations of the residuals of different commodities; a positive correlation was regarded as *prima facie* evidence from complementarity while a negative correlation was taken as indicating substitutability. The first attempt to formalize this connection between the substitution matrix and the variance–covariance matrix of residuals was made by Theil and Neudacker (1957–58) and though this attempt did not entirely achieve its aim, Theil (1971b) has since solved the problem within a general 'theory of the second moments of the disturbance term' and the idea has been exploited by a number of economists in studies of demand. The Theil model makes the variance–covariance matrix proportional to minus the substitution matrix and this result is based on a balance between the loss of satisfaction in not getting the budget precisely correct on the one hand, and the cost of doing so on the other. Most recently, Theil (1973), the model has been generalised with the use of an entropy concept so as to justify multivariate normality of the errors.

In this study, I shall not adopt this model directly; undoubtedly the linear expenditure system ignores some cross effects and basing the error structure on the supposed validity of the underlying utility function is likely only to compound the error. I shall, instead, select a stochastic formulation which would result from a rather more general model in the hope that this can accommodate some of the, mostly second-order, effects ignored by the additivity assumption. Since the specification, while inspired by Theil's model, cannot be justified for the linear expenditure system in terms of it, its *a priori* plausibility is also of considerable importance and I shall emphasize this in its presentation rather than formally deriving it within Theil's framework. Readers interested in the latter will observe the similarity of the stochastic specification proposed here and the structure of the substitution matrix under a weakly separable utility function.

For the basic equation of the linear expenditure system (6.1), I propose the following error structure.

$$\mathcal{E}\{\epsilon_{it}\epsilon_{jt'}\} = \omega_{ij}\delta_{tt'}, \qquad (6.17)$$

as before, but now if $i \in R$ and $j \in S$,

$$\omega_{ij} = \lambda^{RS} b_{iR} b_{jS} + \delta_{RS}\,\omega_{ij}^{R} \qquad (6.18)$$

where $$\sum_R \lambda^{RS} = \sum_S \lambda^{RS} = \sum_j \omega_{ij}^{R} = \sum_i \omega_{ij}^{R} = 0 \qquad (6.19)$$

for all values of R, S, i and j. The matrices of elements λ^{RS} and ω_{ij}^R are denoted Λ and Ω^R respectively.

This combines two ideas: first, that of scaling variances and covariances in proportion to some measure of relative size; and, second, that the covariance structure *within* a branch of the utility tree should be much more general than that between goods in different branches. In Chapter V, the average value shares were used for scaling, here it is the marginal budget shares which take that role. For two goods in different branches the covariance depends on the two branches concerned, but, for all such goods, the covariance is the same but for the scaling factor $b_{iR}b_{jS}$. Within a branch, the presence of the unconstrained matrix, Ω^R, allows a wide range of possible substitution patterns. Singularity of the matrix Λ and of each of the matrices Ω^R is required to make the overall matrix Ω singular as required.

Using equations (6.18) and (6.19) the error structures of both levels of the hierarchy may be derived. Taking the broad groups first, i.e. equation (6.5), the errors are given by

$$\epsilon_R = \sum_{k \in R} \epsilon_k . \tag{6.20}$$

The mean is clearly zero, i.e.

$$\mathcal{E}(\epsilon_R) = \mathcal{E}(\sum_{k \in R} \epsilon_k) = \sum_{k \in R} \mathcal{E}(\epsilon_k) = 0. \tag{6.21}$$

For the covariances

$$\begin{aligned} \mathcal{E}(\epsilon_R, \epsilon_S) &= \mathcal{E}\{\sum_{i \in R} \epsilon_i \cdot \sum_{j \in S} \epsilon_j\} \\ &= \sum_{i \in R} \sum_{j \in S} \lambda^{RS} b_{iR} b_{jS} + \sum_{i \in R} \sum_{j \in S} \delta_{RS} \lambda^{RR} \omega_{ij}^R \\ &= \lambda^{RS}, \end{aligned} \tag{6.22}$$

since $\sum_{i \in R} \omega_{ij}^R = 0$.

Thus, for the top level of the hierarchy, that relating to broad aggregates of goods, the matrix Λ is the variance–covariance matrix of the group errors.

For the second level, writing the ith error of the Rth group v_i^R, we have from (6.9)

$$v_i^R = \epsilon_i - b_{iR}\epsilon_R . \tag{6.23}$$

Once again the mean is zero, i.e.

$$\mathcal{E}(v_i^R) = \mathcal{E}(\epsilon_i) - b_{iR}\mathcal{E}(\epsilon_R) = 0. \tag{6.24}$$

The within group variance–covariance matrix is given by

$$\begin{aligned}\mathcal{E}(v_i^R v_j^R) &= \mathcal{E}(\epsilon_i\epsilon_j) - b_{iR}\mathcal{E}(\epsilon_R\epsilon_j) - b_{jR}\mathcal{E}(\epsilon_i\epsilon_R) + b_{iR}b_{jR}\mathcal{E}(\epsilon_R\epsilon_R)\\ &= \lambda^{RR}b_{iR}b_{jR} + \omega_{ij}^R - b_{iR}\lambda^{RR}b_{jR} - b_{jR}\lambda^{RR}b_{iR} + \lambda^{RR}b_{iR}b_{jR}\\ &= \omega_{ij}^R. \end{aligned} \tag{6.25}$$

So that, for each of the models allocating expenditures within sub-groups the errors have second moments corresponding to the corresponding group matrix Ω^R. Thus, the structure (6.15)–(6.19) not only has a simple and reasonable *a priori* justification, but it also leads to an elegant and simple structure for the error structures of both levels of the hierarchy.

These results produce an intuitively acceptable basis for the estimation of the two levels of the hierarchy using full information maximum likelihood at each stage thus estimating the matrix Λ and the N matrices Ω^R. The resulting parameter estimates of the marginal budget shares can then be used to give an estimate of the full second-moment matrix of the system. Although this procedure will be adopted below, it must be noted that it will not in general yield global maximum likelihood estimates of the whole system even if the specification (6.18)–(6.19) holds good. To calculate such estimators would require maximization of the likelihood function (4.17), subject to the constraints given by the specification. This is not a tractable problem. The alternative offered will hopefully yield much of the benefit of such an estimator without incurring the cost. Once again it should be emphasised, as in the discussion in Chapter V above, that these are matters of the second order of importance especially compared with the specification of the model itself.

A special case of this stochastic formulation is worth pointing out. Consider the following model for Λ and each of the Ω's; for some σ^2,

$$\lambda^{RS} = \sigma^2(\delta_{RS}b_R - b_Rb_S) \tag{6.26}$$

$$\omega_{ij}^R = \sigma^2 b_R(\delta_{ij}b_{iR} - b_{iR}b_{jR}), \tag{6.27}$$

which when substituted in (6.18), gives

$$\omega_{ij} = \sigma^2(b_i\delta_{ij} - b_ib_j). \tag{6.28}$$

This specification makes each good like every other good: in effect, only the scale factors differentiate the various cells of the matrix. This is an important limiting case since it represents the structure of the substitution matrix when preferences are genuinely additive. Thus, if the Theil second-order model is valid, and if the data are representable by the maximization of an additive utility function, then the variance–covariance matrix will have the structure (6.28), though not necessarily with constant σ^2. Note also the similarity between (6.28) and the structure assumed for the maximum likelihood estimation in Chapter V. Recalling equation (5.2), it can be seen that the two structures are identical if the average budget shares substituted for the marginal budget shares of (6.28). Since the *b*'s and *w*'s are comparatively close this difference is unlikely to be of great importance, and the use of the *w*'s has the not inconsiderable advantage of rendering the matrix positive semi-definite independently of the presence of inferior goods.

6.3 Hierarchic estimation and bias

The econometric properties of a hierarchic system of non-linear equations are not easily assessed. Algebraic expressions for the parameter estimates are not derivable and the alternative of numerical experimentation is very expensive. However, there are good grounds for believing that hierarchic estimation of the kind contemplated here will lead to biases of a type similar to those encountered if simultaneous models are estimated on a single equation basis. In this section I shall discuss these by means of a linear analogy. Although this is not an entirely satisfactory procedure, it is probable that non-linear estimation will do at least as badly as linear estimation. On the other hand, I shall be concerned to show that these biases are likely to be small in the cases presented here and thus can be excluded as the source of the major discrepancies which will appear below.

The basic problem is that the within group demand systems, relating the demand for an individual commodity to that for the group as a whole, have the property that the residuals are not independent of the main explanatory variable, i.e. total group expenditure. Consider a simple linear model relating expenditure on each good, μ_i, to total expenditure μ,

$$\mu_i = \alpha_i + \beta_i \mu + \epsilon_i \,. \qquad (6.29)$$

Here the β_i parameters add to unity and the errors ϵ_i to zero as in the linear expenditure system. This equation itself is not necessarily free from simultaneous equation bias since when income is replaced by total expenditure errors in each expenditure ϵ_i, will be reflected in the total μ. This problem has been discussed in an interchange between Summers (1959) and Prais (1959), and is avoided by assuming that μ is predetermined and that the model is only concerned with its allocation; thus the errors sum to zero and the covariance of μ and ϵ_i is zero. Note that this does *not* imply that total expenditure is determined without error in the consumption function, but only that the budgeting process is carried out independently of the consumption-saving decision.

A hierarchic version of this model is derived by summing over each group and substituting for μ in a manner similar to the derivation of equations (6.2) and (6.8). This gives

$$\mu_i = (\alpha_i - \alpha_G/\beta_G) + \beta_{iG}\mu_G + (\epsilon_i - \epsilon_G/\beta_G) \qquad (6.30)$$

and

$$\mu_G = \alpha_G + \beta_G\mu + \epsilon_G, \qquad (6.31)$$

where $\beta_{iG} = \beta_i/\beta_G$ and quantities subscripted by capitals denote sums over groups. The second of these equations, (6.31), the upper level of the hierarchy, presents no problems. The independence between ϵ_i and μ is carried through to an independence between ϵ_G and μ. However, in the lower level systems, (6.30), the compound error contains ϵ_G which, from (6.31), is part of μ_G. Ordinary least squares estimates of the parameters of (6.30) are thus biased and inconsistent.

The ordinary least squares estimate of β_{iG}, $\hat{\beta}_{iG}$, is given by

$$\hat{\beta}_{iG} = \frac{\mu_G'\mu_i}{\mu_G'\mu_G}, \qquad (6.32)$$

where the means have been removed from the observations on μ_i and μ_G. Substituting from (6.31) and (6.29)

$$\hat{\beta}_{iG} = \frac{(\beta_G\mu + \epsilon_G)'(\beta_i\mu + \epsilon_i)}{(\beta_G\mu + \epsilon_G)'(\beta_G\mu + \epsilon_G)} \qquad (6.33)$$

Denoting

$$\operatorname*{plim}_{T\to\infty} \frac{1}{T}\mu'\mu = \sigma_\mu^2 \qquad (6.34)$$

and

$$\operatorname*{plim}_{T\to\infty} \frac{1}{T}\epsilon_i'\epsilon_j = \mathcal{E}(\epsilon_{it}\epsilon_{jt}) = \omega_{ij}, \qquad (6.35)$$

the probability limit of the estimator is given by

$$\operatorname{plim} \hat{\beta}_{iG} = (\beta_{iG} + \xi_{iG})(1 + \xi_G)^{-1} \tag{6.35}$$

where $\xi_{iG} = \sum_{j \in G} \omega_{ij} / \sigma_\mu^2 \beta_G^2$.

Or, since ω_{ij} is small compared with σ_μ^2, we may write

$$\operatorname{plim} \hat{\beta}_{iG} = (\beta_{iG} + \xi_{iG})(1 - \xi_G) \tag{6.36}$$

So that the asymptotic bias is approximated by

$$\text{bias} = \frac{1}{\beta_G^2 \sigma_\mu^2} \{\sum_{j \in G} \omega_{ij} - \beta_{iG} \sum_{k \in G} \sum_{j \in G} \omega_{kj}\}, \tag{6.37}$$

which is not in general zero.

However, there are two good reasons for believing it to be small. In the first place, ω_{ij} is only a very small fraction of the variance of total expenditure σ_μ^2; and, in the second place, reasonable scaling of the matrix will mean that the terms in brackets will tend to cancel each other, thus reducing the bias even further. The first point can be gauged from the observed R^2-statistics for the top level of the hierarchy; from equation (6.31)

$$\operatorname{plim} (1 - R_G^2) = \operatorname{plim} \frac{\epsilon_G' \epsilon_G}{\mu_G' \mu_G} = \frac{\sum_k \sum_j \omega_{kj}}{\beta_G^2 \sigma_\mu^2 + \sum_k \sum_j \omega_{kj}}, \tag{6.38}$$

so that

$$\sum_k \sum_j \omega_{kj} / \beta_G^2 \sigma_\mu^2 = (1 - R_G^2)/R_G^2 . \tag{6.39}$$

As will be shown below, these group R^2 are uniformly high, usually greater than 0.99, so that (6.39) and thus (6.37) will be of the order of 0.01.

The cancelling out of the two terms in (6.37) occurs *exactly* when the stochastic specification is that given by (6.28), i.e. when the utility function is additive. Substituting from (6.28), we have

$$\text{bias} = \frac{\sigma^2}{\beta_G^2 \sigma_\mu^2} \{\beta_i - \beta_i \beta_G - \beta_i (1 - \beta_G)\} = 0. \tag{6.40}$$

Although it is only in this special case that the estimators are consistent, one might expect in general that the two terms in brackets in (6.37) would be, if not of the same sign, at least of the same order of magnitude; and this is all that is needed to support the claim that the bias is small.

This problem would thus seem to be of greater theoretical than practical interest, at least in the context of this book. Nevertheless, given the intellectual effort expended by economists on the conditions needed to construct hierarchic budgeting systems, it is of interest that such models in practice are likely to lead to biased and inconsistent parameter estimates. Neither is it easy to see any simple way out. It is easily shown that using predicted, rather than actual, values for μ_G in the second level of estimation leads to estimators which are still inconsistent, though the biases are different. For the purposes of the rest of this chapter, I wish only to emphasize the *smallness* of the bias; even with the added uncertainty of non-linearity, it is difficult to imagine that the anomalies which are found below can be explained from this cause.

6.4 The grouping of commodities

The analysis so far has assumed that the group to which each commodity should be assigned is known in advance. In this section some attention is paid to the problem of how such categorisation is done in practice and to what extent it is possible to use the data to form 'optimal' groupings.

We have already seen that the linear expenditure system, as an additive model, offers no basis for the distinguishing of groups; each commodity is on a par with every other commodity and, if the model holds good, any arbitrary collection of commodities is as good as any other arbitrary collection. In consequence it is necessary to look to factors disregarded by the model and thus to the error structure of the residuals. This is possible, at least in principle, since we have both an estimate of the variance–covariance matrix of residuals and knowledge of what it should be for any given grouping. The estimate of Ω comes from the maximum likelihood estimation of Chapter V, i.e. Table 5.2. Although the parameters there were estimated on the basis of an assumed structure for Ω, estimates of the parameters are asymptotically independent of estimates of Ω, and so we may use the residuals of the equations already estimated to give a consistent estimator of Ω according to

$$\tilde{\Omega} = \frac{1}{T} \sum_{t=1}^{T} \tilde{\epsilon}_t \tilde{\epsilon}_t' . \qquad (6.40)$$

This matrix can then be examined for patterns of the type predicted by (6.18) to reveal the structure of commodity grouping.

This is much more easily said than done. As already mentioned in another context, (6.40) has a number of defects as an estimator. The matrix Ω has dimensions 37×37 and in theory has rank 36 while the estimator (6.40) computed over 17 observations has rank at most 16. The consistency property is only likely to be of much value here with observations over, say, 100 years. Consequently, working with (6.40) is likely to lead to unreliable results with a high proportion of chance correlations. This problem apart, the examination of a 37×37 matrix for grouping patterns is a task that somehow must be mechanised, especially when exact results cannot be expected. Although very considerable progress has been made in methods of mathematical taxonomy in recent years, in particular, see Jardine and Sibson (1971) and Sibson (1972), a satisfactory algorithm for this type of problem does not yet seem to exist.

Consider the quantity d_{ij} defined for a pair of goods i and j by

$$d_{ij} = \tilde{\omega}_{ij}/\tilde{b}_i\tilde{b}_j, \tag{6.41}$$

which can be calculated from the results in Table 5.2. From (6.18) we can see that if i and j belong to different groups, R and S,

$$d_{ij} = \lambda^{RS} b_R b_S \quad (R \neq S) \tag{6.42}$$

whereas if i and j belong to the same group the formula for d_{ij} is more complex depending on i and j as well as on the group index. Thus for two commodities in different groups the appropriate element of the matrix D can be interpreted as a measure defining the two groups with reference to one another, though this interpretation does not hold if the goods belong to the same group. In consequence, for a pair of goods in the same group all elements of D referring to an arbitrary third good outside of the group will be the same. This, at least in principle, could be used as a basis for classification. Unfortunately, the method involves a closed circle of analysis which cannot be entered at any point. For, in order to allocate goods to groups we must know in advance what interpretation to attach to the elements of D. But this knowledge can come only from a knowledge of the correct grouping, which is the thing that is to be discovered. Or, from a more practical viewpoint, it might be decided that goods i and j belong to the same group on the basis that d_{ik} and d_{jk} were very similar for all k not equal to i or j.

However, if at a subsequent stage it is decided that another good, say good p, also belongs to the group, then d_{ip} and d_{jp} can no longer be interpreted as relevant for the first calculation and the evidence for linking i and j in the first place must be reassessed. In this kind of situation it is not even clear that a method exists which does not involve infinite regress at least as a possibility.

A pairing method not involving going back and recalculating previous groups was tried. The method was inspired by, but simpler than, the techniques proposed by Fisher (1969). Correlations were calculated exclusive of goods already or potentially in the group and those with the highest were merged. Given the difficulties of methodology and the poor qualities of the estimator of Ω it is perhaps not surprising that the results do not seem to make a great deal of sense. Some groupings made sense, others did not and it was never clear that the results corresponded to intuition better than any random partition. But this assessment itself poses conceptual problems since, in the absence of significance tests on the closeness or appropriateness of the clusters, one can only compare the results with *a priori* beliefs, using these latter as a basis of assessment. This tends to make the exercise quite futile since the only outcome which is deemed to be satisfactory is that which leads to the adoption of the course of action which would have been adopted in any case. I have attempted to discover whether there exists some better procedure than that described here and, in the literature of which I am aware, only three published studies contain the results of clustering commodities in consumer demand. The first of these, Bieri and de Janvry (1972), relies on correlations between the purchases themselves arguing that 'if decision-making on quantities demanded is done through preliminary budgeting over groups, items within the same budget category will tend to show high intercorrelations among themselves and also similar profiles of correlations with items outside the group'. It is hard to see why this should be true and I know of no model which gives this result. The second two studies, by Phlips (1971) and by Phlips and Rouzier (1972), use principal components analysis on the errors of estimation to identify particular groups according to their factor loadings. This is rather closer to our approach, especially in the second version which depends upon a formal structure for the Ω matrix. However it does rely on the contention that large correlations between errors, whether positive or negative, are more likely to occur within than across groups. Although it is not immediately obvious why this should be so, except that under their assumptions the corrected correlations will be zero under independence, the results, for eleven groups over some 40 observations, conform to the usual notions of similarity. I have not attempted to apply Phlips' techniques to the problem at hand, mainly because of the multiple singularity of the estimate of Ω. Overall, my impression remains that, given the state of the art of clustering and, probably more importantly, given the quality of the estimate of the covariance matrix in this case, it is best to leave well alone and to rely on groupings which conform to prior notions of what is sensible.

In consequence I have arranged the 37 commodities into eight broad groups corresponding (hopefully) to a likely partition of a weakly separable utility function. Though it is never possible to rule out the possibility of specific interactions between commodities in different groups, I think that the list below reduces this to a minimum, at least, *a priori*. The broad groups with the constituent parts are as follows (the numbers are the same as in the tables in Chapter V).

I Food	=	Goods 1–10	=	1. bread and cereals
				2. meat and bacon
				3. fish
				4. oils and fats
				5. sugar and confectionery
				6. dairy produce
				7. fruit
				8. potatoes and vegetables
				9. non-alcoholic beverages
				10. other manufactured food
II Clothing	=	Goods 11–12	=	11. footwear
				12. clothing
III Housing	=	Goods 13–14	=	13. rents, rates, etc.
				14. maintenance etc.
IV Fuel	=	Goods 15–18	=	15. coal
				16. electricity
				17. gas
				18. other fuel
V Drink and tobacco	=	Goods 19–21	=	19. beer
				20. wines and spirits
				21. cigarettes and tobacco

VI Transport and communication	= Goods 22–26 =	22. postal and telephone charges
		23. running costs of motor vehicles
		24. rail travel
		25. other travel
		26. expenditure abroad
VII Other goods	= Goods 27–33 =	27. textiles and hardware
		28. matches, soap etc.
		29. books
		30. newspapers
		31. recreational goods
		32. chemists' goods
		33. miscellaneous goods
VIII Other services	= Goods 34–37 =	34. domestic service
		35. catering
		36. entertainment
		37. other services

These then are the definitions of the two levels of the hierarchy estimated below.

6.5 The upper hierarchy

The full-information maximum likelihood estimates of the parameters of the linear expenditure system for the upper hierarchy are presented in Table 6.1. Columns 1, 3, and 5 give the estimates of b^0, b^1 and c respectively with asymptotic standard errors below. The accompanying parameter estimates in columns 2, 4 and 6, labelled b^{0*}, b^{1*} and c^*, are the aggregates of the maximum likelihood estimates of the detailed system and are calculated from the values given in Table 5.2. If the model is an adequate representation of the data these should be alternative estimates of the same quantities and thus should be close to one another. As already indicated in section 6.1 above, the aggregation of the c parameters involves an approximation of one price index for another. Columns 7 and 8, as in Table 5.2, list R^2-statistics for expenditures and quantities and income and price elasticities for 1963.

Taken as a whole, these equations are much more satisfactory than the detailed equations of Chapter V. The fits are uniformly

TABLE 6.1
The broad groups

	b^0	b^{0*}	$b^1 \times 10^2$	$b^{1*} \times 10^2$	c	c^*	R^2_{ex}/R^2_q	e_i/e_{ii}
I Food	.1306	.1193	−.5380	−.5896	76.23	80.09	.9994	0.517
	(.0085)		(.0541)		(1.46)		.9824	−.251
II Clothing	.1511	.1430	−.5028	−.4701	21.07	25.14	.9963	1.501
	(.0092)		(.0667)		(1.51)		.9889	−.493
III Housing	.0746	.0919	.6275	.6514	33.11	33.58	.9995	0.651
	(.0138)		(.0617)		(1.11)		.9953	−.236
IV Fuel	.0610	.0694	.1352	.0548	11.96	12.95	.9939	1.208
	(.0129)		(.0926)		(1.27)		.9761	−.365
V Drink and tobacco	.1266	.1243	−.1894	−.2061	34.64	37.72	.9983	0.953
	(.0109)		(.0694)		(1.28)		.9807	−.350
VI Transport and communication	.1532	.1567	.5089	.6078	20.20	23.53	.9993	1.551
	(.0098)		(.0542)		(1.08)		.9974	−.505
VII Other goods	.1549	.1457	−.3429	−.4103	20.64	24.83	.9987	1.542
	(.0076)		(.0487)		(1.49)		.9936	−.504
VIII Other services	.1480	.1498	.3018	.3622	38.45	41.60	.9987	0.990
	(.0140)		(.0877)		(1.60)		.9856	−.374

high and the results are highly plausible. None of the groups has a negative estimated *b*-coefficient so that none of the difficulties over inferiority reoccur. Equally, the income and price elasticities take acceptable values since for broad commodity groups such as these one might reasonably expect to discover a fairly narrow band of income elasticities accompanied by generally low price elasticities. It is results such as these which have led many investigators using the linear expenditure system at a relatively aggregated level to be so pleased with their results. But while in an absolute sense it is obvious that the aggregate model is more satisfactory than its disaggregated counterpart, even in this case the model still suffers from many of the same drawbacks. Again there are difficulties over Pigou's Law. Although it is clear from the table that the proportionality law is not such a close approximation as in the 37 good case, it is still true that the price elasticities are determined by the income elasticities and the supernumerary ratio in a way that is very close to linear, see Figure 6.1 below. Admittedly, such a relationship is more plausible *a priori* for the aggregate model, but it is not obvious that it holds good in practice. Indeed, experiments with a loglinear model, corresponding

Figure 6.1: Income and price elasticities for 8 group system

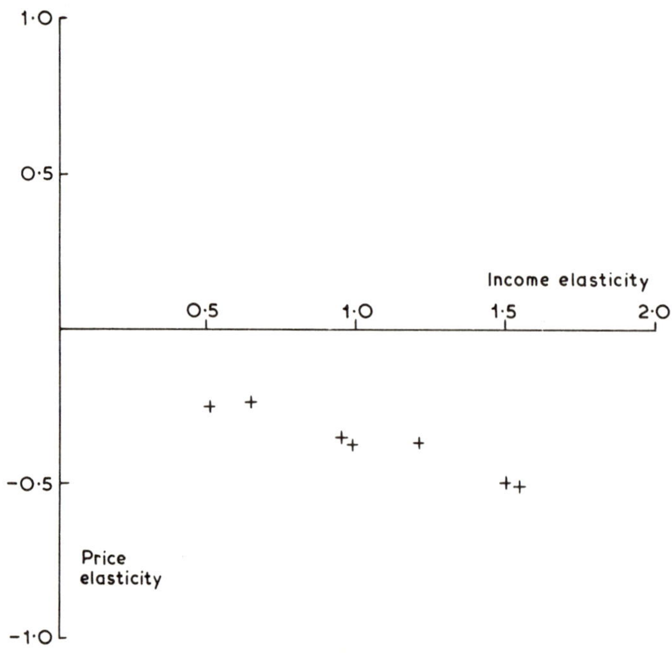

to those in Chapter V, indicated that the law is rejected for just as high a proportion of the goods as it was in the detailed analysis. It may well be that additivity is no better a description of consumer behaviour with respect to aggregated demands than it is for more detailed purchases.

However, this is not the principal issue of this chapter and the empirical validity of the linear expenditure system has already been discussed at length. Here the main problem is whether a hierarchic methodology can be used as a very cheap and convenient substitute for the expensive and more unwieldy simultaneous model. From this point of view the correspondence between the estimates of the aggregates and the aggregated estimates revealed by Table 6.1 is very gratifying. For all three sets of parameters, the two models are very close indeed and show almost no operational difference between the two forms of the model. For defenders of the linear expenditure system this consistency is very satisfactory but we shall see below that is not preserved in each of the second-level models.

6.6 The lower hierarchies

I shall discuss each of the eight groups in turn highlighting only those commodities where the hierarchic model differs significantly in explanation from the simultaneous system. To aid the comparison I shall once again present a number of derived statistics. Firstly, R^2-statistics are given not only for the equations as estimated but also for the equations as they would be used in practice. For, in forecasting, the *actual* group expenditures are not known and those predicted from the first level of the hierarchy must be used. Thus, for a fair comparison with the simultaneous model the 'indirect', as well as direct, R^2-statistics have been calculated for the predictions over the fitted period. Nevertheless, for estimation purposes the *actual* group expenditures were used. This apparent inconsistency was adopted to preserve that independence of the two levels of the hierarchy which is one of its most important properties. If predicted values are used, any change in the parameter estimates of the upper system will always lead to the need for complete re-estimation of all the subsidiary systems and this would destroy much of the convenience of having a hierarchy at all. And, as mentioned in section 3 above, there is little to choose between the methods, from a statistical point of view.

Secondly, for comparison with the previous chapter, the values of the parameters are calculated which would obtain if the model were correct, the parameters given in Table 5.2 were the true values, and the approximations inherent in (6.15) and (6.16) held good. This again is a consistency check between the two alternative methodologies. Thus, besides the values b^0, b^1 and c are listed values for β^0, β^1 and γ, which are calculated by substituting the Table 5.2 values in the approximation formulae (6.15) and (6.16). The values for γ are the same as those for the original c's.

Income and price elasticities for 1963 are also presented. These are calculated in the usual way from the formulae (3.29) and (3.41) except that account is taken of the derivatives of group expenditure with respect to total income and the price of the good being considered. This results in important modifications to the properties of the elasticities and these, as well as the precise formulae will be discussed in the final section, (see (6.47) and (6.50) below).

(i) *Food*

TABLE 6.2
Subsystem I: Food

	b^0	β^0	$b^1 \times 10^2$	$\beta^1 \times 10^2$	c	γ	R^2_{ex}/R^2_q direct	R^2_{ex}/R^2_q indirect	e_i^{63}/e_{ii}^{63}
1. Bread and	.1068	−.1015	−.2194	−.8722	6.88	12.47	.9944	.9954	0.42
cereals	(.0104)		(.0181)		(0.44)		.9325	.9483	−0.39
2. Meat and	.4115	.3732	.1117	.2796	5.32	20.00	.9984	.9972	0.79
bacon	(.0181)		(.0144)		(1.42)		.9682	.9447	−0.56
3. Fish	−.0442	.0654	.0078	−.2976	4.96	2.59	.9226	.9243	−0.68
	(.0130)		(.0032)		(0.56)		−.0819	.0015	0.71
4. Oils and	.0227	.0343	−.0564	−.1565	3.44	4.23	.8944	.8826	0.23
fats	(.0035)		(.0106)		(0.16)		.5910	.5468	−0.23
5. Sugar and	.0825	−.0624	−.2059	−.5967	5.11	9.42	.9765	.9796	0.43
sweets	(.0051)		(.0152)		(0.21)		.7958	.8302	−0.41
6. Dairy produce	.1407	.1786	−.0300	.0420	6.73	11.65	.9935	.9952	0.49
	(.0108)		(.0178)		(0.58)		.9192	.9408	−0.45
7. Fruit	.0612	.1249	.0099	−.0697	2.64	4.38	.9736	.9724	0.52
	(.0087)		(.0168)		(0.43)		.8754	.8649	−0.49
8. Potatoes and	.0590	.1950	.3399	1.1838	7.57	8.57	.9962	.9955	0.26
vegetables	(.0048)		(.0178)		(0.22)		.9794	.9758	−0.26
9. Beverages	.0376	.1062	.1065	.3626	3.84	4.66	.9866	.9840	0.31
	(.0050)		(.0112)		(0.20)		.9523	.9432	−0.30
10. Other manufac-	.1223	.0863	−.0642	.1248	−2.73	2.08	.9640	.9628	2.04
tured food	(.0075)		(.0106)		(0.40)		.8633	.8656	−1.79

There is a greater degree of uncertainty involved in the estimation of this group than is indicated by the small standard errors. The estimation of a ten equation system is very near to the limit of what can be achieved with only seventeen observations, and this means that the variance–covariance matrix of the system is close to being multiply singular. In consequence, a wide range of values of the parameters lead to high values for the likelihood function and the maximum itself is not very well defined. It may thus be that the difference between the two sets of estimates revealed by the table are not so important as may at first appear.

Leaving aside the question of comparison, the table shows that the two-stage procedure can explain the expenditures on foods certainly no worse than the original simultaneous model. The R^2-statistics are mostly higher than in Table 5.2 and the exceptions are not very important ones. Even the indirect predictions, which might be expected to magnify the errors of both levels of the system, are acceptably close to the actuals. Another advantage of the subsystem is the smaller rôle assigned to the time trends; for each of the ten goods the time trend is absolutely smaller than the value predicted by the simultaneous system. To make up for this a more important part is played by prices; the price elasticities are absolutely higher relative to the income elasticities and in one case (the first encountered so far) that of other manufactured food, the price elasticity is absolutely greater than unity. On these grounds, which seem to indicate greater flexibility in the hierarchic model, it might be preferred to the full version. However it must be remembered that this model was derived as a convenient approximation to the larger version and it is not immediately clear whether differences of this sort are acceptable within such a framework. In this particular case, however, the differences may not be significant and we shall postpone discussion of the general issue of compatibility to section 7 below after examining the results for the other groups.

(ii) *Clothing*

TABLE 6.3
Subsystem II: Clothing

	b^0	β^0	$b^1 \times 10^2$	$\beta^1 \times 10^2$	c	γ	R^2_{ex}/R^2_q direct	R^2_{ex}/R^2_q indirect	e_i^{63}/e_{ii}^{63}
1. Footwear	.1894	.1568	−.1501	−.1258	2.52	4.54	.9960	.9904	1.64
	(.0270)		(.0579)		(1.85)		.9790	.9565	−0.57
2. Clothing	.8106	.8432	.1501	.1258	13.81	20.60	.9998	.9965	1.47
	(.0270)		(.0579)		(5.46)		.9995	.9902	−0.50

With only two commodities, the full information estimators are very well defined and, at least in this case, the estimates from both systems are much closer. Once again the hierarchic procedure does not result in any loss of fit; indeed, even the indirect R^2-statistics are higher than those in Table 5.2. Even so, this subsystem presents no difficulty either for the hierarchic model *per se* or for the compatibility between the two versions.

(iii) *Housing*

TABLE 6.4
Subsystem III: Housing

	b^0	β^0	$b^1 \times 10^2$	$\beta^1 \times 10^2$	c	γ	R^2_{ex}/R^2_q direct	R^2_{ex}/R^2_q indirect	e_i^{63}/e_{ii}^{63}
1. Rent, etc.	.6764	.6355	.2234	.6824	26.12	28.84	.9999	.9997	0.54
	(.1014)		(.6080)		(6.82)		.9959	.9894	−0.23
2. Repairs, etc.	.3236	.3645	−.2234	−.6824	3.86	4.74	.9972	.9946	1.18
	(.1014)		(.6080)		(1.84)		.9909	.9869	−0.38

Much the same comments apply here as applied for the previous group. The only major point of difference is the time trend which is insignificant even by the understated standard error given here. Otherwise the two sets of figures are notable for their close correspondence.

(iv) *Fuel*

TABLE 6.5
Subsystem IV: Fuel

	b^0	β^0	$b^1 \times 10^2$	$\beta^1 \times 10^2$	c	γ	R^2_{ex}/R^2_q direct	R^2_{ex}/R^2_q indirect	e_i^{63}/e_{ii}^{63}
1. Coal	.0985	−.0814	−.2223	−4.0095	0.53	6.26	.8652	.8231	0.37
	(.0242)		(.1220)		(0.02)		.9617	.9486	−0.85
2. Electricity	.0207	1.0677	1.0851	−1.4672	5.48	1.44	.9957	.9954	0.07
	(.0141)		(.2880)		(0.52)		.9927	.9924	−0.17
3. Gas	.8490	−.1482	.9322	6.7333	−40.54	3.96	.9062	.9566	5.24
	(.0465)		(.1732)		(14.61)		.8931	.9454	−2.26
4. Other fuel	.0318	.1619	.0694	−1.2560	0.39	1.29	.9752	.9703	0.33
	(.0109)		(.0078)		(0.33)		.7940	.7521	−0.79

The two sets of estimates are here quite startlingly different; the original model and the hierarchic model give quite different explanations of behaviour. And here significance is not in doubt since, as in subsystems II and III, the estimates are well determined. As far as fit is concerned, the hierarchic model is slightly inferior though the difference is not uniform. On the other hand, as was seen to a lesser extent with food in subsystem I, the time trends are very much smaller in the hierarchic model, while prices are very much more important. And as was seen in Chapter V, the fuels were among those commodities where the limited role of prices in the original linear expenditure system was particularly restrictive. So that, once again, at the price of incompatibility the hierarchic model shows a considerable increase in plausibility, if not in fit.

(v) *Drink and tobacco*

TABLE 6.6
Subsystem V: Drink and tobacco

	b^0	β^0	$b^1 \times 10^2$	$\beta^1 \times 10^2$	c	γ	R^2_{ex}/R^2_q direct	R^2_{ex}/R^2_q indirect	e_i^{63}/e_{ii}^{63}
1. Beer	.1542	.1895	1.9972	2.1655	11.59	11.55	.9972	.9957	0.51
	(.0408)		(.2274)		(0.27)		.9811	.9722	−0.16
2. Wines and	.4314	.5071	.8535	.5465	4.73	5.06	.9936	.9938	2.02
spirits	(.0463)		(.2207)		(0.60)		.9822	.9834	−0.43
3. Cigarettes and	.4144	.3034	−2.8511	−2.7116	19.24	21.11	.9975	.9951	0.77
tobacco	(.0648)		(.2727)		(1.38)		.9039	.8110	−0.26

With these estimates there is a return to compatibility between the two versions of the model. The differences in the parameter estimates are all within the bounds of chance and the predicted values correspond almost exactly.

(vi) *Transport and communication*

TABLE 6.7
Subsystem VI: Transport and communication

	b^0	β^0	$b^1 \times 10^2$	$\beta^1 \times 10^2$	c	γ	R^2_{ex}/R^2_q direct	R^2_{ex}/R^2_q indirect	e_i^{63}/e_{ii}^{63}
1. Postal,	.0240	.0696	.1964	.2513	2.22	2.46	.9982	.9980	0.40
telephone	(.0056)		(.0210)		(0.25)		.9924	.9919	−0.32
2. R. costs of	.2950	.8129	1.6413	.6628	0.42	3.93	.9980	.9982	1.23
motor vehicles	(.0398)		(.1606)		(1.64)		.9970	.9972	−0.83
3. Rail travel	.0474	−.1123	−.2052	.7218	1.00	4.32	.9464	.9460	0.85
	(.0081)		(.0159)		(0.41)		.9028	.9035	−0.66
4. Other travel	.2619	−.0200	−.5890	.6998	−1.59	9.60	.9980	.9966	1.48
	(.0303)		(.0979)		(1.33)		.8176	.7090	−1.00
5. Expenditure	.3717	.2498	−1.0436	−2.3358	−9.68	3.22	.9613	.9466	3.32
abroad	(.0453)		(.1521)		(2.09)		.8855	.8460	−1.83

As in the case of fuel, there are larger discrepancies than can be comfortably explained by statistical accident. And, especially for the last three categories where the differences are largest, there are considerable improvements in fit over the simultaneous model. It is also noticeable that in two of these, the hierarchic model allows price elasticities less than minus one and this contributes to the improvement in the explanatory power of the model. At the same time the two domestic travel categories are no longer classed as inferior although, as in many of the cases analysed in Chapter V, the negative time trend is relied upon to explain the secular decline in purchases. Even so, once again the hierarchic model seems to out-perform its parent.

(vii) *Other goods*

TABLE 6.8
Subsystem VII: Other goods

	b^0	β^0	$b^1 \times 10^2$	$\beta^1 \times 10^2$	c	γ	R^2_{ex}/R^2_q direct	R^2_{ex}/R^2_q indirect	e_i^{63}/e_{ii}^{63}
1. Textiles and hardware	.2385 (.0129)	.2689	.0403 (.0363)	.2822	0.75 (0.52)	5.05	.9989 .9961	.9972 .9915	1.66 −0.81
2. Matches, soap, etc.	.0649 (.0086)	.0122	−.1534 (.0264)	.0086	1.92 (0.26)	3.73	.9911 .3714	.9927 .4346	0.92 −0.50
3. Books and magazines	.0400 (.0176)	−.0074	−.0291 (.0067)	−.0460	1.09 (0.54)	2.32	.9872 .3758	.9860 .3002	0.95 −0.52
4. Newspapers	.0548 (.0104)	−.0195	−.0808 (.0230)	.5010	1.46 (0.30)	3.25	.9932 .9022	.9920 .8975	0.97 −0.53
5. Recreational goods	.2115 (.0155)	.3194	.4800 (.0565)	.8882	1.42 (0.58)	4.37	.9983 .9950	.9977 .9935	1.50 −0.75
6. Chemists goods	.2115 (.0113)	.2261	−.0623 (.0317)	−.0399	−0.72 (0.34)	3.20	.9976 .9917	.9977 .9921	2.07 −1.00
7. Other misc. goods n.e.s.	.1789 (.0047)	.2002	−.1947 (.0169)	−.5919	−0.30 (0.23)	2.91	.9975 .9917	.9916 .9733	1.95 −0.96

The differences in this category are relatively unimportant and are concentrated in the commodities which are very badly explained. In broad terms, the hierarchic model reproduces the explanations of the full model and results in no significant loss in explanatory power.

(viii) *Other services*

TABLE 6.9
Subsystem VIII: Other services

	b^0	β^0	$b^1 \times 10^2$	$\beta^1 \times 10^2$	c	γ	R^2_{ex}/R^2_q direct	R^2_{ex}/R^2_q indirect	e_i^{63}/e_{ii}^{63}
1. Domestic	−.0163	−.0902	.3881	.3873	1.91	3.02	.9534	.9677	−0.41
serivce	(.0066)		(.0401)		(0.03)		.9470	.9680	−0.06
2. Catering	−.1342	.4759	−3.1097	−4.2725	19.02	15.03	.9934	.9932	−0.35
	(.0462)		(.2652)		(0.58)		.8849	.8858	−0.01
3. Entertainment	.1770	.1468	−.1795	.0655	7.72	4.79	.9950	.9857	1.45
	(.0090)		(.0794)		(0.32)		.9840	.9512	0.11
4. Other services	.9735	.4674	2.9011	3.8194	31.47	18.76	.9976	.9976	2.11
	(.0459)		(.2792)		(2.14)		.9895	.9899	−0.37

This is a rather curious set of estimates. In particular, unlike any of the other systems so far estimated, group supernumerary expenditure is *negative* for all but the last observation. This stands the system on its head; for example, the *c*'s take values close to the last observed purchases rather than to the first as has so far been the case. It also makes the system very difficult to interpret and one is forced to conclude that, for this group at least, the model is a very bad approximation to reality. Once again we may note that in the discussion on Pigou's Law in the simultaneous system, three of these four commodities were particularly badly served by a model embodying the proportionality restriction. It is thus not surprising that, when isolated, these commodities are predicted even more inaccurately.

6.7 Comparison of hierarchic and disaggregated models

In the previous section it was seen that four of the groupings (clothing, housing, drink and tobacco, other goods) are broadly consistent with the main model; three are inconsistent (fuel, transport and communication, and other services); and one (food) has a doubtful intermediate status. However, even in the incompatible cases, there is no loss of explanatory power and, on the contrary, there are several cases where the equations both fit better and appear more plausible. Thus while the hierarchic methodology is certainly a viable alternative *vis-à-vis* full simultaneous estimation, regarded as an approximation to the latter its good performance is something of an embarrassment, especially since it is clear that the improvement cannot entirely be attributed to chance.

I think it is also fairly obvious that the incompatibilities cannot be explained in terms of the phenomena discussed earlier in the Chapter. The first possibility is the approximation of the theoretical indices which have the c's as weights by Paasche implicit price deflators. Experiments with several of the groups showed very clearly that even in those cases where some c's were negative and where the relative prices had considerable independent movement, the Paasche index was an excellent approximation. The second possibility is the linear approximation for the ratio of two time trends given by (6.15) and (6.16). These can be checked directly and will only go wrong if, for the broad groups, b^1 is not small relative to b^0. But this too does not occur. Lastly, there is the possibility that the estimates are biassed in the manner discussed in section 6.3; this too is very unlikely in the face of the high R^2-statistics quoted in Table 6.1.

The clue to this situation lies in the observation that the incompatibilities are associated largely with those commodities for which Pigou's Law in the form imposed by the simultaneous model is a particularly poor representation. In the rest of this section it will be shown that the hierarchic model, though not dispensing entirely with the law, weakens its force considerably. In so doing, and only in so far as it does so, the model becomes inconsistent with the linear expenditure system and indeed with any model derivable from the maximization of a utility function. The extra flexibility is thus bought at the expense of discarding demand theory. Whether this trade is a bargain or not cannot easily be quantified, but I shall offer a number of observations below.

It is convenient to begin by seeing the extent to which the law is in fact weakened. One aspect of this is illustrated in Figure 6.2 which once again plots income against price elasticity; the values for each good being taken from Tables 6.2–6.9. Clearly, the simple linear relationship evidenced by Figure 5.2 is no longer in evidence. Rather than being replaced by a simple scatter, however, the points now have a tendency to lie along a series of lines, one for each group, with a degree of approximation which also varies from group to group. This is probably most clearly seen from the tables rather than the chart; for example, in Table 6.2, the price elasticities are close to minus the income elasticities for most of the foods. Another important consequence of the operation of the law which was revealed in Chapter V is its tendency to generate inferior goods. Once again, this is much reduced in the hierarchic version; here only three, rather than nine, commodities are treated in this way. Finally, a number of goods are now estimated to be price elastic, a phenomenon which was effectively prevented by the operation of the law in the fully disaggregated model.

Figure 6.2: Income and price elasticities for hierarchy

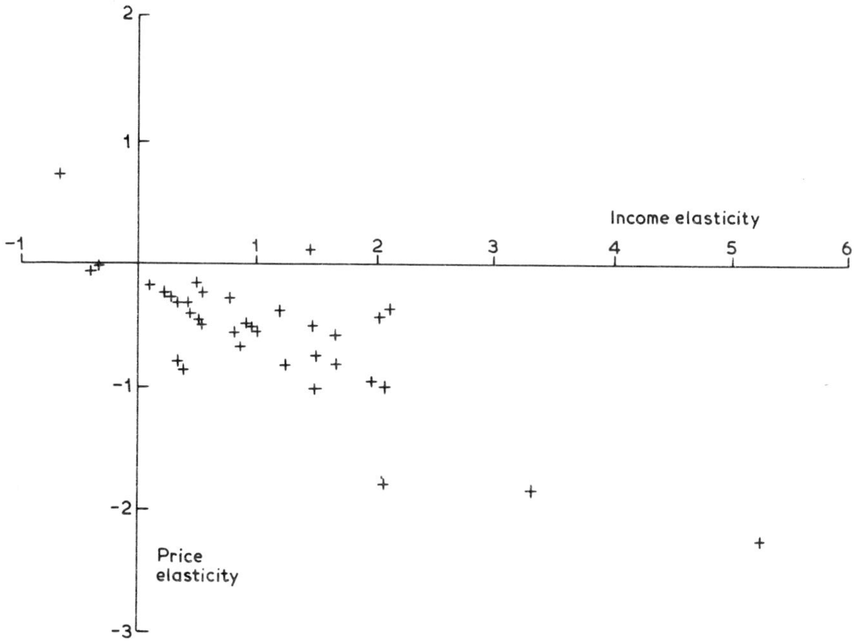

The explanation of these results can best be treated by splitting up the two levels of the hierarchy. At the risk of notational confusion, I shall rewrite the model as

$$p_i q_i = p_i c_i + b_i(\mu_I - \sum_{k \in I} p_k c_k) \qquad (6.43)$$

and

$$\mu_I = \pi_I \gamma_I + \beta_I(\mu - \sum_K \pi_K \gamma_K), \qquad (6.44)$$

where (6.43) is the lower level linking individual to group expenditures and (6.44) is the upper level explaining the broad groups in terms of the total. The notational change is to emphasize the fact that these must now be regarded as independent of one another; they cannot both be derived from the same model. Thus, in general,

$$\sum_{i \in I} p_i c_i \neq \gamma_I \pi_I. \tag{6.45}$$

The general model for the ith commodity must now be written, by substituting (6.44) in (6.43)

$$p_i q_i = p_i c_i + b_i\{\pi_I \gamma_I - \sum_k p_k c_k\} + b_i \beta_I(\mu - \Sigma\, \pi_K \gamma_K) \tag{6.46}$$

which in the special case where (6.45) does not hold, reduces to the linear expenditure system.

This is of course, a completely different model, and it must be analysed as such. In the first place, it is considerably less restrictive than the linear expenditure system since there are $(2N - 1)$ additional independent parameters, the β_I's and γ_I's. These permit some extra flexibility in the relationship between price and income elasticities. Differentiating (6.46) with respect to income yields

$$e_i = \tilde{e}_i \cdot e_I, \tag{6.47}$$

where $\tilde{e}_i$ is the within-group income elasticity or the elasticity of purchases of good i with respect to group expenditure, and e_I is the income elasticity of the quantity index of the group as a whole. These two elasticities can be derived from (6.43) and (6.44) as if each were a separate independent linear expenditure system. For price elasticities, differentiation gives

$$e_{ii} = \tilde{e}_{ii} + b_i(e_{II} + 1)\frac{\mu_I}{\pi_I}\frac{\partial \pi_I}{\partial p_i}\frac{1}{q_i}, \tag{6.48}$$

where $\tilde{e}_{ii}$ is the own-price elasticity of good i when total group expenditure is constant and e_{II} is the own-price elasticity of the group quantity index. In this study, the π_I's are current-weighted Paasche indices, i.e.

$$\pi_I = \sum_{k \in I} p_k q_k^* / \sum_{k \in I} p_k^0 q_k^*, \tag{6.49}$$

where p^0 are base period prices, and q^* are *actual* quantities, to be distinguished from the q as predicted by the model. In this case (6.48) reduces to

$$e_{ii} = \tilde{e}_{ii} + b_i(e_{II} + 1)\frac{q_i^*}{q_i}. \tag{6.50}$$

The relationship between the e_{ii}'s and the e_i's is now more complicated than in the simultaneous model. However, we know that for each group and for the broad groups we have approximately

$$\tilde{e}_{ii} = \phi_I \tilde{e}_i, \tag{6.51}$$

and

$$e_{II} = \phi e_I, \tag{6.52}$$

where the group ϕ_I's are the group supernumerary ratios in the usual way. At the same time, the first term on the right hand side of (6.50) will usually be larger than the second and so, by substitution, the approximation

$$e_{ii} = e_i \phi_I / e_I \tag{6.53}$$

will tend to hold and this is observable in the tables. Note, however, that it is group specific rather than universal, as in the simultaneous model, and furthermore that it is a much less good approximation. This is because, firstly, there are two sources of error rather than one, i.e. both (6.50) and (6.51); and, secondly, though the remainder is still of order n^{-1}, the n now refers to the number of commodities in the group and this is much smaller than the grand total.

The incompatibilities between the two models can be explained in terms of this analysis. If the c_i-parameters are the same within a group as in the full model, by adding up the equations of the original system we may derive

$$\frac{\mu_I - \sum_{k \in I} p_k c_k}{\mu_I} = \frac{\mu - \sum_k p_k c_k}{\mu} \cdot e_I,$$

from which

$$\phi_I = \phi e_I, \tag{6.54}$$

and so (6.53) reduces to Pigou's Law as originally stated. Similarly (6.54) will hold only if the c's in the group add up to the same total as the simultaneous estimates. Thus we may expect compatibility between the hierarchic and simultaneous models if, and only if, the ratio of price to income elasticities within each group is the same as it is for the average of goods as a whole. As was seen in Chapter V, this is most obviously false for the fuel and services groups and these produce the most incompatible estimates. But there are other consequences. Compatibility will depend on which goods are assigned to which groups and, even in the upper level of the hierarchy, if the combination is carried out so that the groups are different on average from the individual goods (say by being much less price elastic) the broad group model will also be inconsistent with the full system. Thus the compatibility which is displayed by Table 6.1 is largely accidental.

If it were true that the linear expenditure system held good and in particular that Pigou's Law was true for each commodity, then there would be nothing to choose between the simultaneous and hierarchic models. But, in reality, many goods do not conform to either the linear expenditure system in general or to Pigou's Law in particular, and thus the consistency of the two models in practice will depend on the grouping of commodities. If anomalous goods are grouped together, then incompatibilities are particularly likely to arise. Alternatively, it might be possible to arrange a grouping procedure which, by putting together commodities with diverse price elasticity to income elasticity ratios, would preserve the original structure. But this is much less interesting than the opposite possibility: that of grouping the commodities so as to exploit the discrepancies and thus do deliberately what was done accidentally above, i.e. to improve explanation and plausibility. If this is to be done, it is necessary to abandon the linear expenditure system as a basis for the model and attempt to find a justification for the hierarchic model (6.43) and (6.44) *per se*.

To do so, let us examine the properties of the new model. First, it is obvious that the system still aggregates: expenditures within the group add to group expenditures which, in turn, add to total expenditure. Second, the model remains homogeneous. A proportional change in prices and total expenditure will effect an equiproportional change in the left-hand side of equation (6.46), leaving the quantities demanded unchanged. This presupposes the entirely reasonable restriction that the price indices π_I are homogeneous of the first degree in the individual prices. It is when we come to symmetry that difficulties arise. In fact, if the indices π_I are linear in the prices (e.g. the Paasche indices above) then (6.46) makes expenditures a linear function of prices and income and, as such, can only exhibit symmetry and thus be consistent with demand theory if it is the linear expenditure system. For in Chapter III we saw that the linear expenditure system is the only linear model consistent with symmetry. And I shall show that, in general, (6.46) is consistent with demand theory if, and only if, the group indices are linear and are the linear expenditure system indices (6.3). In consequence, if we are to exploit the hierarchic version as a remedy for the weaknesses of the original linear expenditure system, to do so involves abandoning not only the original model but also the theory on which it is based.

The Slutsky substitution responses are derived, firstly between two different goods in the same group, and, secondly, between two goods in different groups. If i and j belong to I and $i \neq j$,

$$S_{ij} = \tilde{S}_{ij} - \frac{b_i}{p_i}(1-\beta_I)\left(c_j - \gamma_I \frac{\partial \pi_I}{\partial p_j}\right), \qquad (6.55)$$

where $\tilde{S}_{ij}$ is the substitution response if group expenditure is constant, i.e. as before,

$$\tilde{S}_{ij} = -\frac{b_i b_j}{p_i p_j}(\mu_I - \sum_{k \in I} p_k c_k), \qquad (6.56)$$

and this last is clearly symmetric. But if (6.55) is to be symmetric for arbitrary values of p_i, the last term in brackets must be zero; hence

$$c_j = \gamma_I \frac{\partial \pi_I}{\partial p_j}, \qquad (6.57)$$

or since π_I is homogeneous of the first order,

$$\gamma_I \pi_I = \sum_{k \in I} p_k c_k, \qquad (6.58)$$

and this is the condition that (6.46) be the linear expenditure system. Scaling of π so that it is unity in the base year, gives

$$\gamma_I = \sum_{k \in I} p_k^0 c_k, \qquad (6.59)$$

and so the indices are formally identical to the original indices (6.3). This demonstrates necessity: sufficiency is obvious from inspection of (6.46).

Although it is not strictly necessary to deal with goods in different groups, since the result has been proved, for completeness we show that the same condition can be deduced in this alternative way. For $i \in I$, $j \in J$ and $I \neq J$,

$$S_{ij} = \frac{b_i \beta_I}{p_i}\left\{\left(c_j - \gamma_J \frac{\partial \pi_J}{\partial p_j}\right) + \frac{b_j}{p_j}(\pi_J \gamma_J - \sum_{k \in J} p_k c_k)\right\}, \qquad (6.60)$$

So that for arbitrary p_i and p_j, both terms in round brackets are zero, so that the symmetry of (6.60) implies both (6.57) and (6.58) and thus that (6.46) must be the linear expenditure system.

To some readers, at least, the abandonment of symmetry may not seem to be a serious matter, especially if it is accompanied by an increase in the general acceptability of the predictive equations. The aggregation and homogeneity postulates can reasonably be regarded as more important, and it can always be argued that symmetry is not a property which need hold for aggregate models, though this objection also applies to homogeneity. The trouble with this position is that it allows anything through, offering little *a priori* methodology for discriminating between models. And although one can see possible reasons why symmetry might not hold, it is hard to advance a positive defence for the particular type of asymmetry embodied in this model.

These objections are weakened to the extent that the hierarchic model outperforms the more theoretically satisfactory simultaneous model. If the former is demonstrably superior, the 'safety' or inherent plausibility of the latter, which was seen in practice in Chapter V, carries much less weight. But in the previous section we saw that although the hierarchic model did perform better, the difference was not large. Even so, it could reasonably be argued that this was due to an inappropriate grouping of commodities, and that full advantage of the model can only be taken if they are grouped according to (6.53), i.e. in clusters according to the value of the ratio e_{ii}/e_i. This requires an independent estimate of this ratio, not an entirely satisfactory procedure since this can be done only by using a different and probably inconsistent model. However, as in Chapter V, a double-logarithmic model was estimated and the commodities listed according to the value of the ratio. The results, like the previous attempts to group, are not reported here and for much the same reasons. They make little intuitive sense and, as in the previous case, do not seem to provide a firm enough basis for the revision of prior notions. The case for or against the practical application of the model thus seems to be very much an open one.

In conclusion, we may draw together the various threads of this chapter. The linear expenditure system can be rewritten in a hierarchic form allowing the separate estimation of different parts of the model. Such estimation is viable in the sense that the models fit at least as well as the original, and can be estimated at a considerable saving in cost. However, because of the general invalidity of Pigou's Law, the submodels do not lead to results which are consistent with the original model and the modifications which are necessary to the model to take account of this render it inconsistent with demand theory. These inconsistencies are of course as much due to the deficiencies of the original model as they are to the deficiencies of the hierarchy *per se* and the choice between using one system or the other is by no means an easy one. For, on the one hand, the simultaneous system embodies all the advantages of a theoretically sound model; while, on the other, the hierarchic system is simpler to use as well as fitting better. However, it is hard to see why, if we are to abandon the linear expenditure system and with it the use of utility analysis for aggregate data, we should adopt instead a rather hybrid model such as the hierarchy instead of a more pragmatic and more flexible system.

Chapter 7

THE FORECASTING MECHANISM: A TRIAL RUN TO 1975

The main purpose of this chapter is to present an analysis of the performance in forecasting of the various models discussed in earlier chapters. This is done by using each of the four models to predict the pattern of demand in a future year relatively close to the sample period. The year 1975 was chosen, partly because it is a target year for the Cambridge Growth Model which can thus provide useful supplementary information, and partly because it is far enough beyond the last year of the sample period to allow divergence between the models while being close enough to the time of writing to allow some assessment of the realism of alternative projections. The information gleaned from this preliminary comparison can then be used to select appropriate equations for more distinct projections, in particular for 1980.

In order to calculate projections at all, it is necessary to have values for the independent variables: namely, total expenditure, and prices. In sections 7.1 and 7.2 below, each of these is treated in turn. In the first of these sections, an aggregate consumption function is presented and used to predict total expenditures in 1975; in the second section, we give an outline of the way in which the Cambridge growth model generates prices and this is applied, once again, for 1975. In section 7.3, these results are fed into the various models to derive alternative expenditure patterns for the predicted year; these projections are discussed on a commodity by commodity basis. Lastly, in section 7.4, the substantive conclusions of the comparisons are brought together and summarized.

7.1 The consumption function

The link between personal disposable income and consumers'

expenditure is provided by the consumption function developed by Stone in a series of papers, Stone and Rowe (1962), Stone (1964, 1966) and Stone (1973). In this model, consumption is made to depend upon income and upon wealth, with differential marginal propensities to consume out of the permanent and transient components of each. Denoting permanent components by the subscript 1, and transient components by the subscript 2, the function is taken to be linear homogeneous, so that we may write

$$\epsilon = \alpha_1\omega_1 + \alpha_2\omega_2 + \beta_1\mu_1 + \beta_2\mu_2, \tag{7.1}$$

where ϵ is total expenditure, ω is wealth, and μ is personal disposable income. All variables are taken *per capita* and in constant prices. Note that, for the first time in this book, a distinction is being made between total expenditure on the one hand, and income on the other. In this chapter, the symbol μ is reserved for income which is not synonymous with total expenditure.

Permanent and transient components together add to measured income or wealth; thus

$$\omega_1 + \omega_2 \equiv \omega \tag{7.2}$$

$$\mu_1 + \mu_2 \equiv \mu. \tag{7.3}$$

The permanent component of income is defined by an adaptive mechanism of the form

$$\mu_1 = \lambda\mu + (1-\lambda)\Lambda^{-1}\mu_1, \tag{7.4}$$

where Λ is the shift operator, i.e.

$$\Lambda^\theta x_\tau = x_{\tau+\theta}. \tag{7.5}$$

The distinction between the two components of wealth may be drawn in a number of different ways; either an adaptive mechanism similar to (7.4) may be used, or the two components may be linked directly to observable components of the wealth stock, e.g. accumulated saving, revaluations, and so on. These alternatives, in conjunction with the wide range of possible definitions of wealth itself, give rise to a large number of possible permutations; these have been discussed by Stone (1973). To summarize, he found that, no matter which definition was used, the marginal propensity to consume transient wealth was never significantly different from zero; i.e., the statement that $\alpha_2 = 0$ can never be disproved. Secondly, he found that defining permanent wealth as accumulated saving provided as good or better an explanation of consumption as any of the more sophisticated alternatives. In consequence, we may define ω_1 by

$$\omega_1 = \sum_{\theta=1}^{\infty} \Lambda^{-\theta}(\mu - \epsilon). \tag{7.6}$$

For estimation purposes, the infinite sum can be dealt with by selecting a base year $\bar{\theta}$, in which wealth is $\bar{\omega}$, so that for any year τ,

$$\omega_1 = \bar{\omega} + \sum_{\theta=1}^{\tau-\bar{\theta}} \Lambda^{-\theta}(\mu - \epsilon). \tag{7.7}$$

The second term on the right-hand side, ω^*, say, can be calculated and becomes data, while the first is a constant, which may be estimated.

The original equation (7.1) may now be written

$$\epsilon = \alpha_1\bar{\omega} + \alpha_1\omega^* + (\beta_1 - \beta_2)\mu_1 + \beta_2\mu, \tag{7.8}$$

which when multiplied by the Koyck transform $\{1-(1-\lambda)\Lambda^{-1}\}$, becomes

$$\epsilon = \alpha_1\lambda\bar{\omega} + (1-\lambda)\Lambda^{-1}\epsilon + \alpha_1\omega^* - \alpha_1(1-\lambda)\Lambda^{-1}\omega^*$$
$$+ \{\beta_1\lambda + \beta_2(1-\lambda)\}\mu - \beta_2(1-\lambda)\Lambda^{-1}\mu. \tag{7.9}$$

This equation, as written, cannot be estimated since there is an exact linear dependency between the independent variables; this comes about because last year's saving is always the change in permanent wealth, i.e.

$$\omega^* = \Lambda^{-1}(\omega^* + \mu - \epsilon). \tag{7.10}$$

If we use this to substitute for $\Lambda^{-1}\omega^*$ in (7.9), we reach, after some re-arrangement, the following equation which is now exactly identified:

$$\Delta^*\epsilon = \alpha_1\lambda\bar{\omega} + \alpha_1\lambda\omega^* + \{\beta_1\lambda + \alpha_1(1-\lambda)\}\mu$$
$$+ (\beta_2 - \alpha_1)(1-\lambda)\Delta^*\mu - \{\lambda + \alpha_1(1-\lambda)\}\Lambda^{-1}\epsilon, \tag{7.11}$$

where $\Delta^* \equiv 1 - \Lambda^{-1}$, is the backward first-difference operator. This, then, is the estimating equation.

In a consumption function which emphasizes wealth, as this one does, it is important to use data which includes the post-war period of dissaving since this, it may be hoped, can be explained in terms of the model. In consequence, annual data was used from 1948–1972. This was taken principally from the 1973 edition of *National Income and Expenditure*, though earlier volumes were used as necessary. The

TABLE 7.1
Consumers' expenditure, income, and wealth 1948–72, £1963 *per capita*

	ϵ	μ	ω^*
1948	279.0	272.0	7.0
49	280.8	278.2	0.0
1950	286.6	283.9	−2.6
51	281.5	276.6	−5.3
52	280.1	282.4	−10.1
53	289.5	296.6	−7.8
54	299.0	306.3	−0.7
55	310.3	318.9	6.6
56	314.9	325.5	15.2
57	318.9	330.0	25.9
58	324.0	335.2	37.0
59	334.1	350.8	48.3
1960	345.9	369.5	64.9
61	353.6	381.7	88.5
62	358.0	381.0	116.6
63	369.5	395.8	139.6
64	372.7	401.4	165.8
65	385.8	416.2	194.5
66	393.6	423.1	224.9
67	399.4	427.3	254.4
68	407.5	432.7	282.2
69	411.7	433.6	307.5
1970	420.2	447.1	329.4
71	426.0	459.6	356.3
72	447.5	489.1	389.9

data are laid out in Table 7.1 above: all variables are *per capita* and at 1963 prices; income has been adjusted for capital consumption and stock appreciation, while total consumption has been adjusted so as to exclude *net* investment in durable goods (i.e. it includes only that part of the annual purchase of durable goods which can be accounted as depreciation of existing and new stocks). 1949 was taken as the base year for permanent wealth, so that $\omega^* = 0$ in that year.

It is worth noting the time-profile of ω^* from this table. The dissaving before 1952 causes a dip in the series before it begins to rise; it cannot then be compared in its effects to a linear time trend as has sometimes been suggested.

On these data, ordinary least squares estimation of equation (7.11) gives, with standard errors in brackets,

$$\Delta^*\epsilon = \underset{(22.359)}{55.524} + \underset{(0.020988)}{0.042431\omega^*} + \underset{(0.11539)}{0.42981\mu} + \underset{(0.14068)}{0.12006\Delta^*\mu}$$

$$- \underset{(0.18658)}{0.62105\Lambda^{-1}\epsilon}. \quad \text{s.e.} = 1.85,\ R^2 = 0.8970.$$

The actual and predicted values of this equation are sketched in Figure 7.1. It can be seen that the model predicts rather well, and it is clear that the addition of two additional observations, beyond those used by Stone (1973), does not appreciably affect the performance of the model. This impression is further reinforced by calculation of the structural parameters; these are

$$\alpha_1 = 0.0717 \qquad \beta_2 = 0.366$$

$$\beta_1 = 0.677 \qquad \lambda = 0.592$$

$$\bar{\omega} = 1308$$

which values are well within the ranges reported by Stone.

In order to use this model to project to 1975, we need to make some assumption about personal disposable income after 1972. At the time of writing, the full data for 1973 are not available, but it is fairly clear from what information exists that there was a considerable expansion in disposable income during that year. On partial evidence, I have taken this growth to be 4.7% in real terms between 1972 and 1973. In the present situation, it is obviously unlikely that this rate of increase will be maintained; some attempt is almost certain to be made to cut back the growth of consumption through reductions in disposable income. Two possibilities for 1974 and 1975 are laid out in Table 7.2; the first, (i), assumes that real disposable income grows at 1.5% *per annum* after 1973, while the second, (ii), assumes no growth whatever between 1973 and 1975. The resulting figures for consumption are shown on the left of the table;

TABLE 7.2
Income and expenditure 1972–1975, £1963 *per capita*

	Consumption		Income	
	(i)	(ii)	(i)	(ii)
1972	447.5 (5.0)		489.1 (6.4)	
1973	466.3 (4.2)		512.1 (4.7)	
1974	476.8 (2.3)	472.6 (1.4)	519.8 (1.5)	512.1 (0.0)
1975	486.0 (1.9)	476.7 (0.9)	527.6 (1.5)	512.1 (0.0)

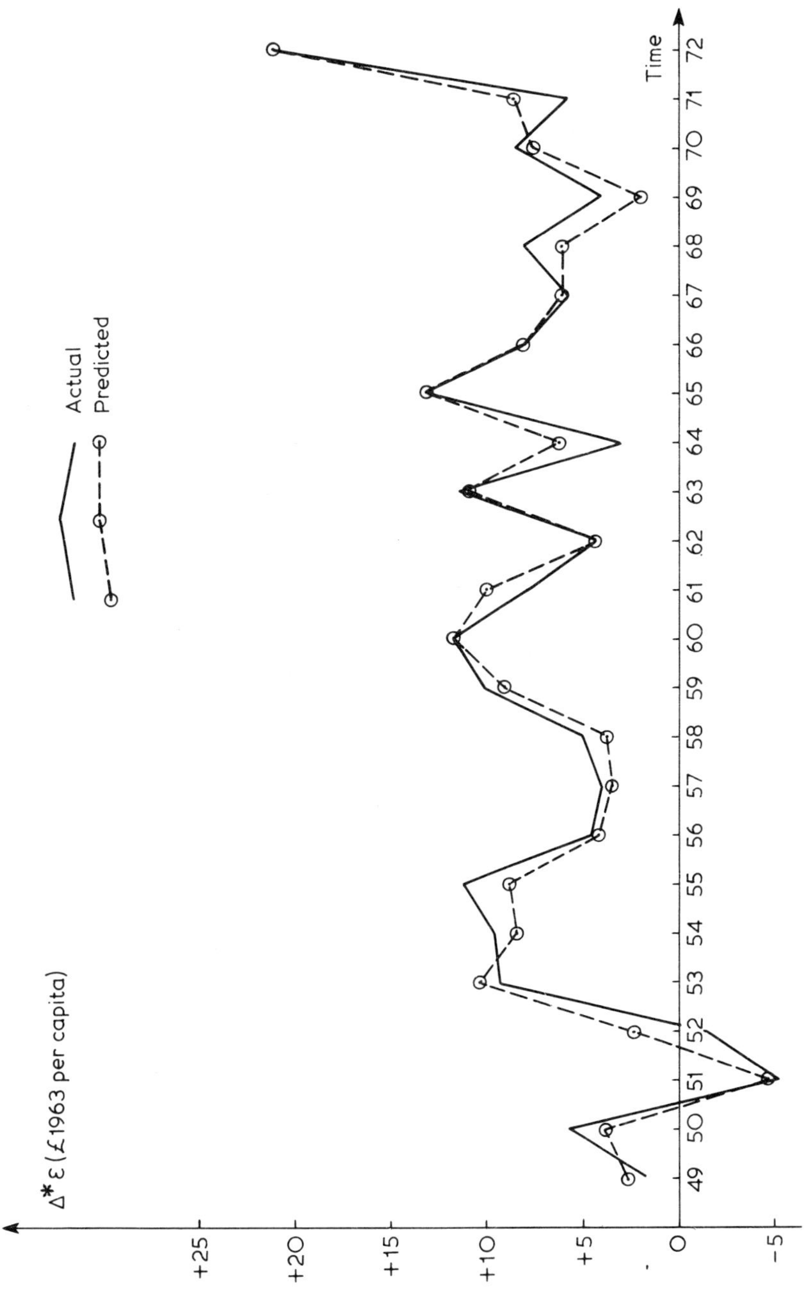

Figure 7.1: Actual and predicted changes in consumption 1949–72

levels are given first, followed by growth rates over the previous year in brackets. The table shows clearly the effects of the lags in the model. These effects are clear; even when income stops growing completely, consumption continues to rise. Of these two projections the second, with zero growth in personal disposable income, seems the likelier of the two and is selected as the basis for the projections which follow.

One further adjustment must be made. Total consumption in this model includes the depreciation of durable goods which is not part of consumers' expenditure as defined in previous chapters. Although durable purchases themselves are notoriously volatile, the depreciation series, which is based on constant proportional depreciation of stocks, is relatively smooth. It may thus be projected straightforwardly to 1975. This gives a figure of £36.6 *per capita* in 1963 prices which when subtracted from the figure in TABLE 7.2, yields a non-durable total of £440.1 *per capita* to be allocated among the other elements of consumers' expenditure.

7.2 The projection of consumer goods' prices

For this section, the predictions of the Cambridge Growth Model for 1975 were used as a starting point for the calculations. However, projections at this time are particularly hazardous; not only has the absolute price level risen very rapidly over the last few years compared with general post-war experience, but this has been accompanied by remarkable changes in the patterns of relative prices. So that while, for much of the post-war period, many of the relative prices of consumers' goods and services followed quite well-defined trends, this has not been true since 1970. In consequence, it is inevitable that even models which have predicted relative prices well in the past will require substantial *ad hoc* modification in order to yield realistic projection for 1975.

I shall begin by giving an outline of how the Cambridge model generates prices; this calculation is not independent of other parts of the model but may still be sufficiently isolated to give a fairly good idea of how the process works. The model postulates a cost mark-up theory of price determination which works through the input–output system. If we simplify to bare essentials, we may write the price vector, p, as

$$p = A'p + t + w + r, \qquad (7.12)$$

where A is the input–output matrix and t, w, and r are vectors of taxes, wages, and profits per unit of output. This has the familiar solution

$$p = (I - A')^{-1}(t + w + r). \qquad (7.13)$$

In practice, this simple model has to be modified to allow for the difference between absorption prices and production prices caused by the presence of imports as well as to allow for classification differences between commodities, industries, and consumers' expenditures.

Apart from taxes, other important exogenous variables in the calculation are the prices of imports and the average domestic wage level. The following diagram, Figure 7.2, adapted from *A Programme for Growth, Vol. 9*, Cambridge, Department of Applied Economics (1970), illustrates how these interact to produce consumer prices.

Figure 7.2: The determination of consumers' expenditure prices

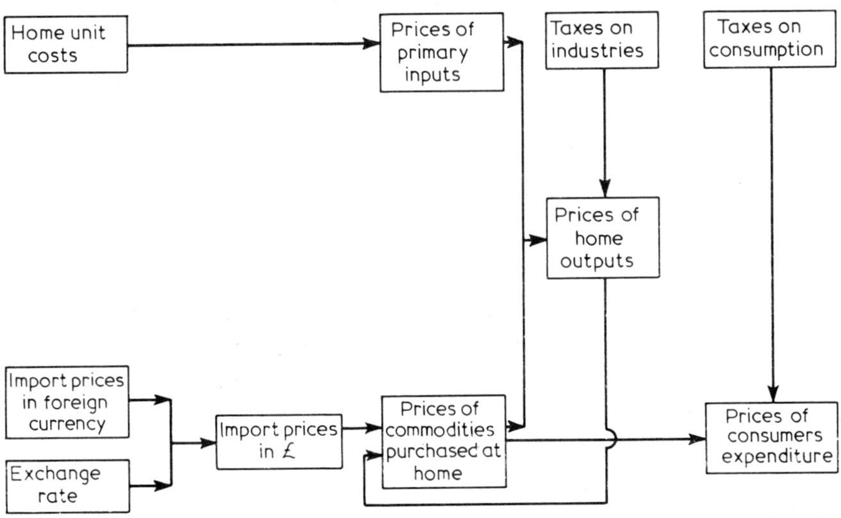

More formally, we may proceed by deriving an expression for the price vector of commodities purchased domestically, p_h. For industries, we may write a modified version of (7.12),

$$p_y = A'p_h + w + r + t_y + m_y, \qquad (7.14)$$

where p_y is a vector of prices of industrial outputs, classified differently from commodities, and A is the commodity into industry input–output matrix. The vector t_y is a vector of indirect taxes levied on industries, including value-added tax, rates, *ad valorem* and specific duties, while m_y allows certain imports to be charged directly to industries, mainly charter payments for shipping. The industry wage and gross-of-tax profit rates per unit of output are linked directly to the assumed level of the average wage, ω, by means of the two relationships

$$w = \hat{a}_1 \hat{q}_y^{-1} e_y \omega \tag{7.15}$$

$$r = \hat{a}_2 w$$

where q_y and e_y are vectors of industry outputs and employment levels respectively. The vector a_1 represents industrial wage differentials; these are projected from past experience, as are the elements of a_2, the industrial ratios of profits to wages. The industry productivities q_y/e_y are affected by the level of investment so that increases in the capital to labour ratio in an industry lowers the wage per unit of output and, *ceteris paribus*, the relative price of the corresponding output. Note that this last assumption, taken with (7.14), implies that while indirect taxes are passed on, direct taxes are not.

In order to use (7.14) to determine p_h, we must complete the links between the prices of industrial outputs and the prices of commodity inputs. At the commodity level, there must be a balance in money terms between use and production, so that

$$\hat{m}p_m + \hat{q}p_q = (\hat{m} + \hat{q} - \hat{x})p_h + \hat{x}p_x, \tag{7.17}$$

where m, q, and x are vectors of quantities of commodities imported, produced, and exported, their prices being denoted by appropriate subscripts. The import price vector, p_m, is adjusted for customs duties and for value added tax, but is essentially exogenous. This equation, on the simplifying but inessential assumption that production and export prices are identical, i.e. $p_x \equiv p_q$, may be rearranged to give p_h as a weighted sum of p_q and p_m, *viz.*

$$p_h = \hat{a}_3 p_q + (I - \hat{a}_3)p_m, \tag{7.18}$$

with

$$a_3 = (\hat{m} + \hat{q} - \hat{x})^{-1}(q - x). \tag{7.19}$$

The prices of commodity outputs are related to the prices of industry outputs – not every industry makes a single commodity, and some commodities are produced by more than one industry – by means of a classification converter C_1, i.e.

$$p_q = C_1 p_y . \tag{7.20}$$

The equations (7.14)–(7.16), (7.18), and (7.20) can now be combined to give the practical analogue of the original simplified equation (7.12);

$$p_h = [I - \hat{a}_3 C_1 A']^{-1} [\hat{a}_3 C_1 \{(I - \hat{a}_2)\hat{a}_1 \hat{q}_y^{-1} e_y \omega + t_y + m_y\} + (I - \hat{a}_3) p_m]. \tag{7.21}$$

This expression is rather clumsy, but it illustrates very directly the way in which commodity prices depend upon wages, taxes, and import prices and how their influence is modified by the industrial wage and profit differentials and by the input–output system. Note that, although p_h appears explicitly only on the left-hand side of (7.21), the equation is not analytically soluble. The levels of imports, exports and outputs appear on the right-hand side, mainly as weights, and these are themselves functions of the various prices in the model. These effects are mainly of the second-order of magnitude since the model is not overall highly price sensitive and since the expressions involved do not depend crucially on variations in weights. From a computational viewpoint, the non-existence of an analytical solution is of no importance: the model is solved iteratively in any case and the individual equations (7.14)–(7.21) can be followed through at each iteration, updating the prices from step to step.

The prices of consumers' expenditures are derived from the commodity prices by allowing for taxes charged to consumption and by allowing for the different composition of consumers' expenditure in some cases, e.g. engineering goods are heavy mechanical engineering as an investment input into industry but are light electrical durables to consumers. Thus

$$p_c = C_2 p_h + t_c , \tag{7.22}$$

where C_2 is a classification converter and t_c is a vector of taxes per unit.

In projecting 1975, the model was particularly useful for assessing the effects of taxes and of working through the likely implications of increased import prices, particularly of oil. Equally, for a number of other commodities it became clear, in view of price changes which had already occurred by end-1973, that the price projections were not at all realistic. It was felt important not to sacrifice reality for consistency with the main model, especially in view of the large number of parameters in equations (7.21)–(7.22), each of which has to be projected accurately. Corrections were thus made where appropriate, so as to bring into line with the most recent information those prices where there was no definite view to the contrary. This was done by working with the price relatives, i.e. the ratios of price indices to the price deflator of consumers' expenditure as a whole. These have no trend and allow us to deal separately with the problems of projecting the *structure* and *level* of prices.

It is neither possible nor desirable to discuss here full details of the assumptions underlying the current projections of the Cambridge Model; interested readers may refer to the forthcoming monograph in this series edited by Barker (1975). However, there are a number of assumptions which relate directly to price determination and are thus of considerable importance for the following discussion.

The first of these relates to the *absolute* level of prices. While it is true that the quantities predicted by each of the models depend only upon real income and relative prices, these relative prices themselves are directly and importantly influenced by the absolute rate of price inflation. It may well be true in some general sense that relative prices change in a systematic way as the absolute price level changes, but one phenomenon which can easily be identified and modelled is the effect on the prices of those items subject to heavy specific duties. For these goods (most obviously wines and spirits, beer, and cigarettes and tobacco) the money tax to be paid is determined by the physical content of the good concerned so that when the general price level is rising and the level of duties is fixed, the relative prices of these items fall. This phenomenon is reflected in the prices of the goods already mentioned as well as in the index of running costs of motor vehicles where, in addition to the specific tax on petrol, there are road fund licences also fixed in money terms. The price of entertainment and recreational services is also affected, in this case because of the fixed element accounted for by television licences. Until recently, the projection of these effects would not have been of any great importance; however, at current rates of inflation, the opposite is true. We are currently estimating that, by 1975, the implicit price deflator of consumers' expenditure will be exactly twice its 1963 level and we shall see below the considerable effects of this assumption on the prices of those goods affected.

It is also necessary to make some assumption about the price of oil. Basically we are assuming a threefold increase over 1963 by 1975 in the import price of oil; this is an increase from £6.8 per ton (c.i.f.) in 1963 to £20.4 per ton (c.i.f.) in 1975. As far as consumer expenditures are concerned, this comes through most noticeably in the price of 'other fuels', a high proportion of which is fuel oil, and in the running costs of motor vehicles. For this latter, the effects of the increases in the price of oil more than offset the downward effects of the high rate of inflation.

The information used to supplement and correct the prices produced by the Cambridge model came from two sources. The first was the latest set of estimates of consumer expenditure published in the *National Income and Expenditure* Blue Book for 1973, C.S.O. (1973a). This information extends the data use in the earlier chapters by two observations, those for 1971 and 1972. Unfortunately there has been a change of price base, so that the new statistics are based on 1970 prices rather than the 1963 base used heretofore. And, as is usual on such occasions, many fundamental revisions and definitional changes have been worked into the data. However, attempts were made to correct for these revisions in order to get some idea of the changes of the original price relatives in these two years. The second source was the retail price index, which at time of writing is available in the *Monthly Digest of Statistics*, C.S.O. (1973b), up to and including November 1973. Most of the categories of consumers' expenditure are covered and so this source provided some indication of the latest changes. Although much of the information from both of these sources is clearly not strictly comparable with the earlier data, it was thought important to use as much of it as possible given the large changes in relative prices which have been taking place and are likely to take place over the next few years.

It is, of course, impossible to project all the *relative* prices independently of one another so that, having attempted to do so, some reconciliating adjustment must be carried out. Let us denote the (inconsistent) trial vector of relative prices by r, each element of r having been derived independently by the methods described above. We also know the total of consumers' expenditure at constant prices from the consumption function, as well as the implicit price deflator of consumers' expenditure. This is clearly one piece of information too many. To discover the size of the inconsistency, we need a set of quantities to use as weights and these will be different for each of the models. A simple method of adjustment was chosen using the linear expenditure system.

If we deflate each side of the linear expenditure system by π, the average price index, we may write the linear expenditure system as

$$q = c + \hat{r}^{-1}b\left(\frac{\mu}{\pi} - r'c\right) \tag{7.23}$$

so that quantities are chosen with reference only to relative prices r and the constant price total. If we set b to its 1975 level, and use (7.23) to predict a q vector on the basis of our assumed level of r and μ/π, then there is no reason to suppose that the vector q will add to μ/π, as it should. In consequence, we can remove the discrepancy by choosing a new vector of relative prices, say r^*, so that the new vector of quantities q, satisfies $\iota'q = \mu/\pi$. One obvious and very simple way to do this is to set $r^* = \phi r$, where, by substitution, ϕ is given by

$$\phi = \frac{\iota'\hat{r}^{-1}b\dfrac{\mu}{\pi}}{\dfrac{\mu}{\pi} - \iota'c + \iota'\hat{r}^{-1}b\dfrac{\mu}{\pi}}. \tag{7.24}$$

With $\pi = 2$ and $\mu/\pi = 440.1$ (see above), this gave a value of ϕ only very slightly less than one, indicating that the trial set of relative prices were almost consistent. This is the sort of result one would expect whatever adjustment method had been adopted; it would take some very inappropriate method of projecting price relatives to generate any major discrepancy.

The indices of relative and absolute prices are given in Table 7.3; both are based on 1963. The relative prices are illustrated in the graphs in Chapter V above: the solid line indicates the values over the data period 1954–1970; the two asterisks indicate the values for 1971 and 1972 based on the 1973 Blue Book, and the point marked by a cross indicates the 1975 projection. The broken line joins 1970, the last data point, to the projection; this emphasises that the two asterisks are often not strictly comparable with the other points. Even so, it is obvious that the broken line *does not* indicate the likely path from 1970 to 1975, it is included only to accentuate the important information, the change between 1970 and 1975.

TABLE 7.3
Price projections to 1975 (1963 = 100)

	Level	Relative
1. Bread and cereals	2.2216	1.1108
2. Meat and bacon	2.2416	1.1208
3. Fish	3.5706	1.7853
4. Oils and fats	1.6266	0.8133
5. Sugar and confectionery	1.7852	0.8926
6. Dairy produce	1.9836	0.9918
7. Fruit	2.0234	1.0117
8. Potatoes and vegetables	1.8844	0.9422
9. Beverages	1.2894	0.6447
10. Other manufactured food	1.6266	0.8133
11. Footwear	1.7456	0.8728
12. Clothing	1.7258	0.8629
13. Rents, rates, etc.	2.5788	1.2894
14. Household maintenance	2.2216	1.1108
15. Coal	2.4796	1.2398
16. Electricity	1.6862	0.8431
17. Gas	1.1902	0.5951
18. Other fuels	2.3804	1.1902
19. Beer	1.7456	0.8728
20. Wines and spirits	1.7852	0.8926
21. Cigarettes and tobacco	1.5870	0.7935
22. Post, telephone etc.	2.1226	1.0613
23. Running costs of motor vehicles	2.1820	1.0910
24. Rail travel	2.4796	1.2398
25. Other travel	1.9044	0.9522
26. Expenditure abroad	2.1226	1.0613
27. Household textiles and hardware	1.8646	0.9323
28. Matches, soap, etc.	1.7060	0.8530
29. Books and magazines	2.5788	1.2894
30. Newspapers	3.1738	1.5869
31. Recreational goods	1.7852	0.8926
32. Chemists' goods	1.6266	0.8133
33. Other goods n.e.s.	1.6862	0.8431
34. Domestic service	2.4200	1.2100
35. Catering	2.4200	1.2100
36. Entertainment	1.9242	0.9621
37. Other services	2.1424	1.0712
All goods	2.0000	1.0000

I shall not discuss these indices in detail here; wherever comment seems necessary it will be included in the discussion of the individual projections below.

7.3 The alternative projections

The results of the two preceding sections give us enough information to calculate projections to 1975 for the linear expenditure and loglinear systems as discussed in Chapter V above. For the hierarchic model of Chapter VI, we need price indices for the eight commodity groups. These could conceivably be calculated by iterating between the two levels of the hierarchy, but this is tedious and unnecessary since the deflators will change little from iteration to iteration. Accordingly, weighted averages of the figures in Table 7.3 were used and only one calculation performed.

To these three sets of projections, one more was added. In Chapter V, where attention was focused on the effects of Pigou's Law on the performance of the linear expenditure system, the loglinear system was used as a simple alternative which did not embody the Law. Since the linear expenditure system has time trends in the income elasticities and thus in the price elasticities, the system used for comparison also had to allow such trends. Within the loglinear model the only way of doing this was to allow for time trends in both income and price elasticities, and this allowed the investigation of the validity of a proportionality relationship on an equation by equation basis. For purposes of projection, however, such a model is less appropriate. It was clear from the discussion of the detailed results in Chapter V, that many of the least satisfactory and least convincing explanations were given by equations which leant heavily upon time trends, particularly in the price elasticities. These difficulties can only be expected to become more serious in projection where, apart from the usual uncertainties, the time trends are all the more important. The loglinear system was thus re-estimated without time trends in the price elasticities, i.e. by setting $\gamma^1 = 0$ in equation (5.5). This gives an estimating equation

$$\log q_i = \alpha_i + (\beta_i^0 + \beta_i^1 \theta) \log \frac{\mu}{\pi} + \gamma_i \log \frac{p_i}{\pi}. \qquad (7.25)$$

This was estimated for each commodity by ordinary least squares using the same thirty-seven goods from 1954 to 1970 as before. The results are presented in Table 7.4 with the usual summary statistics. In many cases, notably when γ_i^1 was not significantly different from zero in the original equation, the new equation is very similar to the old. In cases where time trend was significant, there is some loss of explanatory power but, as we shall see below, this often leads to a more credible equation.

The four sets of projections are listed in Table 7.5. The projection from each system has been transformed to yield a quantity in each case; for the linear expenditure systems, this involves dividing by the corresponding price, for the loglinear models, taking antilogs. The heading LES, as before, denotes the linear expenditure system as discussed in Chapter V; HLES, the hierarchic linear expenditure system discussed in Chapter VI; LLS1, is the loglinear system with a single time trend, i.e. in the income elasticity, while LLS2 is the original loglinear system with time trends in both income and price elasticities.

Before discussing the individual predictions, it is worth examining the total expenditures given in the last row of Table 7.5. These are derived by converting each of the quantities to expenditures and then summing. This total should, of course, be the total from which one starts, i.e. £880.2 = £(63)440.1 × 2. However, only the two linear expenditure systems will add up in this way by construction; the loglinear models will, in general, produce some error since they do not and cannot be made to add up exactly. Within the sample period, the constraint on each of the equations to fit well will keep this total discrepancy under control, but as soon as the models are used to project, this factor ceases to operate and there is nothing to guarantee that the error will be small. In this case, after only five years beyond the sample, the discrepancies are large enough to be disturbing for both of the loglinear models. For the LLS1, the discrepancy is £44.8 *per capita*, in total more than £2.5 billion at 1975 prices which is more than 5% of consumers' expenditure; for the LLS2, the corresponding figures are £58.9 *per capita*, £3.4 billion, and 6.5% of consumers' expenditure.

It would, of course, be possible to allocate this discrepancy, say *pro rata*, to the individual expenditures. This, though hiding the problem, does not remove it, since such a procedure would not add to the credibility of the individual estimates. There is also good reason to suppose that the discrepancy will worsen over time. Since the majority of goods show patterns of increasing purchases over time, estimating loglinear equations will lead to a preponderance of predictions which increase exponentially with income. The sum of these will then tend to exceed the (linear) income constraint by an ever increasing amount. Such a situation would arise eventually

TABLE 7.4
Loglinear system with one time trend

	α_i	β_i^0	β_i^1	γ_i	R^2
1. Bread & cereals	−0.9972	0.5893	−0.0033	−0.2118	0.9705
	(1.4606)	(0.2497)	(0.0008)	(0.1042)	
2. Meat & bacon	−4.1662	1.2484	−0.0030	−0.3209	0.9058
	(2.5518)	(0.4361)	(0.0014)	(0.1974)	
3. Fish	−2.3379	0.5874	−0.0016	0.8514	0.3528
	(8.4889)	(1.4515)	(0.0047)	(0.4439)	
4. Oils & fats	−1.4017	0.4939	−0.0028	−0.3025	0.4737
	(4.0002)	(0.6836)	(0.0025)	(0.1041)	
5. Sugar & confectionery	3.5415	−0.2348	−0.0009	−0.4136	0.9312
	(2.1196)	(0.3625)	(0.0012)	(0.0012)	
6. Dairy produce	−4.2103	1.1575	−0.0039	−0.5548	0.9548
	(1.5729)	(0.2689)	(0.0010)	(0.1419)	
7. Fruit	−10.424	2.0678	−0.0057	−0.2910	0.8681
	(4.771)	(0.8153)	(0.0025)	(0.2315)	
8. Potatoes & vegetables	−0.6179	0.5029	0.0012	−0.1559	0.9750
	(2.7373)	(0.4680)	(0.0015)	(0.0952)	
9. Beverages	0.0686	0.2812	0.0027	0.2409	0.9599
	(3.1914)	(0.5455)	(0.0021)	(0.1724)	
10. Other man. food	−12.132	2.2408	−0.0085	−2.1510	0.8684
	(7.823)	(1.3366)	(0.0053)	(0.9136)	
11. Footwear	−14.128	2.7202	−0.0062	−0.2527	0.9333
	(5.738)	(0.9792)	(0.0038)	(0.5380)	
12. Clothing	−11.331	2.5084	−0.0073	−1.0860	0.9925
	(1.956)	(0.3344)	(0.0013)	(0.2322)	
13. Rents, rates, etc.	7.3008	−0.6496	0.0051	−0.0060	0.9967
	(1.1510)	(0.1966)	(0.0005)	(0.0511)	
14. Household maintenance, etc.	−2.0108	0.6801	0.0044	−1.7338	0.9814
	(5.8612)	(1.0020)	(0.0034)	(0.6435)	
15. Coal & coke	−28.467	5.1607	−0.0254	0.7273	0.9410
	(9.050)	(1.5468)	(0.0050)	(0.4140)	
16. Electricity	−33.755	6.0791	−0.0055	−0.3109	0.9849
	(10.313)	(1.7627)	(0.0056)	(0.5189)	
17. Gas	24.254	−3.9434	0.0171	−1.6849	0.9940
	(5.331)	(0.9106)	(0.0031)	(0.0961)	
18. Other fuels	−6.5011	1.2378	−0.0032	1.0425	0.6886
	(14.848)	(2.534)	(0.0076)	(0.6608)	
19. Beer	3.6685	−0.1838	0.0040	0.0012	0.9529
	(4.5509)	(0.7777)	(0.0025)	(0.1348)	

TABLE 7.4 continued

	α_i	β_i^0	β_i^1	γ_i	R^2
20. Wines & spirits	−19.794 (4.876)	3.7633 (0.8327)	−0.0054 (0.0026)	−0.3978 (0.1908)	0.9889
21. Cigarettes & tobacco	−10.470 (3.981)	2.3283 (0.6807)	−0.0069 (0.0022)	−0.6850 (0.2475)	0.5553
22. Postal & telephone charges	6.5464 (3.3003)	−0.9168 (0.5642)	0.0094 (0.0018)	−0.2199 (0.0947)	0.9906
23. R.c. of motor vehicles	−9.8317 (6.2830)	2.1143 (1.0731)	0.0089 (0.0033)	−1.5290 (0.3106)	0.9975
24. Rail travel	5.7736 (8.4950)	−0.8002 (1.4501)	0.0015 (0.0040)	−0.6689 (0.2747)	0.9291
25. Other travel	3.4103 (2.3999)	−0.1989 (0.4103)	0.0039 (0.0014)	−1.5778 (0.2803)	0.8174
26. Expenditure abroad	−23.471 (11.458)	4.3108 (1.9576)	−0.0105 (0.0064)	−1.3250 (0.4544)	0.8810
27. Household textiles & hardware	−9.5620 (2.6592)	1.9827 (0.4545)	−0.0031 (0.0014)	−1.0302 (0.2154)	0.9934
28. Matches, soap, etc.	0.5543 (2.7565)	0.1354 (0.4709)	−0.0001 (0.0016)	−0.0789 (0.1065)	0.5507
29. Books & magazines	1.5666 (5.2310)	−0.1294 (0.8943)	0.0020 (0.0033)	−0.6658 (0.3811)	0.4007
30. Newspapers	1.8650 (4.0700)	−0.1288 (0.6956)	−0.0001 (0.0028)	−0.3401 (0.1597)	0.9407
31. Recreational goods	−17.871 (6.436)	3.3991 (1.0993)	−0.0041 (0.0030)	−0.3223 (0.5109)	0.9905
32. Chemists' goods	−11.456 (4.697)	2.2461 (0.8026)	−0.0034 (0.0025)	−1.0507 (0.2741)	0.9820
33. Other goods	−13.142 (4.587)	2.5166 (0.7834)	−0.0062 (0.0024)	−0.9988 (0.1186)	0.9767
34. Domestic service	10.098 (7.055)	−1.5944 (1.2056)	0.0028 (0.0049)	−0.7593 (0.6970)	0.9319
35. Catering	−15.699 (6.009)	3.1899 (1.0271)	−0.0082 (0.0038)	−0.4164 (0.6698)	0.6592
36. Entertainment	6.0137 (8.3297)	−0.7083 (1.4232)	0.0051 (0.0042)	−1.0902 (0.4638)	0.9369
37. Other services	1.7417 (4.9842)	0.2424 (0.8518)	0.0070 (0.0027)	−1.8970 (0.4231)	0.9793

TABLE 7.5
Alternative projections to 1975 (£1963 *per capita*)

	LES	HLES	LLS1	LLS2
1. Bread and cereals	10.06	10.28	10.26	10.46
2. Meat and bacon	23.04	23.24	24.04	24.39
3. Fish	2.50	3.82	5.02	1.33
4. Oils and fats	4.13	4.35	4.32	4.28
5. Sugar and confectionery	7.42	8.15	8.13	8.44
6. Dairy produce	13.09	13.22	12.88	13.23
7. Fruit	5.15	5.54	5.73	5.62
8. Potatoes and vegetables	12.88	12.53	12.73	12.64
9. Beverages	7.13	7.50	6.49	5.95
10. Other manufactured food	3.21	3.88	3.79	2.89
11. Footwear	6.55	6.49	7.46	7.02
12. Clothing	34.00	33.23	35.37	35.33
13. Rents, rates, etc.	42.63	42.46	41.15	40.76
14. Maintenance, etc.	12.29	11.87	9.68	7.28
15. Coal and coke	1.35	2.92	3.49	2.61
16. Electricity	14.01	12.85	18.11	13.95
17. Gas	15.55	10.44	10.76	12.09
18. Other fuels	1.53	1.78	2.67	1.27
19. Beer	20.56	19.84	17.14	22.66
20. Wines and spirits	15.16	15.67	15.85	22.32
21. Cigarettes and tobacco	19.13	20.90	28.71	36.97
22. Postal and telephone	5.46	5.23	5.17	4.35
23. Running costs of motor vehicles	31.99	30.72	34.96	40.54
24. Rail travel	2.80	2.24	2.39	2.01
25. Other travel	10.99	11.91	13.01	11.81
26. Expenditure abroad	5.17	5.92	6.86	6.82
27. Household textiles and hardware	10.14	9.37	10.48	10.56
28. Matches, soap, etc.	3.97	3.72	4.00	3.82
29. Books and magazines	2.14	2.03	2.13	2.18
30. Newspapers	2.22	2.40	2.50	2.41
31. Recreational goods	12.35	11.37	12.85	11.63
32. Chemists' goods	7.19	7.57	8.90	6.41
33. Other goods	4.54	5.79	6.67	5.61
34. Domestic service	1.69	2.12	1.57	2.01
35. Catering	16.96	15.57	20.83	15.13
36. Entertainment	9.52	9.05	8.33	9.49
37. Other services	41.60	41.60	36.53	47.19
Total	440.1	437.6	460.9	473.5
Total (current £)	880.2	880.2	925.0	939.1

even if all goods were inferior save one; as it is, the difficulties appear to be significant and immediate. This, then, would seem to be an important point against the use of loglinear models, at least without some modification.

A brief description of the projection of each of the commodities is given below. These comments are an extension of the remarks in section 6 of Chapter V and should be read in conjunction with them and with the illustrations. As with the price relatives, the quantities for 1971 and 1972 are marked by asterisks and once again it must be emphasized that these points are in many cases not strictly comparable with the earlier information. Since only the LES predictions are illustrated over the sample period, the broken line has been used to link the 1970 figure with the LES projection; again this does not represent a predicted path. The predictions for the LLS1 are illustrated by a square.

In assessing the realism or otherwise of these projections, the projections for total expenditure must continually be borne in mind. Note from Table 7.2 that the rate of growth of total expenditure is expected to fall considerably from the levels enjoyed in the recent past. The 1971 and 1972 values illustrated correspond to years in which total expenditure in constant prices had grown 1.4% and 5% respectively. Between 1972 and 1975, the consumption function predicts an average rate of growth of 2.1% per annum, so that even if changing relative prices were to have no effect, the 1975 projection would be unlikely to lie on the extrapolation of the 1970–71–72 path.

1. *Bread and cereals*

Most of the models explain this category in terms of the time trend; the LES is inferior, and by Pigou's Law, Giffen, so that the projected increase in the price relative actually keeps purchases higher than they would otherwise have been. The LLS1 has a price elasticity of the right sign but it is small and has little influence. All the projections look too high relative to the 1971 and 1972 observations; perhaps the price elasticity is understated in the sample. As between the projections, there is little to choose.

2. *Meat and bacon*

Once again it seems possible that the price elasticity is underestimated within the sample since the surge in relative price, though seeming to affect the 1971 and 1972 actuals, has little effect on the projection. The LES is the lowest and perhaps the best, but is only so because it has the largest time-trend in the income coefficient.

3. *Fish*

This category shows one of the most dramatic rises in relative prices, seemingly due to supply shortages. This has unfortunate consequences for the LLS1 which finds a perverse price effect over the sample and thus projects huge increases in demand. The LLS2, on the other hand has a normal but increasing (absolutely) price elasticity, so that its projection looks too low. The LES looks about right, although once again this is only a trend projection.

4. *Oils and fats*

The supply shortages which caused the high prices in 1971 and 1972 seem to be lessening, and only a small relative increase over 1970 is projected for 1975. In consequence, the projections differ less than they would given a larger change. The LES again looks best, but it is doubtful whether this is much more than a chance occurrence.

5. *Sugar, preserves and confectionery*

In this case the LES produces a nonsensical result; the projection is low partly because of the Giffen paradox and partly because of the increasingly important negative time trend. The 1971 and 1972 observations occurred without much change in the price relative so that if the latter is not very important and if the rate of growth of total expenditure slows down as predicted, then either the LLS1 or LLS2 prediction could be well within range.

6. *Dairy produce*

As indicated in Chapter V, the models offer similar explanations of this category and the similarity between the projections reflects this. The 1975 figures look perfectly reasonable given the sample information but are made to look more doubtful by the 1971 and 1972 observations. It is hard to see how these latter can be explained except perhaps by the small change in definition which has taken place; in any case they do not help us to discriminate between the models.

7. *Fruit*

The 1971 and 1972 observations are rather hard to explain since the price relative has risen in both years and the rise in income was larger in the second when purchases actually fell. The LES looks best in the light of these points but is being helped by the time trend rather than any genuine price sensitivity. The higher predictions of the LLS models are at least as convincing.

8. *Potatoes and vegetables*

The price index is predicted to increase between 1972 and 1975 in order to allow restoration of the profitability of this type of farming *vis-à-vis* the production of those commodities whose prices are determined on the world market and have risen rapidly over the last few years. The models are quite similar for this good although the projections, which are influenced by positive time trends all look rather high. There is little between the models on this score, however.

9. *Beverages*

Both the LLS models have perverse price elasticities so that the fall in the price relative keeps demand low. There seems little reason to disbelieve the LES, although the 1971 and 1972 observations are again difficult to explain.

10. *Other manufactured food*

The LLS2, which perhaps looks best, achieves its projection from a perverse price elasticity. The LES continues on trend while the LLS1 has a sharp normal response to the fall in the price relative. This last looks too high and the model does not fit well enough over the sample period to give the projection much credibility. Thus, the

LES is to be preferred, but again not on any very strong positive grounds.

11. *Footwear*

The declining time trend in the income coefficient of the LES gives a very low projection; both LLS models are more income elastic but the LLS2 has a perverse price response. Consequently, the LLS1 gives the best projection, though it is probably too high given the projected slow-down in total expenditure.

12. *Clothing*

The projections are similar, as are the explanations offered by the models, although the LES is perhaps a little low. The high 1972 figure is reasonably well explained by the high growth of disposable income in that year.

13. *Rent, rates and water charges*

The LES has considerable difficulty explaining this rather straightforward category, as is explained in Chapter V. The LLS1 projection, which looks perfectly sensible, is thus to be preferred.

14. *Household maintenance and improvements*

The trend explanation of the LES fits well over the sample but cannot deal with the effects of a reversal of trend in the price relative and so generates an absurdly high prediction. The LLS2, on the other hand, has much too high a price elasticity by 1975 and yields a projection which is much too low. This leaves the LLS1 which looks very good. Even so, the difficulties over measuring the price index discussed in Chapter V must be borne in mind; it is always possible that the fall in purchases is due to upward bias in the price index and is at least partly spurious. It is hard to see how one could make any allowance for this.

15. *Coal*

The LLS1 projection is high because of the perverse price elasticity which holds demand up. The LLS2 figure is better and is based on a sensible figure for the price elasticity; even so this last has too large a time trend for comfort. The LES projection fits in well with the latest observations but it purely a trend extrapolation and will become negative within a few years. None of the models is thus really satisfactory and this highlights the need for a separate model for fuels, especially in view of the incentives for substitution in the next few years.

16. *Electricity*

As expected from their performance over the sample period, the LES and LLS2 have very similar projections which there seems little reason to doubt. The LLS1 gives an enormous income elasticity which sends the system into exponential growth after 1969. The LES is probably best in view of the perverse price elasticity of the LLS2.

17. *Gas*

The LES, which over the sample is forced to have a large positive time trend because of the difficulties over Pigou's Law, suffers accordingly outside the sample. The LLS2 is probably overpredicting too, this time because of the time trend in the price elasticity. The LLS1 projection is quite sensibly based and looks plausible.

18. *Other fuels*

Projection of this category in terms of the models considered is an impossible task. The sample information provides little clear-cut evidence about responses and so it is not surprising that, faced with a very large off-trend movement in the price relative, the different models give quite different results. Clearly the LLS1 is wrong, but nothing else is very clear.

19. *Beer*

It is rather surprising that none of the models can make much sense of this commodity. The projections are trend extrapolations for the LLS1 and LES while the LLS2 has the highest prediction of all, based on a very large price elasticity induced by the time trend on that parameter. The truth must lie between the LLS1 and

LES projections and, though this says little, the evidence seems to permit no nore.

20. *Wines and spirits*

The LLS2 projection is absurdly high, again because of an inappropriate parameter. The LES and LLS1 are in reasonable agreement and are probably accurate. The high observation for 1972 is consistent with the considerable income elasticity of this item.

21. *Cigarettes and tobacco*

There is a wider range of projections for this item than for any other. The LES, as stated in Chapter V, picks up the propaganda effect by means of the time trend in the income coefficient and accords little influence to price. This naturally leads to a low projection; the propaganda effects continue and the decrease in relative price has little influence. The LLS models, on the other hand, accord considerable influence to fluctuations in price. Clearly the LLS2 overstates this effect by 1975 but it is not obvious that the LLS1 does so. We thus have two plausible but entirely different explanations and projections and the 1971 and 1972 observations are ambivalent. A resolution of this problem would require a more serious attempt than has been made here to disentangle the propaganda from price effects. In any case, there is obviously a strong case for raising the specific duty on this item so as to restore the price relative.

22. *Postal and telephone charges*

The LLS2 has much too large a price elasticity by 1975 and so gives a very low projection. In both the LES and LLS1 the time trends are doing a good deal of work, although the latter makes some allowance for the rising price relative. Either projection could well be correct.

23. *Running costs of motor vehicles*

The LLS2 has a perverse price elasticity by 1975 and for that reason gives an absurdly high projection. In both LES and LLS1 projections the rising time trend offsets the effects of rising price and both look too high. It is hard to believe that the higher price will not have more effect than is predicted here.

24. *Rail travel*

The LES has severe difficulties here due to the effects of Pigou's Law and its projection is worth very little. The LLS2 has too high a price elasticity and the projection is too low. The LLS1 does not fit very well and uses the price relative to do most of the explanations; even so its projection looks reasonable if the price relative does not rise further than predicted.

25. *Other travel*

Pigou's Law prevents the LES giving any useful explanation of this item and the projection is of no value. The time trend in the LLS2 means that the price effect is very attenuated by 1975 so that the LLS1, with a fixed elasticity of −1.6, gives the highest projection which, on the face of it, is not impossible. However, there has been a considerable change in the product mix of this category over the period in favour of air travel and chartered holidays. This latter must have a high income elasticity which may have been disguised over the sample by compensating movements in the other components. On this interpretation, the 1972 observation is high because of the high level of income in that year given that the air travel component had become large; in which case, the LLS1 projection for 1975 is too high. On these rather speculative grounds, the LLS2 figure of 11.8 may be more reasonable.

26. *Expenditure abroad*

The LES projection is absurd and is due to its attempt to model price and direct control effects with a time trend. Both LLS1 and LLS2 give reasonable projections, if a little low. Again, the 1972 observation is high because of the boom in personal disposable income in that year.

27. *Household textiles and hardware*

The difference between the LES and LLS models is not very marked, nor would one expect it to be given the similarities over the sample. The LLS1 and LLS2 are slightly more price sensitive and give a slightly higher projection which looks quite plausible given the slowing down of total expenditure to 1975.

28. *Matches, soap, and other cleaning materials*

All the models follow one trend or another; nothing is explained and the projections are purely extrapolative.

29. *Books and magazines*

As for the previous category, the LES simply projects the trend. The LLS1 and LLS2 have some price sensitivity but give similar results to one another and to the LES. The 1971 and 1972 observations appear to belong to the earlier (unexplained) cycle so that the trend projection may not be far out. Note that the amplitude of the fluctuations of this category is very small so that the projection error is unlikely to be large in any case.

30. *Newspapers*

The LES has Pigou's Law and inferiority problems. The LLS1 and LLS2 give similar projections; the latter has a higher price elasticity and is thus a bit lower. Either of these two could be correct.

31. *Miscellaneous recreational goods*

The LLS2 projection is too low because of a perverse price effect; there is little to choose between the LES and LLS1 although the lower price elasticity of the former appears to give the more credible projection.

32. *Chemists' goods*

The LLS2 is absurdly low, again because of a perverse price elasticity. The LES relies more heavily on the time trend and less on the price than does the LLS1; for once this seems to give a better result, both within the sample and outside of it.

33. *Other miscellaneous goods*

The LES relies on the time trend to explain the slowing down and fall of purchases over the sample whereas both LLS1 and LLS2 make much more use of the price relative. The sharp drop in the price relative after 1970 thus shows up only in the LLS projections which are thus much superior.

34. *Domestic service*

Both the LES and the LLS2, although for different reasons, have perverse price elasticities in 1975. This has little effect on the projections since the price relative continues on trend. Even so the LLS1, which makes sense, looks plausible and is to be preferred.

35. *Catering*

Here again we have dramatically divergent projections. The LES and LLS2 projections are given by the time trends involved in each and there seems little reason to believe them. The LLS1 projection looks equally bad in the opposite direction and seems to be largely random since the model fits very badly over the sample. There is no satisfactory projection here.

36. *Entertainment and recreational services*

The LES and LLS2 give almost identical, high, projections; the former because of a rising time trend and the latter because it is increasingly price elastic. The LLS1 is relatively inelastic and, though more credible than either of the others, appears to be too low.

37. *Other services*

The LLS2 and LES are again much too high; the LES again because of the time trend, the LLS2 because of a perverse price elasticity. The LLS1 projection is again quite credible.

7.4 *A general assessment*

It will have been noted that in the discussion above little mention was made of the hierarchic linear expenditure system even though, in many cases, its projections were at least as credible as those of the other models. This omission is based on the arguments presented at the end of Chapter VI above; the hierarchic model cannot be regarded as an acceptable variant of the linear expenditure system since it involves abandoning the utility approach to demand analysis which is the basis of that model. Although there obviously is a case for abandoning this methodology, and this will be further discussed in Chapter IX below, if we do so we should choose an alternative model such as the loglinear system which makes the most of abandoning the difficulties of estimation and interpretation which bedevil models derived from the theory. It is hard to see the attractions of a model which abandons the theory while retaining many of its difficulties.

Reverting to the other models, it is clear that these trial projections have revealed serious difficulties for each of them. In mitigation, it must be said that these models are highly simplistic, and that the test to which they have been subjected in this chapter is a severe one. The models were required to project into a period where the configuration of independent variables, particularly that of relative prices, is in many cases quite different from that of the sample period. It is a fairly safe prediction that if, instead of the remarkable changes which have taken place, relative prices and incomes had continued roughly on trend, the alternative predictions would have been closer to one another and a much lower proportion would have been obviously wrong. From a positive point of view however, this change of environment is to be welcomed since the information revealed should enable substantial emendation and improvement.

Before attempting these changes, it is worth identifying several specific sources of difficulty. The first is the operation of Pigou's Law in the linear expenditure system; this has been discussed at length in Chapter V and the problems revealed there reappear in the projections. The most common symptom of distortion is the underestimation of price elasticities with compensating over-reliance on time trends. The second difficulty relates to the time trends themselves; it is obvious that whenever a model depends heavily upon them to perform the role normally expected to be fulfilled by income or prices, the prediction will not respond to off-trend changes in the latter. To some extent, then, it is worth sacrificing some fit over the sample period to achieve increased plausibility since this will frequently give better predictions outside the sample. This was seen above, for example, in the generally superior projections of the loglinear system with a single time trend over its counterpart with two, even though the latter's performance over the sample was often significantly better.

Thirdly, there is a general difficulty in estimating credible and sensible price responses. In the first instance, this is an information problem; the data do not contain a great deal of relative price variation nor are the responses to what there is always clearly detectable. This deficiency of the data has to be repaired by the use of a plausible *a priori* theory, so that the models do not have more independent responses to be estimated than can be determined by the information available. In this respect, the linear expenditure system contains too much such information, much of it inconsistent with the sample; while both loglinear models, and particularly that with double time trends, contain too little and so we find a high proportion of random absurd results. Here, however, there exists a partial remedy. The two extra observations, 1971 and 1972, which caused so much difficulty for projection, contain a great deal of extra variation, for some commodities more than in the whole of the rest of the sample. We can thus use this information in the hope of gaining substantial improvements in precision and credibility, especially for the loglinear model. This will be done in the next chapter before final predictions are presented and before any attempt is made to go beyond 1975.

How then should one best proceed? One possibility would be to accept the theoretical and empirical results presented so far as a catalogue of the failure of simple demand models in a practical context. However, while the deficiencies must be admitted, some model must be used for projection and it is no easy task to provide superior alternatives. In consequence, albeit with some hesitation, we shall go on in the next chapter to provide some compromise estimates for 1975 and 1980. To try to keep manageable the range of possibilities I shall use only the linear expenditure system and the single-trend loglinear system and I shall begin by updating the estimates using the new information.

Chapter 8

PROJECTIONS FOR 1975 and 1980

The purpose of this chapter is to try to take the best of the previous results to predict the patterns of demand in 1975 and 1980. This is done with some trepidation. The many difficulties met in the earlier chapters would prevent any overconfidence in the predictions of the models examined in this book. Nevertheless predictions will always be made somehow and those presented below may have some value as a guide to the kind of changes to expect in the medium-term future.

It was decided, in view of the considerable changes in relative prices over the last few years, that there could be substantial gains in precision in using the 1954 to 1972 data to update the results of Chapter V before proceeding. This was done at the cost of a change of price base and of a number of definitional alterations in the data. Some of these are of considerable importance; for example, electricity and gas sold under different tariffs are now treated as different goods whereas, until 1973, the quantity indices for these fuels were based on thermal content. The full details are given in the notes to the tables on pages 100–102 of the 1973 *National Income and Expenditure Blue Book*, (C.S.O. 1973a).

The new estimates for the loglinear model and the linear expenditure system corresponding to those in Tables 5.2 and 7.4 are given in Table 8.1, for the linear expenditure system, and Table 8.2 for the loglinear model. Due to the change of base the different sets of results are not always comparable. For the linear expenditure system, the c values are now at 1970 prices, while θ, the time index, is now zero in 1970 so that $b = b^0$ in that year rather than in 1963 as before. The elasticities of the loglinear model are unit free so that the price elasticities γ_i are estimates of the same quantities as those listed in Table 7.4; the time trends in the income elasticities have been rebased on 1970 as for the linear expenditure system. The intercept terms are of course in different units.

Most of these results do not differ in any major respect from the parameter estimates over the earlier, shorter period. As is to be expected from its high *a priori* content, this is particularly true for the linear expenditure system. Most of the changes to this model are confined to the values of the b^1 parameters associated with the time trends. This confirms the earlier result that these parameters absorb many of the price effects which cannot otherwise be allowed for within the model. In consequence the b^1's show most impact when the relative prices in the data are altered. The loglinear model shows rather more instability reflecting the greater number of parameters involved and their comparative imprecision. In the majority of cases, this shows up as an improvement in the results. For example, only two commodities, non-alcoholic beverages and beer, have perverse price elasticities, neither of which is significantly different from zero, as opposed to five such commodities in the previous regressions. Two of these latter have been subject to redefinition, however, since the *Blue Book* aggregation of coal with coke has been adopted here rather than allocating coke to other fuels as was done earlier; both categories then become normally rather than perversely price responsive. Overall, the precision of the price elasticities shows a tendency to increase with t-values going up more than would be expected simply from the lengthening of the sample period. For a number of commodities, e.g. fish, household maintenance, other fuels, cigarettes and running costs of motor vehicles, there are considerable changes in the nature of the explanation offered. These correspond either to definitional changes or to cases where changes in relative prices have been particularly marked post-1971. It is of particular interest to note that both cigarettes and running costs of motor vehicles, both modelled as significantly price sensitive over the earlier data, now cease to be so.

As a first step, projections to 1975 were generated for each model using the price and income assumptions laid out in Chapter VII. The relative prices were converted to 1970 base by appropriate scaling although, in a few cases, changes of definition necessitated further compensating corrections. A consistent set of relatives was then calculated using the linear expenditure system as before. The predictions at constant (1970) prices and at current prices, both

TABLE 8.1
Linear expenditure system 1954–1972

	c_i	b_i^0	$b_i^1 \times 10^2$	R^2_{ex}/R^2_q	e_i^{70}/e_{ii}^{70}
1. Bread and cereals	16.65	−0.0126	−0.0879	0.9949	−0.451
	(0.69)	(0.0043)	(0.0369)	0.9407	0.153
2. Meat and bacon	25.96	0.0360	−0.1727	0.9972	0.602
	(0.99)	(0.0052)	(0.0486)	0.9349	−0.215
3. Fish	3.21	0.0040	−0.0753	0.9795	0.554
	(0.35)	(0.0021)	(0.0161)	0.6542	−0.174
4. Oils and fats	4.36	0.0020	−0.0413	0.9636	0.224
	(0.21)	(0.0014)	(0.0178)	0.4579	−0.071
5. Sugar and confectionery	12.91	−0.0114	0.0358	0.9850	−0.550
	(0.52)	(0.0029)	(0.0289)	0.8197	0.183
6. Dairy produce	13.98	0.0179	−0.0091	0.9951	0.564
	(0.52)	(0.0030)	(0.0358)	0.9392	−0.189
7. Fruit	5.08	0.0100	−0.0466	0.9876	0.791
	(0.33)	(0.0019)	(0.0238)	0.8957	−0.252
8. Potatoes and vegetables	9.44	0.0254	−0.0356	0.9950	0.993
	(0.58)	(0.0031)	(0.0369)	0.9738	−0.324
9. Beverages	4.87	0.0130	−0.0400	0.9813	0.986
	(0.32)	(0.0018)	(0.0250)	0.9319	−0.314
10. Other manufactured food	1.87	0.0109	−0.0657	0.9711	1.583
	(0.30)	(0.0015)	(0.0174)	0.8812	−0.495
11. Footwear	5.14	0.0179	−0.0561	0.9931	1.178
	(0.44)	(0.0023)	(0.0270)	0.9583	−0.376
12. Clothing	22.67	0.1057	−0.2201	0.9956	1.406
	(1.19)	(0.0045)	(0.0536)	0.9841	−0.495
13. Rent, rates, etc.	47.98	0.0792	0.5651	0.9998	0.692
	(2.26)	(0.0146)	(0.0671)	0.9944	−0.276
14. Household maintenance	5.27	0.0461	0.0724	0.9876	1.910
	(0.55)	(0.0030)	(0.0271)	0.9653	−0.609
15. Coal and coke	8.75	−0.0144	−0.3769	0.8898	−1.200
	(1.03)	(0.0067)	(0.0238)	0.9695	0.391
16. Electricity	0.55	0.0708	−0.0877	0.9920	3.090
	(0.84)	(0.0029)	(0.0255)	0.9779	−0.958
17. Gas	5.42	0.0082	0.3313	0.9962	0.645
	(0.68)	(0.0045)	(0.0292)	0.9893	−0.206
18. Other fuels	0.43	0.0068	−0.0432	0.9429	2.339
	(0.21)	(0.0011)	(0.0142)	0.8734	−0.725
19. Beer	18.08	0.0372	0.3003	0.9978	0.819
	(0.69)	(0.0049)	(0.0333)	0.9820	−0.281

TABLE 8.1 continued

	c_i	b_i^0	$b_i^1 \times 10^2$	R_{ex}^2/R_q^2	e_i^{70}/e_{ii}^{70}
20. Wines and spirits	7.13	0.0640	0.2039	0.9946	1.930
	(0.52)	(0.0036)	(0.0328)	0.9888	−0.623
21. Cigarettes and tobacco	26.40	0.0277	−0.4208	0.9923	0.477
	(1.60)	(0.0083)	(0.0641)	0.7452	−0.171
22. Communications	4.17	0.0124	0.1629	0.9956	1.063
	(0.47)	(0.0031)	(0.0220)	0.9826	−0.337
23. Running costs of motor vehicles	2.57	0.1679	0.3619	0.9899	2.960
	(1.04)	(0.0053)	(0.0370)	0.9836	−0.929
24. Rail travel	6.14	−0.0139	0.0152	0.9626	−1.933
	(0.53)	(0.0032)	(0.0173)	0.7921	0.620
25. Other travel	15.52	−0.0063	0.1359	0.9799	−0.230
	(0.93)	(0.0054)	(0.0381)	0.2941	0.078
26. Expenditure abroad	4.15	0.0295	−0.1033	0.9581	1.745
	(0.58)	(0.0026)	(0.0213)	0.8326	−0.553
27. Household textiles and hardware	6.91	0.0368	0.0999	0.9972	1.512
	(0.43)	(0.0027)	(0.0268)	0.9909	−0.487
28. Matches, soap, etc.	4.45	0.0012	−0.0067	0.9966	0.142
	(0.37)	(0.0022)	(0.0264)	0.4322	−0.045
29. Books and magazines	4.02	−0.0028	0.0122	0.9919	−0.424
	(0.43)	(0.0026)	(0.0136)	0.2569	0.134
30. Newspapers	5.86	−0.0053	−0.0650	0.9935	−0.565
	(0.57)	(0.0035)	(0.0083)	0.8741	0.181
31. Recreational goods	5.24	0.0462	0.0132	0.9986	1.917
	(0.55)	(0.0026)	(0.0272)	0.9954	−0.611
32. Chemists' goods	4.11	0.0280	−0.0193	0.9971	1.712
	(0.44)	(0.0022)	(0.0228)	0.9881	−0.543
33. Other goods n.e.s.	3.95	0.0202	−0.0986	0.9805	1.481
	(0.44)	(0.0020)	(0.0191)	0.9261	−0.469
34. Domestic service	4.35	−0.0095	0.0003	0.9679	−1.809
	(0.36)	(0.0021)	(0.0144)	0.9121	0.574
35. Catering	21.07	0.0414	−0.3563	0.9954	0.792
	(1.57)	(0.0080)	(0.0420)	0.8559	−0.276
36. Entertainment	7.34	0.0179	0.0256	0.9845	0.929
	(0.49)	(0.0028)	(0.0248)	0.8115	−0.300
37. Other services	22.47	0.0918	0.0922	0.9979	1.302
	(1.27)	(0.0059)	(0.0509)	0.9799	−0.457

TABLE 8.2
Loglinear model 1954–1972

	α_i	β_i^0	β_i^1	γ_i	R^2
1. Bread and cereals	−1.8196	0.7171	−0.0036	−0.2509	0.9443
	(2.1006)	(0.3341)	(0.0010)	(0.1569)	
2. Meat and bacon	−4.3552	1.2457	−0.0029	−0.4965	0.8986
	(2.3777)	(0.3781)	(0.0011)	(0.1889)	
3. Fish	−19.620	3.3418	−0.0099	−0.3322	0.3019
	(8.541)	(1.3586)	(0.0040)	(0.3171)	
4. Oils and fats	0.5725	0.1588	−0.0015	−0.2804	0.4680
	(3.6105)	(0.5741)	(0.0017)	(0.0790)	
5. Sugar and confectionery	4.4579	−0.3294	−0.0003	−0.1867	0.8452
	(2.7286)	(0.4340)	(0.0013)	(0.1791)	
6. Dairy produce	−1.9392	0.7587	−0.0007	−0.0640	0.9561
	(1.9197)	(0.3052)	(0.0009)	(0.1543)	
7. Fruit	−6.7669	1.3822	−0.0035	−0.4263	0.8964
	(3.4386)	(0.5467)	(0.0016)	(0.1679)	
8. Potatoes and vegetables	−0.8268	0.5490	0.0010	−0.1453	0.9773
	(2.4357)	(0.3873)	(0.0012)	(0.0854)	
9. Beverages	−3.3692	0.8483	0.0027	0.6054	0.9293
	(4.3085)	(0.6850)	(0.0029)	(0.4443)	
10. Other manufactured food	−19.009	3.2335	−0.0107	−2.0479	0.8496
	(8.683)	(1.3806)	(0.0046)	(0.7867)	
11. Footwear	−17.505	3.1195	−0.0077	−0.7666	0.9599
	(4.648)	(0.7398)	(0.0029)	(0.4448)	
12. Clothing	−10.441	2.2492	−0.0053	−0.9389	0.9945
	(1.750)	(0.2782)	(0.0008)	(0.1260)	
13. Rent, rates, etc.	6.6247	−0.3998	0.0049	−0.1729	0.9978
	(0.8081)	(0.1286)	(0.0003)	(0.0389)	
14. Household maintenance	2.9652	−0.0639	0.0063	−1.9366	0.9867
	(4.5193)	(0.7186)	(0.0022)	(0.3866)	
15. Coal and coke	−36.619	6.1261	−0.0238	−0.4217	0.8805
	(15.759)	(2.5057)	(0.0068)	(0.8106)	
16. Electricity	−39.308	6.6598	−0.0084	−0.5996	0.9705
	(12.544)	(1.9935)	(0.0057)	(0.5724)	
17. Gas	24.176	−3.5399	0.0162	−1.9964	0.9795
	(7.835)	(1.2469)	(0.0038)	(0.2557)	
18. Other fuels	−45.786	7.3586	−0.0168	−0.3086	0.8366
	(15.692)	(2.4965)	(0.0084)	(0.7222)	
19. Beer	8.0405	−0.7732	0.0059	0.0207	0.9590
	(4.8636)	(0.7738)	(0.0023)	(0.1520)	

TABLE 8.2 continued

	α_i	β_i^0	β_i^1	γ_i	R^2
20. Wines and spirits	−8.5905	1.8228	0.0022	−0.3762	0.9866
	(5.5822)	(0.8880)	(0.0025)	(0.3441)	
21. Cigarettes and	−11.247	2.3373	−0.0070	−0.0224	0.5301
tobacco	(3.737)	(0.5942)	(0.0017)	(0.1514)	
22. Communications	7.8994	−0.9699	0.0098	−0.3437	0.9713
	(6.1832)	(0.9834)	(0.0029)	(0.1935)	
23. Running costs of	−27.759	4.9694	0.0011	−0.1220	0.9885
motor vehicles	(12.961)	(2.0632)	(0.0055)	(0.8728)	
24. Rail travel	12.212	−1.7223	0.0034	−0.3902	0.8994
	(8.053)	(1.2825)	(0.0032)	(0.2720)	
25. Other travel	−0.6488	0.5264	0.0016	−1.5153	0.8660
	(2.4128)	(0.3837)	(0.0011)	(0.1550)	
26. Expenditure abroad	−22.081	3.8595	−0.0079	−1.2894	0.9211
	(8.342)	(1.3277)	(0.0038)	(0.3278)	
27. Household textiles	−4.7456	1.1636	0.0023	−0.1118	0.9907
	(3.5037)	(0.5577)	(0.0015)	(0.2526)	
28. Matches, soap, etc.	−1.0609	0.4142	−0.0011	−0.1061	0.4163
	(2.3240)	(0.3698)	(0.0012)	(0.0892)	
29. Books and	3.1644	−0.3032	0.0010	−0.2000	0.2689
magazines	(5.0768)	(0.8073)	(0.0027)	(0.3911)	
30. Newspapers	1.3582	0.0400	−0.0010	−0.2957	0.9578
	(3.2959)	(0.5241)	(0.0019)	(0.1260)	
31. Recreational goods	−14.992	2.7939	−0.0020	−0.4417	0.9931
	(4.407)	(0.7019)	(0.0017)	(0.3842)	
32. Chemists' goods	−11.381	2.1563	−0.0021	−0.8370	0.9905
	(3.132)	(0.498)	(0.0014)	(0.1900)	
33. Other goods n.e.s.	−15.329	2.7511	−0.0063	−0.9377	0.9798
	(3.9351)	(0.6268	(0.0017)	(0.1180)	
34. Domestic service	10.457	−1.5009	0.0016	−0.4287	0.9571
	(4.176)	(0.6640)	(0.0020)	(0.1977)	
35. Catering	−14.222	2.7968	−0.0045	−1.9616	0.7487
	(4.340)	(0.6900)	(0.0024)	(0.5984)	
36. Entertainment	8.6367	−1.0116	0.0056	−1.6881	0.9111
	(5.5927)	(0.8901)	(0.0026)	(0.3218)	
37. Other services n.e.s.	−3.8654	1.1932	0.0008	−0.3618	0.9789
	(3.2571)	(0.5178)	(0.0015)	(0.3506)	

per capita, are given in the appropriate columns of Table 8.3. The price relatives for each good are given in the first column; the aggregate expenditure *per capita* in 1975 is £880.1 at current prices with an aggregate price deflator of 1.4549 compared with the 1970 figure of unity.

Since all the available information has been absorbed into the sample, it is now relatively more difficult to judge between the alternative projections. Nevertheless the results of Chapter VII indicate which particular numbers are likely to be suspect and a cursory examination of the table quickly identifies a number of peculiar estimates. In arriving at compromise estimates I have tried wherever possible to use one model or the other and I have done this using the evidence of the previous chapter as well as rather informal ideas of what does or does not look reasonable. Such a procedure is clearly biassed towards conservatism and this may have something to do with the fact that the linear expenditure system projection has been chosen in the majority of cases, twenty-four out of thirty-seven. This however also reflects the relative 'safeness' of many of these projections over those of the loglinear model which is less well determined and contains less *a priori* information. For a number of cases, neither model yielded a plausible projection. Fortunately, in all of these, reasonable values seemed to lie somewhere between the alternatives, suggesting the crude method of averaging. There is little to justify this, in principle, but without any further information no alternative is immediately apparent. Which model was chosen is indicated in the last column of the table, the number $\frac{1}{2}$ indicating averaging. Estimates derived in this way do not in general satisfy the adding-up constraint; in this case only a small residual emerged and this was allocated *pro rata* over the commodities. These final adjusted compromise estimates are given in the columns labelled C in the table. Note that the constant price figures do not add exactly to the constant price total which is exogenously given, but this difference is too small to justify any further adjustments.

Finally, we present the results of using these compromise demand equations to project ahead to 1980. Since prior information for this year is less available than that for 1975, it was decided to accept the Cambridge Model input–output projections for relative prices in 1980 with minimal alteration. For many commodities this gives a return from the abnormal values post-1970 to the sort of levels which have been more common over most of the post-war period. This may

TABLE 8.3
Alternative and compromise estimates for 1975
(£ *per capita* or £1970 *per capita*)

		Constant prices			Current prices			
	Price relative	LES	LLS	C	LES	LLS	C	Basis
1. Bread and cereals	1.601	13.1	13.9	13.7	21.0	22.3	21.9	½
2. Meat and bacon	1.627	31.6	32.3	32.0	51.5	52.6	52.1	LES
3. Fish	2.580	3.2	3.6	3.3	8.4	9.3	8.5	LES
4. Oils and fats	1.510	4.3	4.6	4.4	6.6	7.0	6.6	LES
5. Sugar, etc.	1.345	10.5	10.5	10.6	14.1	14.1	14.3	LES
6. Dairy produce	1.608	17.6	18.0	17.9	28.4	28.9	28.7	LES
7. Fruit	1.686	6.6	6.8	6.7	11.1	11.4	11.3	LES
8. Potatoes and veg.	1.557	14.5	15.1	14.7	22.7	23.5	22.9	LES
9. Beverages	1.107	8.2	7.3	7.9	9.1	8.1	8.7	½
10. Other man. food	1.309	3.8	4.8	3.9	5.0	6.3	5.1	LES
11. Footwear	1.439	8.7	9.4	8.8	12.5	13.5	12.6	LES
12. Clothing	1.429	45.0	45.2	45.6	64.3	64.6	65.1	LES
13. Rent, rates, etc.	1.591	70.8	67.0	67.8	112.6	106.6	107.9	LLS
14. Maintenance	1.629	15.6	12.7	12.8	25.3	20.6	20.9	LLS
15. Coal and coke	1.622	1.9	6.1	1.9	3.0	9.9	3.0	LES
16. Electricity	1.456	15.9	21.8	16.1	23.2	31.7	23.5	LES
17. Gas	1.355	11.6	8.7	10.3	15.7	11.8	13.9	½
18. Other fuel	1.666	1.4	2.2	1.8	2.3	3.6	3.0	½
19. Beer	1.165	33.2	26.4	26.7	38.7	30.8	31.1	LLS
20. Wines and spirits	1.254	27.1	24.8	25.1	33.9	31.1	31.5	LLS
21. Cigs. and tobacco	1.140	28.4	33.3	31.2	32.3	37.9	35.6	½
22. Communication	1.559	8.6	7.2	8.7	13.4	11.2	13.6	LES
23. R.c. of motor v.	1.567	42.6	60.2	43.1	66.7	94.3	67.6	LES
24. Rail travel	1.752	3.6	3.4	3.7	6.3	5.9	6.4	LES
25. Other travel	1.282	15.7	19.4	17.7	20.1	24.9	22.7	½
26. Exp. abroad	1.440	9.8	11.0	11.2	14.2	15.9	16.1	LLS
27. H'hold text., etc.	1.407	16.9	16.2	17.1	23.8	22.8	24.1	LES
28. Matches, soap, etc.	1.417	4.7	4.8	4.7	6.6	6.7	6.7	LES
29. Books & magazines	1.604	3.6	3.4	3.6	5.7	5.5	5.8	LES
30. Newspapers	1.676	4.1	4.7	4.2	6.9	7.8	7.0	LES
31. Recr. goods	1.283	17.6	18.1	17.8	22.5	23.2	22.8	LES
32. Chemists' goods	1.194	11.8	12.6	11.9	14.0	15.0	14.2	LES
33. Other goods n.e.s.	1.126	8.5	10.3	9.5	9.6	11.6	10.7	½
34. Domestic service	1.580	2.3	2.4	2.4	3.7	3.7	3.7	LES
35. Catering	1.617	26.0	28.3	28.6	42.0	45.7	46.3	LLS
36. Entertainment	1.369	12.1	11.5	12.2	16.5	15.7	16.7	LES
37. Other services	1.509	44.0	44.2	44.6	66.4	66.7	67.2	LES
Totals	1.455	604.9	632.2	604.3	880.1	922.3	880.1	

be thought of as being due to the reinstatement in importance of long-run cost factors in price determination over short-run demand pressures and supply difficulties. As to the development of consumers' expenditure in total over the five years 1975 to 1980, the Cambridge Model predicts quite rapid growth, the central estimate being 4.9% per annum in real terms. This is permitted by a massive relaxation of the balance of trade constraint due to supplies of North Sea oil; it is assumed – quite conservatively – that 120 million tons a year will be available in 1980, and at projected world prices for oil, this implies an improvement in the trade balance of some £5,000 million over the situation which would have occurred by 1980 without the oil. At the same time, the available labour force is expected to expand relatively quickly from 1975 to 1980, and it is necessary to expand investment and consumption to absorb this.

I have taken the 4.9% growth rate as a standard but to give a range of values I have calculated projections for 0.5% on either side of this, i.e. for 4.4% and 5.4% per annum growth rates respectively; these three alternatives give constant price total consumers' expenditure as £1621, £1660, and £1700 *per capita*, all at 1970 prices. The consumer price index is assumed to reach 2.161 by 1980 so that present rates of inflation are assumed to moderate somewhat, running at between 8% and 9% per *annum* from 1975 to 1980. This assumption is particularly hazardous but the pattern of expenditures in constant prices is independent of the absolute level of prices and thus of the rate of inflation except in so far as it affects relative prices.

The results of repeating the 1975 compromise calculations for 1980 are presented in Table 8.4. Columns headed L, S, and H refer to the low, standard, and high projections respectively. It will be noticed that the four fuels have been aggregated into a single group; this has been done since neither of the models gives plausible estimates. The most obvious problem with the linear expenditure system projection relates to underprediction for coal – the figure is negative – and overprediction for gas. Taken together the figures are not unreasonable and for this reason the compromise estimate for fuels is based on the sum of the linear expenditure system projections and is presented in aggregate only.

More generally, I shall make no attempt to offer a detailed appraisal of these results since the basis for this does not exist. None of the figures appears absurd; nevertheless the shortcomings of the models detailed in the earlier chapters should always be borne in mind.

TABLE 8.4
Alternative projections for 1980
(£1970 or £ *per capita*)

	Price relative	Constant prices L	Constant prices S	Constant prices H	Current prices L	Current prices S	Current prices H
1. Bread and cereals	1.112	12.0	12.0	11.9	28.8	28.7	28.5
2. Meat and bacon	1.198	31.9	32.2	32.4	82.6	83.3	83.9
3. Fish	1.282	2.2	2.2	2.1	6.1	6.0	5.8
4. Oils and fats	1.060	3.6	3.6	3.5	8.3	8.2	8.1
5. Sugar and confectionery	0.886	9.7	9.5	9.3	18.5	18.2	17.9
6. Dairy produce	0.834	21.7	22.0	22.3	39.0	39.6	40.2
7. Fruit	0.877	7.4	7.5	7.5	13.9	14.1	14.3
8. Potatoes and vegetables	0.692	21.3	21.8	22.3	31.7	32.6	33.4
9. Beverages	0.709	9.4	9.6	9.8	14.4	14.8	15.1
10. Other manufactured food	0.917	3.6	3.7	3.8	7.2	7.4	7.5
11. Footwear	0.938	10.1	10.3	10.5	20.4	20.8	21.3
12. Clothing	0.941	56.0	57.5	59.0	113.8	117.0	120.1
13. Rents, rates, etc.	1.269	71.1	70.4	69.7	194.7	192.9	191.2
14. Maintenance etc.	1.108	15.9	15.9	15.8	38.0	37.9	37.9
15–18. Fuels	1.100	43.7	45.0	46.3	75.4	77.4	79.4
19. Beer	0.805	27.5	27.0	26.5	47.8	47.0	46.1
20. Wines and spirits	0.866	39.8	41.5	43.3	74.4	77.7	81.0
21. Cigarettes	0.785	31.6	32.6	33.6	53.5	55.3	57.1
22. Communication	1.077	14.1	14.6	15.0	32.8	33.9	35.0
23. R.c. of motor vehicles	1.067	74.0	77.3	80.6	170.5	178.3	186.1
24. Rail travel	1.259	2.5	2.3	2.1	6.8	6.3	5.8
25. Other travel	0.856	21.4	21.6	21.8	39.6	40.0	40.3
26. Expenditure abroad	1.007	19.0	20.7	22.6	41.3	45.1	49.2
27. H'hold textiles, etc.	0.886	26.7	27.6	28.5	51.0	52.8	54.6
28. Matches, soap, etc.	0.889	4.7	4.7	4.7	9.1	9.1	9.1
29. Books and magazines	1.410	3.6	3.6	3.6	11.0	10.9	10.9
30. Newspapers	1.460	2.9	2.7	2.6	9.0	8.6	8.1
31. Recreational goods	0.979	23.4	24.2	25.1	49.5	51.3	53.1
32. Chemists' goods	0.902	14.9	15.4	15.9	29.1	30.1	31.1
33. Other goods n.e.s.	0.916	10.5	11.1	11.6	20.9	21.9	22.9
34. Domestic service	1.259	1.6	1.4	1.3	4.3	3.9	3.5
35. Catering	1.117	44.2	47.1	50.1	106.5	113.6	121.0
36. Entertainment	1.039	14.7	15.1	15.4	33.1	33.8	34.6
37. Other services	1.172	54.8	56.2	57.7	138.6	142.4	146.3

Chapter 9

CONCLUSIONS: METHODOLOGY OF APPLIED DEMAND ANALYSIS

In Chapter II, in the discussion of the historical development of the subject, it was shown how, during the last two decades, a new methodology of demand analysis has developed. This, which may be thought of as having begun in earnest with the publication in 1954 of Stone's *Economic Journal* paper, consists of the unmodified applica- of the utility theory of the *individual* consumer to the task of explaining consumption behaviour of the *average* consumer. The factors which led to this development have already been discussed; in this final chapter, I should like to step back from the detailed analysis, and try to use some of the material of this study to make an assessment of the success and usefulness of this approach.

While demand theory *per se* is capable of generating a wide range of alternative models, it is nevertheless true that the vast majority of models which have been estimated and which are based on the theory are either directly or indirectly additive. Direct additivity, which is assumed by the linear expenditure system and which, more generally, is the basis of Pigou's Law, has already played an important part in the analysis of the earlier chapters. *Indirect* additivity is a similarly restrictive assumption which relates to the functional form of utility defined in the dual space, i.e. utility defined over prices and money income. This latter assumption, like the former, implies a relationship between price and income elasticities; the exact nature of this will be discussed below, but the two relationships are close enough to justify discussing indirectly and directly additive models together.

In section IV of the survey article, Brown and Deaton (1972), I attempted to compile as comprehensive a list as possible of those studies of demand which used a model based on demand theory. A very high proportion of these related to the model used in this book, namely the linear expenditure system. The Cambridge Growth Model has used this system for the United Kingdom for a considerable time, see in particular, Stone and Croft-Murray (1959), Stone, Brown and Rowe (1964), Stone (1965), and the series, *A Programme for Growth*, e.g. Vols. V and IX, Cambridge, Department of Applied Economics (1964), (1970). In addition to this, Paelinck (1964) has analysed Belgian consumption using the model, Parks (1969) has applied it to Swedish data, Pollak and Wales (1969) to post-war United States data, Yoshihara (1969) to Japanese data, Leoni (1967) to Italian data, and Dahlman and Klevmarken (1971) to Swedish data. Cross-country comparative studies on OECD data have been undertaken by Baschet and Debreu (1971), Goldberger and Gamaletsos (1970), Solari (1971), and Parks and Barten (1973); and more recently, Lluch and Powell (1973) have studied differences in the parameter estimates of the model fitted over nineteen developed and underdeveloped countries, while Muellbauer (1974) has used the linear expenditure system to study the effects of price changes on the distribution of real income in the United Kingdom. Nor have other models based on direct additivity lacked applications. Powell's (1966) model of additive preferences has been applied to Canada, Powell (1965), to the United States, Powell, van Hoa, and Wilson (1968), and to inter-regional and welfare problems in Australia, van Hoa (1968) and (1969). Frisch's (1959) complete scheme for computing elasticities has been, and as far as I am aware still is, used for planning in Norway, see Johansen (1968). Indirect additivity has been somewhat less used but Houthakker's (1960a), (1960b) indirect addilog model has been used alongside the linear expenditure system by a number of the authors already quoted, i.e. Parks (1969), Solari (1971) and Baschet and Debreu (1971) and it has been much vaunted as a tool of demand analysis in applications to Holland by a number of Dutch writers, e.g. Somermeyer, Hilhorot and Wit (1962), Wit (1960) and Somermeyer and Langhout (1972). Finally, direct additivity has found a new application in dynamic models of demand, see in particular, Houthakker and Taylor (1970), Chapter 5, Phlips (1971) and (1972), and Taylor and Weiserbs (1972).

I have quoted this literature at some length because it is important to realise how much of it there is, and the extent to which empirical analysis has taken as a starting point the (mostly uncritical) acceptance of one or other of the additivity assumptions. Other studies which have attempted to analyse and test the additivity restriction within a more general model are not included in the list above and will be dealt with below.

This dominance of additivity is based upon powerful practical considerations. If demand analysis is to begin from a utility function, it must be given a precise functional form. The most natural and easiest way to do this is to write the function as a sum of identical functions, one for each commodity, with only the values of the parameters being allowed to vary; indeed all theorists prior to Pareto thought of utility functions in this way. To do otherwise requires knowledge of how different commodities relate to one another in the provision of welfare and, even if this can be done reliably, such specifications tend to lead to models which, for estimation purposes, have too many parameters. This argument applies with equal force to those investigators who take demand functions as their starting point. In most cases only a small number of parameters can be estimated; the general theory of demand leaves too much unspecified and direct and indirect additivity are the only obvious assumptions strong enough to yield models of general applicability. (Interestingly, the indirect addilog system was derived by Leser (1942) from just such considerations nearly twenty years before Houthakker defined it from the appropriate indirect utility function.) And the way in which additivity is usually stated as restricting behaviour is exactly the sort of empirical constraint which is needed, i.e. one which deals with the cross-price elasticities leaving the model to measure the responses which are of major interest, the income and own-price elasticities.

However, additivity has much more severe implications than this. As was shown in Chapter III, direct additivity implies Pigou's Law, that the ratio of price to income elasticity is the same for each good. And I have shown elsewhere, Deaton (1974a), that under indirect additivity the sum of price and income elasticities is constant for each good. Yet, as far as I am aware, in no one of the studies cited is either of these relationships noted, let alone justified. This certainly cannot be because they have little effect: in Chapters V and VI, the the consequences of Pigou's Law were examined in detail for the linear expenditure system and it was clear that they were highly significant in determining the performance of the model, both as a device for measuring and modelling behaviour and as a basis for projection. It would be very surprising if such difficulties were to be confined to the linear expenditure system; Pigou's Law is bound to cause difficulty in any directly additive model. Of indirect additivity

I have attempted no direct test, but in other work it has not done well in comparison with directly additive models, and this is consistent with the plausible view that the constant sum restriction between price and income elasticities is even more unlikely to be true than Pigou's Law. Thus, there can be little doubt that, in view of the relationships implied between income and own-price elasticities, both direct and indirect additivity lack general validity on the evidence available nor indeed would one expect such validity *a priori*.

One might still however doubt the importance of looking at the consequences of additivity in this way. It has been known for some time that additivity is inconsistent with most evidence; studies by Barten (1964) and (1969), Byron (1968) and (1970a), Theil (1971a), Lluch (1971) and Deaton (1974b) have all reached this conclusion using formal tests of competing models often based on some likelihood criterion. However there are difficulties in drawing practical conclusions from the results of such tests. Firstly, these studies use relatively small samples and the use of tests valid in large sample situations can often lead to the rejection of valid hypotheses. Secondly, and more importantly, formal tests of this nature absorb all the available evidence into one test statistic; so that, even if the rejection is correct, we have no idea what has gone wrong. Too much evidence is brought to bear on a single issue. For example, the inappropriate modelling of one, perhaps uninteresting, cross-price elasticity, will lead to the rejection of the whole model even though the investigator may well be prepared to accept such small transgressions to obtain the other benefits yielded by additivity. Minor data inaccuracies could lead one into a similar situation. And since the majority of the investigators who have been cited as using additive models professed themselves satisfied with their results, one might be entitled to suppose that there were no serious contradictions between additivity and the data. Such a supposition would be manifestly false; the truth is that many investigators have subjected their results neither to very close nor to very critical scrutiny. This is perhaps understandable; in many applications estimation problems have been very severe, especially until recently, and to formulate and estimate a model has been in itself a formidable task. In consequence many of the results of this research are susceptible to reinterpretation in the light of Pigou's Law, and I shall argue that the rejections of additivity here and elsewhere are given a new force. Let us deal with reinterpretation first by way of some particularly striking examples.

As has become clear in many examples in this book, the estimation of a directly additive model yields a value for the quantity $\ddot{\omega}$, Frisch's income flexibility of the marginal utility of money. In consequence of this, and of the voluminous literature on additivity, $\ddot{\omega}$ has been estimated in a wide variety of circumstances and, with a few exceptions, these estimates have been close, clustering around a value of -2. This uniformity has been much commented upon, see for example, Brown and Deaton (1972), section IV.5, and Clark (1973). Now such constancy over different countries and different times may seem surprising for a quantity which is defined as the elasticity of the marginal utility of money with respect to income, where marginal utility is rendered non-cardinal by relating it to the (unique) strictly additive utility function of the class underlying the model. Pigou's Law offers a very simple alternative. For if direct additivity is assumed, the measured value of ϕ, the reciprocal of $\ddot{\omega}$, can be interpreted as an average of the ratio of price to income elasticities, the weights of the average depending on the particular model and estimation technique used. It must be emphasized that this is *not* inconsistent with the Frisch interpretation; but it is considerably simpler, it gives an intuitively acceptable explanation of an observed phenomenon (the constancy), and it permits a less restrictive view of reality, since it would not be necessary to believe in the applicability of utility theory to aggregate data in order to accept the plausibility of rough uniformity in the average ratio of price to income elasticities for different countries.

Another good example of the possibilities for re-interpretation is provided by a fascinating, but yet unpublished conference paper by Lluch and Powell (1973). These authors estimated the linear expenditure system for nineteen widely assorted countries separately and then examined the predicted elasticities for cross-country regularities. Their results show a significant negative relationship between the income elasticity for food and *per capita* income and a rather weaker, but still distinct, positive relationship between the food *price* elasticity and *per capita* income. The first of these relationships has often been suggested, but the data base tended to yield ambiguous results, see e.g. Houthakker (1957); while the second relationship is, as far as I am aware, a new one. Indeed the lack of any such association has been reported by Houthakker (1965) and by Goldberger and Gamaletsos (1970). We can immediately see that Pigou's Law has much to do with these findings. Since the values for the flexibility are roughly constant across countries, Lluch and Powell's price elasticity/*per-capita*-income relationship is simply the mirror image of their income elasticity/*per-capita*-income relationship. Both Houthakker and Goldberger/Gamaletsos used loglinear systems which do not enforce Pigou's Law so that we might reasonably suppose that Lluch and Powell's second result is an assumption rather than an empirical finding. Even the income elasticity result might owe something of its clarity of definition to the enforcement of the proportionality constraint.

Questions of interpretation aside, the major contradictions found between Pigou's Law and the evidence in Chapter V must give rise to serious doubts about the whole methodology of demand analysis using additive models. This is not because the rejection of additivity is itself new, but because the prior implausibility of the proportionality relation much enhances the force of the rejection. For if additivity is regarded as a convenient way of dealing with cross-price responses, the finding that the assumption is false can be taken to mean that there exists more interaction between commodities than has been explicitly modelled. This is neither very surprising nor very important since, in most cases, the difficulties of accounting for such behaviour consistently with the data (which may in any case be subject to error) are large enough to outweigh any minor degree of verisimilitude lost by the inappropriate modelling of the cross-price responses. But in view of Pigou's Law, this position is no longer tenable; it is the own-price responses which additivity is distorting and it is the income and own-price elasticities which are the very stuff of the modelling and analysis of demand behaviour. Thus the difficulties with additivity which have been reported in this book, as well as the formal rejections in the studies quoted above, should be taken seriously by anyone considering the construction models of consumer behaviour using directly or indirectly additive utility functions. This is not to say such models should not be used. We saw, over both sample and prediction periods, how often even false prior information was helpful in preventing something worse. The main point is that investigators should be aware of the effects of their assumptions on their results, an awareness which has been inconspicuous in much of the recent literature.

It may quite plausibly be argued that the considerations so far advanced are valid objections to the use of additive systems for modelling disaggregated commodity demands, but that they do not apply to the analysis of broad groups of goods. Certainly it is true that, *a priori*, the assumption of independent wants is more reasonable when applied to broad aggregates, although there is considerable scope for disagreement as to the number of categories at which 'broad' disaggregation becomes 'detailed'. It is also fair to point out that most of the studies so far discussed have distinguished relatively few commodities, rarely more than ten, and often as few as four. There seem to be two good arguments for not accepting this defence of additivity. In the first place, the proportionality approximation must still be satisfied. Now, while it is true that the range of both income and price elasticities tends to narrow as aggregation is extended and substitutes are absorbed, I see no reason to suppose that Pigou's Law is any more likely to be true after aggregation than before. Furthermore, the formal rejections of additivity show no evidence of weakening as aggregation increases. It may well be that if, in fact, independent wants exist, they do not correspond to a simple partition of the commodities, so that several commodities, if not all, go toward satisfying more than one want. The second objection is more practical. The analysis of four, eight, or ten, commodities is all very well as a statistical exercise or as a testing ground for a new model. But, eventually, if a model is to be used as a tool of policy and prediction it must be able to deal with the sort of level of disaggregation used in this book. Otherwise such models remain technical *curiosa*.

The results presented in this study have revealed clearly many of the limitations of models based on directly additive utility functions. Equally, simple pragmatic models did no better. And although the competing models were certainly not the best possible alternatives, it became clear that models with too little prior information are usually worse than those with too much, where, in this context, too much implies that some is false. So that, in order to progress, we must use models which are less restrictive than additive systems but which contain more prior structure than can be generated by the casual pragmatic empiricism embodied in loglinear models.

What then should be the role of the theory in this process? If additivity were as necessary a part of the theory as the applied literature seems to suggest, then we might be forced to answer that its role is limited. But it is not so; and some studies, principally Barten (1967), Parks (1969), Byron (1968), (1970a) and (1970b), Lluch (1971), Theil (1971a, Chapter 11), and Deaton (1972) and

(1974b) have attempted a more general assessment of the usefulness of the theory. A variety of different models were used and there is considerable apparent diversity and disagreement in the results. Even so, I feel that, taken with a good deal of statistical scepticism, the results are not entirely inconsistent with the validity of utility analysis. This judgement is subject to one important *caveat*. In every case where it has seriously been tested the homogeneity postulate has been rejected; i.e. there appears to be considerable evidence that the 'average' consumer suffers from money illusion. This finding is so extraordinary and yet so universal that it is very tempting to abandon the fiction of the average consumer obeying a theory of the individual consumer, and recognise the aggregation problem explicitly. Inappropriate aggregation certainly seems the most likely source of such difficulties, and there seems no reason to suppose that explicit integration over different consumers using various models of taste and income distribution should not give perfectly good results. The approach has been used in the analysis of production functions, see Houthakker (1956–6) and Johansen (1972), and should be just as useful if applied to utility functions.

Even without this, the difficulties with additivity and the small number of viable alternatives should not make us turn back to the old pragmatic methodology but only to a more realistic and modest expectation of the possibilities of the new. While the belief that maximization of an additive utility function yields sensible global demand functions has been shown to be untenable, this does not mean that the theory is incapable of generating empirically useful restrictions on patterns of behaviour. Such restrictions we shall always heed from somewhere. Admittedly, the results of Sonnenschein and of Debreu, quoted in Chapter II, remove the basis for an absolute unqualified belief in such a position, yet the construction of arbitrary demand functions requires arbitrary manipulation of the income distribution and of preferences, and it is unlikely that the fates manipulate real income with the sole object of frustrating demand analysis. Further, as was discussed in Chapter II, there are grounds for believing that there may exist realistic restrictions on changes in income distribution which will allow aggregation if only for broad groups of commodities. So that what is fundamentally required is a good model of income redistribution which, if we take the theory as axiomatic for homogeneous income groups, will generate aggregate demand equations which are either consistent with the theory or differ from it in a predictable way. In the meantime, though it may be tempting to take the theory as axiomatic for aggregate or *per capita* behaviour (as for example is done in the excellent forthcoming text by Phlips (1974)) given the evidence available to date, such an approach has obvious dangers.

Independently of the aggregation problem, the theory will still be inapplicable unless there exists some non-additive demand system suitable for empirical analysis. Such a model must be both estimable and cast in a form in which prior information may be easily incorporated. It has often enough been said that utility theory offers a framework for the expression and organization of prior knowledge, yet it has rarely been used for this in practice. (Barten's (1964) paper is a notable exception.) On the contrary, it has been the pragmatic formulations which have allowed their users greatest flexibility in the selection of variables. Yet this approach ignores equally valuable theoretical information and, ideally, it should be possible to design a system with both flexibility and a suitable theoretical backing.

A number of non-additive utility functions have been suggested, for example, the quadratic utility function or 'linear preference scale' put forward by Allen and Bowley as early as 1935. But this has been analysed by Goldberger (1967) and is both difficult to estimate and of exceedingly implausible interpretation. This latter is particularly infelicitous for our purpose, since plausibility and ease of interpretation are essential if sensible prior restrictions are to be thought of. Another possible model is the S-branch utility tree, a generalization of the linear expenditure system suggested by Brown and Heien (1972). In this model the complications, especially of estimation, over and above the original linear expenditure system are very large and the reward, in terms of increased flexibility of the price responses, is very low. Indeed many of the consequences of Pigou's Law still hold, see the Appendix of Deaton (1974a). More promising, perhaps, is work by Nasse (1970) who has made the c-parameters of the linear expenditure price sensitive in a way which allows considerable relaxation of the assumptions of the model, while still allowing scope for the prior restriction of unwanted parameters. Application of the model so far has been disappointing, but the approach bears considerable promise. Alternatively it may be possible to generate non-additive demand systems from consideration of appropriate cost functions; these have been used relatively little in applied work to date and there exists a number of functional forms which do not embody either of the additivity assumptions. A first attempt in this direction is contained in Deaton (1974c) where a fairly general model, containing the linear expenditure system as a subcase, is presented and estimated. This model has relatively few parameters and does allow completely independent measurement of income and price responses.

Undoubtedly research will continue in these and other directions, and the discovery of an empirically sensible and theoretically sound demand system with the flexibility and some of the freedom of the loglinear model, would mark a considerable step forward. Even so, I see at best only a supplementary rôle for such a model. Detailed and careful study of individual commodities, perforce on a single equation basis, is likely to remain necessary for the foreseeable future. Complete systems of demand equations can usefully serve as a framework in which such studies can be placed, partly to guarantee overall consistency, and partly to yield sensible, if not ideal, explanations and predictions of those commodities which are of insufficient interest at any given time to justify the effort of detailed modelling.

APPENDIX: THE PROGRAM RIDGE

This appendix brings together the formulae of Chapter IV which are actually used in the estimation procedure and provides a bridge between the estimation theory of that chapter and the actual computer program.

At each iteration, we begin with an established set of values for the c-parameters. Values for b^0 and b' are then calculated according to (4.41), i.e.

$$\begin{pmatrix} b^{0\prime} \\ b^{1\prime} \end{pmatrix} = \begin{pmatrix} \xi_t\xi_t & \theta_t\xi_t\xi_t \\ \theta_t\xi_t\xi_t & \theta_t^2\xi_t\xi_t \end{pmatrix}^{-1} \begin{pmatrix} \xi_t(y_t - p_t c)' \\ \xi_t\theta_t(y_t - p_t c)' \end{pmatrix} \tag{A.1}$$

where $\xi_t = \mu_t - p_t'c$, and the repetition of a t-suffix in a product implies summation. These values can then be used with the c-parameters in the calculation which follow. A new step for c, δc, is then calculated according to a Marquardt (1963)-type modification of the ridge-walking algorithm, i.e.

$$\delta c = (A^* + \lambda I)^{-1} g_c^*, \tag{A.2}$$

where

$$A = -(H_{22} - H_{21}H_{11}^{-1}H_{12}), \tag{A.3}$$

and the matrix H is that given by (4.52), so that

$$H_{11} = \begin{pmatrix} \xi_t\xi_t\tilde{V}^{-1} & \theta_t\xi_t\xi_t\tilde{V}^{-1} \\ \theta_t\xi_t\xi_t\tilde{V}^{-1} & \theta_t^2\xi_t\xi_t\tilde{V}^{-1} \end{pmatrix} \tag{A.4}$$

and

$$H_{12} = H_{21} = \begin{pmatrix} \xi_t\tilde{V}^{-1}(p_t - b_t p_t) \\ \theta_t\xi_t\tilde{V}^{-1}(p_t - b_t p_t') \end{pmatrix} \tag{A.5}$$

The vector g_c is the gradient of the likelihood function in the c-directions, so that, from (4.37),

$$g_c = (\hat{p}_t - p_t b')\tilde{V}^{-1}(y_t - f_t), \tag{A.6}$$

where f_t is the current value of the predictions, i.e.

$$f_t = \hat{p}_t c + b_t(\mu_t - p_t' c), \tag{A.7}$$

where, as before, $b_t = b^0 + b^1\theta_t$. The asterisks in (A.2) indicate that A has been scaled to give a unit diagonal and a similar compensating transformation has been carried out on g, see Marquardt (1963). The quantity λ is a nonnegative number which, as estimation proceeds, the program tries to make smaller, but which may be increased locally to ensure that δc gives rise to an increase in likelihood.

The matrix H_{11} may be easily inverted. Denote the elements of the inverse of the matrix on the right-hand side of (A.1) by α_{11}, α_{12}, α_{21} and α_{22}. Then we must evaluate these in any case to derive b^0 and b', so that H_{11}^{-1} is given by

$$H_{11}^{-1} = \begin{pmatrix} \alpha_{11}\tilde{V} & \alpha_{12}\tilde{V} \\ \alpha_{21}\tilde{V} & \alpha_{22}\tilde{V} \end{pmatrix} \tag{A.8}$$

Thus, apart from the inversion of $\tilde{V}$ which must be carried out in any case, only one $n \times n$ matrix has to be inverted at each iteration. The algorithm really does avoid the necessity of repeatedly inverting a $3n \times 3n$ matrix; this is much more than a trick of partitioning.

A parameter TEM appears in the argument list of RIDGE; this takes one of four values, 'FIML', 'OLSE', 'APML', or 'WMML' and controls the type of estimation undertaken. For FIML, full information maximum likelihood, the formulae apply as above and the matrix V is estimated according to (4.30), i.e.

$$\tilde{V} = \frac{1}{T}\sum_t \tilde{e}_t\tilde{e}_t' + \kappa ii' \tag{A.9}$$

For OLSE, ordinary least squares estimation, according to (4.23) and (4.25)

$$\tilde{V} = \tilde{\sigma}^2 I$$

$$\tilde{\sigma}^2 = \frac{1}{T(n-1)}\sum_t \tilde{e}_t'\tilde{e}_t\,. \tag{A.10}$$

For APML, 'a-priori maximum likelihood' and WMML, 'weighted-mean maximum likelihood', V is given by

$$\left.\begin{aligned} \tilde{V} &= \tilde{\sigma}^2 V_0 \\ \tilde{\sigma}^2 &= \frac{1}{T(n-1)} \sum_t \tilde{e}_t' V_0^{-1} \tilde{e}_t \,. \end{aligned}\right\} \qquad \text{(A.11)}$$

In APML, V_0 is given by the user, while for WMML, V_0 is formed from the averages of the value shares over the sample period as described in Chapter V, e.g. (5.2).

```
      SUBROUTINE RIDGE(TEM,NN,NT,NITS,LAP,IREADV)
      IMPLICIT REAL*8 (A-H,O-$)
      DIMENSION ITHETA(50),Y(10),P(10)
      COMMON W(100),YINC(50),THETA(50),RPP(100),RPTP(100),
     1RPT2P(100),RPY(100),RPTY(100),RYY(100),RMP(10),RMY(1
     20),RMTY(10),RMTP(10),RMT2P(10),RMM,RMTM,RMT2M,CP(10)
     3C(10),BC(10),B1(10),RVBC(10),RVB1(10),A(100),R(10),R
     4PZ(10),RYZ(10),RYTZ(10),RPTZ(10),RPT2Z(10),RZZ,RZTZ,
     5RZT2Z,AL11,AL12,AL22,V(100),ID1,N,G(10),DELTA(10),T,
     6KZ,D
      EQUIVALENCE (ITHETA(1),RPP(1)),(Y(1),BC(1)),(P(1),B1
     1(1))
      INTEGER T
      REAL*8 LAT,LAP,NU,AN*4(4),TEM*4
      DATA AN(1),AN(2),AN(3),AN(4)/4HFIML,4HOLSE,4HAPML,4H
     1WMML/
      N=NN
      T=NT
      ID1=10
      CVC=1.D-06
      NU=10.D0
    1 FORMAT(3I2,D7.1)
    2 FORMAT(6D12.6)
    3 FORMAT(D8.3,2X,I3)
    6 FORMAT(10D7.3)
    7 FORMAT(10D7.5)
   53 FORMAT(6D12.4)
C READ STARTING VALUES
      DO 19 I=1,4
   19 IF(TEM.EQ.AN(I))KZ=I-2
      READ(5,2) (CP(I),I=1,N)
      ALKHD=DFLOAT(T)*(DLOG(DFLOAT(N))-DFLOAT(N-1)*2837877
     10664D-10)
      IF(KZ-1)50,51,50
   51 IA=-ID1
      DO 52 J=1,N
      IA=IA+ID1
   52 READ(IREADV,53) (V(IA+I),I=1,N)
C READ DATA AND ACCUMULATE
   50 DO 4 I=1,T
      READ(4,3) YINC(I),ITHETA(I)
    4 THETA(I)=DFLOAT(ITHETA(I))
      IA=-ID1
      DO 8 J=1,N
      IA=IA+ID1
      IB=IA
      DO 9 I=1,N
      IB=IB+1
      RPP(IB)=0.D0
      RPTP(IB)=0.D0
      RPT2P(IB)=0.D0
      RPY(IB)=0.D0
      RPTY(IB)=0.D0
    9 RYY(IB)=0.D0
      RMP(J)=0.D0
      RMY(J)=0.D0
```

```
          RMTY(J)=0.D0
          RMTP(J)=0.D0
          RMT2P(J)=0.D0
      8   C(J)=0.D0
          DO 5 L=1,T
          READ(4,6)  (Y(K),K=1,N)
          READ(4,7)  (P(K),K=1,N)
          IA=-ID1
          DO 5 J=1,N
          IA=IA+ID1
          DO 10 I=1,N
          IB=IA+I
          RPP(IB)=RPP(IB)+P(I)*P(J)
          RPTP(IB)=RPTP(IB)+P(I)*P(J)*THETA(L)
          RPT2P(IB)=RPT2P(IB)+P(I)*P(J)*THETA(L)*THETA(L)
          RPY(IB)=RPY(IB)+P(I)*Y(J)
          RPTY(IB)=RPTY(IB)+P(I)*Y(J)*THETA(L)
       10 RYY(IB)=RYY(IB)+Y(I)*Y(J)
          C(J)=C(J)+Y(J)/YINC(L)
          RMP(J)=RMP(J)+P(J)*YINC(L)
          RMY(J)=RMY(J)+Y(J)*YINC(L)
          RMTY(J)=RMTY(J)+Y(J)*YINC(L)*THETA(L)
          RMTP(J)=RMTP(J)+P(J)*YINC(L)*THETA(L)
        5 RMT2P(J)=RMT2P(J)+P(J)*YINC(L)*THETA(L)*THETA(L)
          RMM=0.D0
          RMTM=0.D0
          RMT2M=0.D0
          DO 11 L=1,T
          RMM=RMM+YINC(L)*YINC(L)
          RMTM=RMTM+YINC(L)*YINC(L)*THETA(L)
       11 RMT2M=RMT2M+YINC(L)*YINC(L)*THETA(L)*THETA(L)
C SET UP FIRST TIME
          IF(KZ) 54,55,56
       55 IA=-ID1
          DO 57 J=1,N
          IA=IA+ID1
          DO 57 I=1,N
          V(IA+I)=0.D0
          IF(I-J) 57,58,57
       58 V(IA+I)=1.D0
       57 CONTINUE
          GO TO 54
       56 IF(KZ-2) 63,59,54
       59 IA=-ID1
          DO 66 I=1,N
      66  C(I)=C(I)/DFLOAT(T)
          WRITE(6,40) (C(I),I=1,N)
          DO 61 J=1,N
          IA=IA+ID1
          DO 61 I=1,N
          V(IA+I)=-(C(I)*C(J))/(DFLOAT(T)*DFLOAT(T))
          IF(I-J)61,62,61
       62 V(IA+I)=V(IA+I)+C(I)/DFLOAT(T)
       61 CONTINUE
      63  IA=-ID1
          DO 64 J=1,N
          IA=IA+ID1
          DO 64 I=1,N
```

```
   64 V(IA+I)=DFLOAT(N)*V(IA+I)+1.D0
      CALL MD01AD(V,N,D,ID1)
      ALKHD=ALKHD-DFLOAT(T)*(DLOG(D)-DFLOAT(N)*DLOG(DFLOAT
     1(N)))
      CALL MB03AD(V,N,NS,ID1)
      IA=-ID1
      DO 70 J=1,N
      IA=IA+ID1
      DO 70 I=1,N
   70 V(IA+I)=V(IA+I)*DFLOAT(N)
  54  DO 12 I=1,N
   12 C(I)=CP(I)
      CALL MAKEBV
      ALKHDP=ALKHD-DFLOAT(T)*D
      WRITE(6,49)
      WRITE(6,39) LAP,ALKHDP
      WRITE(6,40) (CP(I),I=1,N)
      WRITE(6,40) (B0(I),I=1,N)
      WRITE(6,40) (B1(I),I=1,N)
  49  FORMAT(//1H ,15HSTARTING VALUES)
      ITSOUT=0
C MAIN LOOP STARTS HERE
   13 ITSOUT=ITSOUT+1
      ITSIN=0
      WRITE(6,14) ITSOUT
   14 FORMAT(1H0,30HENTER MAIN LOOP: ITERATION NO ,I2)
      LAT=LAP/NU
      IF(KZ)65,46,46
  65  CALL MB03AD(V,N,NS,ID1)
      IF (NS) 45,46,45
  45  STOP 0001
C CONSTRUCT A AND G
  46  IA=-ID1
      DO 15 I=1,N
      RVB0(I)=0.D0
      RVB1(I)=0.D0
      IA=IA+ID1
      DO 15 K=1,N
      RVB0(I)=RVB0(I)+V(IA+K)*B0(K)
   15 RVB1(I)=RVB1(I)+V(IA+K)*B1(K)
      RBVB0=0.D0
      RBVB1=0.D0
      RBVB01=0.D0
      DO 17 K=1,N
      RBVB0=RBVB0+B0(K)*RVB0(K)
      RBVB1=RBVB1+B1(K)*RVB1(K)
   17 RBVB01=RBVB01+B0(K)*RVB1(K)
      IA=-ID1
      DO 16 J=1,N
      IA=ID1+IA
      IB=-ID1
      T1=(RBVB0-RVB0(J))*RPZ(J)+RBVB01*RPTZ(J)
      T2=(RBVB01-RVB1(J))*RPZ(J)+RBVB1*RPTZ(J)
      T3=(RBVB0-RVB0(J))*RPTZ(J)+RBVB01*RPT2Z(J)
      T4=(RBVB01-RVB1(J))*RPTZ(J)+RBVB1*RPT2Z(J)
      IB=-ID1
      DO 20 I=1,N
      IB=IB+ID1
```

```
      T5=RPZ(J)*(RVB0(I)-V(IA+I))+RVB1(I)*RPTZ(J)
      T6=RPTZ(J)*(RVB0(I)-V(IA+I))+RVB1(I)*RPT2Z(J)
      IC=IA+I
      A(IC)=RPZ(I)*(AL11*(T5-T1)+AL12*(T6-T3))+RPTZ(I)*(A
     112*(T5-T1-T4)-AL11*T2+AL22*(T6-T3))
      A(IC)=A(IC)-RPT2Z(I)*(AL12*T2+AL22*T4)+RPP(IC)*(V(I
     1)-RVB0(I)-RVB0(J)+RBVB0)
   20 A(IC)=A(IC)-RPTP(IC)*(RVB1(I)+RVB1(J)-2.D0*RBVB01)+
     1PT2P(IC)*RBVB1
      G(J)=-RPZ(J)*(RVB0(J)-RBVB0)-RPTZ(J)*(RVB1(J)-2.D0*
     1BVB01)+RPT2Z(J)*RBVB1
      IC=-ID1
      DO 16 L=1,N
      IC=IC+ID1
   16 G(J)=G(J)+RPY(IC+J)(L))-RPP(IC+J)*C(L)*(V(IC+J)-RVB
     1*V(IC+J)-RVB0(L))+RVB1(L)*(RPTP(IC+J)*C(L)-RPTY(IC+
     1))
C SCALING OF A AND G
      IA=-ID1
      DO 21 I=1,N
      IA=IA+ID1+1
   21 R(I)=DSQRT(A(IA))
      IA=-ID1
      DO 22 J=1,N
      IA=IA+ID1
      DO 23 I=1,N
   23 A(IA+I)=A(IA+I)/(R(I)*R(J))
   22 G(J)=G(J)/R(J)
C CALCULATE DELTA: INNER LOOP STARTS HERE
   36 IA=-ID1
      DO 24 J=1,N
      IA=IA+ID1
      DO 24 I=1,N
      IF(I-J)25,26,25
   26 W(IA+I)=A(IA+I)+LAT
      GO TO 24
   25 W(IA+I)=A(IA+I)
   24 CONTINUE
      CALL MB03AD(W,N,NS,ID1)
      IF (NS) 27,28,27
   27 STOP 0002
   28 DO 29 J=1,N
      IA=J-ID1
      DELTA(J)=0.D0
      DO 30 K=1,N
      IA=IA+ID1
   30 DELTA(J)=DELTA(J)+W(IA)*G(K)
      DELTA(J)=DELTA(J)/R(J)
   29 C(J)=CP(J)+DELTA(J)
C COMPUTE NEW LIKELIHOOD AND COMPARE
      CALL MAKEBV
      ALKHDT=ALKHD-DFLOAT(T)*D
      IF(ALKHDT-ALKHDP)31,32,32
   31 ITSIN=ITSIN+1
      IF(ITSIN-9)33,33,34
   33 WRITE(6,35) ITSIN
   35 FORMAT(1H0,31HENTER INNER LOOP: ITERATION NO ,I2)
      LAT=LAT*NU
```

```
      GO TO 36
   34 WRITE(6,37)
   37 FORMAT(1H0,32H9 CYCLES COMPLETED IN INNER LOOP)
      DO 67 I=1,N
   67 C(I)=CP(I)
      CALL MAKEBV
      RETURN
   32 WRITE(6,38) ITSOUT
   38 FORMAT(//1H ,13HITERATION NO ,I2)
      DIFF=ALKHDT-ALKHDP
      WRITE(6,39) LAT,ALKHDT,DIFF
   39 FORMAT(1H ,1PD7.1,1P2D16.9)
      WRITE(6,40) (DELTA(I),I=1,N)
   40 FORMAT(1H0,10F12.8)
      WRITE(6,40) (C(I),I=1,N)
      WRITE(6,40) (B0(I),I=1,N)
      WRITE(6,40) (B1(I),I=1,N)
      ALKHDP=ALKHDT
      LAP=LAT
      DO 44 I=1,N
   44 CP(I)=C(I)
      DO 41 I=1,N
      IF(DABS(DELTA(I))-CVC) 41,41,42
   41 CONTINUE
      WRITE(6,68)
   68 FORMAT(1H ,'CONVERGENCE CRITERION SATISFIED')
      RETURN
   42 IF(ITSOUT-NITS)13,43,43
  43  WRITE(6,69)
   69 FORMAT(1H ,'LIMITS ON MAIN LOOP REACHED')
      RETURN
      END


      SUBROUTINE MAKEBV
      IMPLICIT REAL*8 (A-H,O-$)
      COMMON W(100),YINC(50),THETA(50),RPP(100),RPTP(100),
     1RPT2P(100),RPY(100),RPTY(100),RYY(100),RMP(10),RMY(1
     20),RMTY(10),RMTP(10),RMT2P(10),RMM,RMTM,RMT2M,CP(10)
     3C(10),B0(10),B1(10),RVB0(10),RVB1(10),A(100),R(10),R
     4PZ(10),RYZ(10),RYTZ(10),RPTZ(10),RPT2Z(10),RZZ,RZTZ,
     5RZT2Z,AL11,AL12,AL22,V(100),ID1,N,G(10),DELTA(10),T,
     6KZ,D
      INTEGER T
      IA=-ID1
      IB=ID1+ID1
      IC=IB+ID1
      ID=IC+ID1
      DO 1 I=1,N
      W(I)=0.D0
      W(I+ID1)=0.D0
      W(IB+I)=0.D0
      W(IC+I)=0.D0
      W(ID+I)=0.D0
      IA=IA+ID1
      DO 2 K=1,N
      W(I)=W(I)+RPP(IA+K)*C(K)
      W(ID1+I)=W(ID1+I)+RPY(IA+K)*C(K)
```

```
      W(IB+I)=W(IB+I)+RPTY(IA+K)*C(K)
      W(IC+I)=W(IC+I)+RPTP(IA+K)*C(K)
    2 W(ID+I)=W(ID+I)+RPT2P(IA+K)*C(K)
      RPZ(I)=RMP(I)-W(I)
      RYZ(I)=RMY(I)-W(I+ID1)
      RYTZ(I)=RMTY(I)-W(I+IB)
      RPTZ(I)=RMTP(I)-W(I+IC)
    1 RPT2Z(I)=RMT2P(I)-W(I+ID)
      RZZ=RMM
      RZTZ=RMTM
      RZT2Z=RMT2M
      DO 3 K=1,N
      RZZ=RZZ+C(K)*(W(K)-2.D0*RMP(K))
      RZTZ=RZTZ+C(K)*(W(IC+K)-2.D0*RMTP(K))
    3 RZT2Z=RZT2Z+C(K)*(W(ID+K)-2.D0*RMT2P(K))
      DEL=RZZ*RZT2Z-RZTZ*RZTZ
      AL11=RZT2Z/DEL
      AL12=-RZTZ/DEL
      AL22=RZZ/DEL
      DO 4 I=1,N
      TEM1=RYZ(I)-RPZ(I)*C(I)
      TEM2=RYTZ(I)-RPTZ(I)*C(I)
      B0(I)=AL11*TEM1+AL12*TEM2
    4 B1(I)=AL12*TEM1+AL22*TEM2
      IA=-ID1
      D=0.D0
      DO 5 J=1,N
      IA=IA+ID1
      IB=-ID1+J
      DO 5 I=1,N
      IB=IB+ID1
      IC=IA+I
      TEM=RYY(IC)-RPY(IC)*C(I)-RPY(IB)*C(J)-RYZ(I)*B0(J)-
     1YZ(J)*B0(I)+RPP(IC)*C(I)*C(J)
      TEM=TEM+RPZ(I)*C(I)*B0(J)+RPZ(J)*C(J)*B0(I)+RZZ*B0
     1)*B0(J)-RYTZ(I)*B1(J)
      TEM=TEM-RYTZ(J)*B1(I)+RPTZ(I)*C(I)*B1(J)+RPTZ(J)*C
     1)*B1(I)
      TEM=TEM+RZTZ*(B0(I)*B1(J)+B0(J)*B1(I))+RZT2Z*B1(I)*
     11(J)
      IF(KZ)7,8,8
    7 V(IC)=DFLOAT(N)*TEM/DFLOAT(T)+1.D0
      GO TO 5
    8 D=D+TEM*V(IC)
    5 CONTINUE
      IF(KZ)11,9,9
    9 D=DLOG(D/(DFLOAT(N-1)*DFLOAT(T)))*DFLOAT(N-1)
      RETURN
   11 CALL MDC1AD(V,N,D,ID1)
      D=DLOG(D)-DFLOAT(N)*DLOG(DFLOAT(N))
      IA=-ID1
      DO 10 J=1,N
      IA=IA+ID1
      DO 10 I=1,N
   10 V(IA+I)=V(IA+I)/DFLOAT(N)
      RETURN
      END
```

```
      SUBROUTINE SEBC
      IMPLICIT REAL*8 (A-H,O-$)
      COMMON W(100),YINC(50),THETA(50),RPP(100),RPTP(100),
     1RPT2P(100),RPY(100),RPTY(100),RYY(100),RMP(10),RMY(1
     20),RMTY(10),RMTP(10),RMT2P(10),RMM,RMTM,RMT2M,CP(10)
     3C(10),B0(10),B1(10),RVB0(10),RVB1(10),A(100),R(10),R
     4PZ(10),RYZ(10),RYTZ(10),RPTZ(10),RPT2Z(10),RZZ,RZTZ,
     5RZT2Z,AL11,AL12,AL22,V(100),ID1,N,G(10),DELTA(10),T,
     6KZ,D
      INTEGER T
      IA=-ID1
      DO 4 J=1,N
      IA=IA+ID1
      DO 4 I=1,N
    4 A(IA+I)=A(IA+I)*R(I)*R(J)
      IF(KZ)1,2,2
    2 IA=-ID1
      D=DEXP(D/DFLOAT(N-1))
      DO 3 J=1,N
      IA=IA+ID1
      DO 3 I=1,N
    3 A(IA+I)=A(IA+I)/D
    1 CALL MB03AD(A,N,NS,ID1)
      IF(NS)5,6,5
    5 STOP 0006
    6 IA=-ID1
      DO 7 I=1,N
      IA=IA+ID1+1
    7 RVB1(I)=DSQRT(A(IA))
      DO 8 I=1,N
      G(I)=AL11*RPZ(I)+AL12*RPTZ(I)
    8 RVB0(I)=AL11*RPTZ(I)+AL12*RPT2Z(I)
      DO 10 I=1,N
      R(I)=0.D0
      IA=-ID1
      DO 9 J=1,N
      IA=IA+ID1
      T1=-B0(I)*G(J)-B1(I)*RVB0(J)
      IF(I.EQ.J) T1=T1+G(I)
      DO 9 K=1,N
      T2=-B0(I)*G(K)-B1(I)*RVB0(K)
      IF(I.EQ.K) T2=T2+G(I)
    9 R(I)=R(I)+T1*T2*A(IA+K)
   10 R(I)=DSQRT(R(I))
      DO 11 I=1,N
      G(I)=AL12*RPZ(I)+AL22*RPTZ(I)
   11 RVB0(I)=AL12*RPTZ(I)+AL22*RPT2Z(I)
      DO 13 I=1,N
      DELTA(I)=0.D0
      IA=-ID1
      DO 12 J=1,N
      IA=IA+ID1
      T1=-B0(I)*G(J)-B1(I)*RVB0(J)
      IF(I.EQ.J) T1=T1+G(J)
      DO 12 K=1,N
      T2=-B0(I)*G(K)-B1(I)*RVB0(K)
      IF(I.EQ.K) T2=T2+G(I)
```

```
   12 DELTA(I)=DELTA(I)+T1*T2*A(IA+K)
   13 DELTA(I)=DSQRT(DELTA(I))
      WRITE(6,14)
   14 FORMAT(1H1,'STANDARD ERRORS OF C,BO,AND B1')
      WRITE(6,15)  (RVB1(I),I=1,N)
      WRITE(6,15)  (R(I),I=1,N)
      WRITE(6,15)  (DELTA(I),I=1,N)
   15 FORMAT(1H0,10F12.8)
      RETURN
      END
```

A LIST OF WORKS CITED

Allen, R.G.D. and A. Bowley (1935). *Family Expenditure*. P.S. King and Son, London.

Barker, T.S. (editor), (forthcoming). *Modelling Economic Structure*, Chapman and Hall, London.

Barten, A.P. (1964). Consumer demand functions under conditions of almost additive preferences. *Econometrica*, Vol. 32, pp. 1–38.

Barten, A.P. (1967). Evidence on the Slutsky conditions for demand equations. *Review of Economics and Statistics*, Vol. 49, pp. 77–84.

Barten, A.P. (1969). Maximum likelihood estimation of a complete system of demand equations. *European Economic Review*, Vol. 1, pp. 7–73.

Barten, A.P. (1970). Réflexions sur la construction d'un système empirique des fonctions de demande. *Cahiers du Séminaire D'Économetrie*, No. 12, pp. 67–80.

Barten, A.P. and H. Theil (1964). Simultaneous estimation of a complete system of demand equations. Netherlands School of Economics, Econometric Institute, Report 6405.

Barten, A.P. and S.J. Turnovsky (1966). Some aspects of the aggregation problem for composite demand equations. *International Economic Review*, Vol. 7, pp. 231–259.

Baschet, J. and P. Debreu (1971). Systèmes de lois de demande: une comparison internationale. *Annales de l'I.N.S.E.E.*, No. 6, pp. 3–39.

Benini, R. (1907). Sull'uso delle formole empiriche nell'economia applicata. *Giornale degli economisti*, 2nd series, Vol. 35, pp. 1053–63.

Bieri, J. and A. de Janvry (1972). *Empirical Analysis of Demand Under Consumer Budgeting.* Giannini Foundation Monograph, Number 30.

Brown, J.A.C. and A.S. Deaton (1972). Models of consumer behaviour: a survey. *Economic Journal*, Vol. 82, pp. 1145–1236.

Brown, M. and D.M. Heien (1972). The *S*-branch utility tree: a generalization of the linear expenditure system. *Econometrica*, Vol. 40, pp. 737–747.

Byron, R.P. (1968). Methods for estimating demand equations using prior information: a series of experiments with Australian data. *Australian Economic Papers*, Vol. 7, pp. 227–248.

Byron, R.P. (1970a). A simple method for estimating demand systems under separable utility assumptions. *Review of Economic Studies*, Vol. 37, pp. 261–274.

Byron, R.P. (1970b). The restricted Aitken estimation of sets of demand relations. *Econometrica*, Vol. 38, pp. 816–830.

Cambridge, Department of Applied Economics (1964). *A Programme for Growth, Vol. V.* Chapman & Hall, London.

Cambridge, Department of Applied Economics (1970). *A Programme for Growth, Vol. IX.* Chapman & Hall, London.

Central Statistical Office (1971a). *National Income and Expenditure 1971.* Her Majesty's Stationery Office, London.

Central Statistical Office (1971b). *Annual Abstract of Statistics 1971.* Her Majesty's Stationery Office, London.

Central Statistical Office (1973a). *National Income and Expenditure 1973.* Her Majesty's Stationery Office, London.

Central Statistical Office (1973b). *Monthly Digest of Statistics, December 1973.* Her Majesty's Stationery Office, London.

Clark, C. (1973). The marginal utility of income, *Oxford Economic Papers*, Vol. 25, pp. 145–159.

Clarkson, G.P.E. (1963). *The Theory of Consumer Demand: A Critical Appraisal.* Prentice Hall, Engelwood Cliffs, New Jersey.

Dahlman, C.J. and A. Klevmarken (1971). *Den Privata Konsumtionen 1931–1975.* Uppsala.

Davenant, C. (1699). *An Essay upon the Probable Methods of Making a People Gainers in the Balance of Trade.* London, 1699.

Deaton, A.S. (1972). The estimation and testing of systems of demand equations. *European Economic Review*, Vol. 3, pp. 390–411.

Deaton, A.S. (1974a). A reconsideration of the empirical implications of additive preferences. *Economic Journal*, Vol. 84, pp. 338–348.

Deaton, A.S. (1974b). The analysis of consumer demand in the United Kingdom, 1900–1970. *Econometrica*, Vol. 42.

Deaton, A.S. (1974c). A simple non-additive model of demand. Presented to European Meeting of the Econometric Society, Grenoble, 1974.

Debreu, G. (1973). Excess demand functions. Center for Research in Management Science, University of California, Berkeley. (mimeo.).

Edgeworth, F.Y. (1881). *Mathematical Psychics.* Keegan Paul, London.

Ezekiel, M. (1930). *Methods of Correlation Analysis.* John Wiley, New York.

Fisher, W.D. (1969). *Clustering and Aggregation in Economics.* Johns Hopkins. Baltimore.

Frisch, R. (1932). *New Methods of Measuring Marginal Utility.* J.C.B. Mohr, Tübingen.

Frisch, R. (1959). A complete scheme for computing all direct and cross demand elasticities in a model with many sectors. *Econometrica*, Vol. 27, pp. 177–196.

Geary, R.C. (1949–50). A note on 'A constant utility index of the cost of living'. *Review of Economic Studies*, Vol. 18, pp. 65–66.

Goldberger, A.S. (1964). *Econometric Theory.* John Wiley, New York.

Goldberger, A.S. (1967). Functional form and utility: a review of consumer demand theory. Social Systems Research Institute, University of Wisconsin: Systems Formulation, Methodology, and Policy Workshop paper No. 6703. mimeo.

Goldberger, A.S. and T. Gamaletsos (1970). A cross-country comparison of consumer expenditure patterns. *European Economic Review*, Vol. 1, pp. 357–400.

Goldfeld, S.M. and R.E. Quandt (1972). *Non-linear Methods in Econometrics*. North-Holland.

Gorman, W.M. (1953). Community preference fields. *Econometrica*, Vol. 21, pp. 63–80.

Gorman, W.M. (1959). Separable utility and aggregation. *Econometrica*, Vol. 27, pp. 469–481.

Gossen, H.H. (1854). *Entwickelung der Gesetze des menschlichen Verkers, und der daraus fliessenden Regeln für menschliches Handeln*. Druck und Verlag von Friedrich Vieweg und Sohn, Braunschweig.

Green, H.A.J. (1964). *Aggregation in Economic Analysis*. Princeton University Press.

Hicks, J.R. (1936). *Value and Capital*. Oxford University Press.

Hicks, J.R. (1956). *A Revision of Demand Theory*. Oxford University Press.

Hicks, J.R. and R.G.D. Allen (1934). A reconsideration of the theory of value. *Economica*, Vol. 1, pp. 52–75, 196–219.

Houthakker, H.S. (1955–6). The Pareto distribution and the Cobb/Douglas production function in demand theory. *Review of Economic Studies*, Vol. 23, pp. 27–31.

Houthakker, H.S. (1957). An international comparison of household expenditure patterns commemorating the centenary of Engel's Law. *Econometrica*, Vol. 25, pp. 532–551.

Houthakker, H.S. (1960a). Additive preferences. *Econometrica*, Vol. 28, pp. 244–256.

Houthakker, H.S. (1960b). The influence of prices and incomes on household expenditures. *Bulletin of the International Institute of Statistics*, Vol. 37, pp. 9–22.

Houthakker, H.S. (1965). New evidence on demand elasticities. *Econometrica*, Vol. 33, pp. 277–288.

Houthakker, H.S. and L.D. Taylor (1970). *Consumer Demand in the United States 1929–70, Analysis and Projections*. Harvard University Press, second edition.

Jardine, N. and R. Sibson (1971). *Mathematical Taxonomy*. John Wiley, London.

Jevons, W.S. (1863). *A Serious Fall in the Value of Gold*. London.

Jevons, W.S. (1871). *The Theory of Political Economy*. Macmillan, London.

Johansen, L. (1968). Explorations in long-term projections for the Norwegian economy. *Economics of Planning*, Vol. 8, pp. 70–117.

Johansen, L. (1972). *Production Functions*. North-Holland.

Katzner, D.W. (1970). *Static Demand Theory*. Collier-Macmillan, New York.

Keynes, J.M. (1936a). *The General Theory of Employment, Interest and Money*. Macmillan, London.

Keynes, J.M. (1936b). William Stanley Jevons, 1835–1882. *Journal of the Royal Statistical Society*, Vol. 99, Part III, pp. 516–548.

Klein, L.R. and H. Rubin (1947–48). A constant utility-index of the cost of living. *Review of Economic Studies*, Vol. 15, pp. 84–87.

Konüs. A.A. (1939). On the theory of means. *Acta Universitatis Asiae Mediae (Tashkent)*, Series Va, Mathematica, Fasc. 24, pp. 3–10.

Kornai, J. (1971). *Anti-Equilibrium. On economic systems theory and the tasks of research*. North-Holland.

Lehfeldt, R.A. (1914). The elasticity of the demand for wheat. *Economic Journal*, Vol. 24, pp. 212–217.

Lenoir, M. (1913). *Etudes sur la Formation et le Mouvement des Prix*. Paris.

Leoni, R. (1967). An analysis of expenditures on private consumption. *Rivista di Politica Economica*, (selected papers), pp. 179–199.

Leontief, W. (1936). Composite commodities and the problem of index numbers. *Econometrica*, Vol. 4, pp. 39–59.

Leser, C.E.V. (1941–42). Family budget data and price elasticities of demand. *Review of Economic Studies*, Vol. 9, pp. 40–57.

Lluch, C. (1971). Consumer demand functions, Spain, 1958–64. *European Economic Review*, Vol. 2, pp. 277–302.

Lluch, C. and A.A. Powell (1973). International comparisons of expenditure and saving patterns. Presented to European Meeting of the Econometric Society, Oslo, 1973.

Malinvaud, E. (1972). *Lectures on Microeconomic Theory*. North-Holland.

Marquardt, D.W. (1963). An algorithm for least-squares estimation of non-linear parameters. *Journal of the Society of Industrial and Applied Mathematics*, Vol. 11, pp. 431–441.

Marshall, A. (1890). *Principles of Economics*. Macmillan, London.

Maurice, R. (1968). *National Accounts Statistics: Sources and Methods*. Her Majesty's Stationery Office, London.

Mishan, E.J. (1961). Theories of consumer behaviour: a cynical review. *Economica*, Vol. 28, pp. 1–11.

Moore, H. (1929). *Synthetic Economics*. Macmillan, New York.

Muellbauer, J. (1974). Recent U.K. experience of prices and inequality: an application of true cost of living and real income indices. *Economic Journal*, Vol. 84, pp. 32–55.

Muellbauer, J. (1974). Aggregation, income distribution and consumer demand. Birkbeck College, Discussion Paper No. 25.

Nasse, P. (1970). Analyse des effets de substitution dans un système complet de fonctions de demande. *Annales de l'Insee*, No. 5, pp. 81–110.

Paelinck, J. (1964). *Fonctions de Consommation pour la Belgique, 1948–59*. Facultés Universitaires N-D de la Paix, Namur.

Parks, R.W. (1969). Systems of demand equations: an empirical comparison of alternative functional forms. *Econometrica*, Vol. 37, pp. 629–650.

Parks, R.W. (1971). Maximum likelihood estimation of the linear expenditure system. *Journal of the American Statistical Association*, Vol. 66, pp. 900–3.

Parks, R.W. and A.P. Barten (1973). A cross-country comparison of the effects of prices, income, and population composition on consumption patterns. *Economic Journal*, Vol. 83, pp. 834–852.

Pearce, I.F. (1964). A *Contribution to Demand Analysis*. Oxford University Press.

Phlips, L. (1971). Substitution, complementarity, and the residual variation around dynamic demand equations. *American Economic Review*, Vol. 61, pp. 586–597.

Phlips, L. (1972). A dynamic version of the linear expenditure model. *Review of Economics and Statistics*, Vol. 54, pp. 450–458.

Phlips, L. (1974). *Applied Demand Analysis*. North-Holland.

Phlips, L. and P. Rouzier (1972). Substitution, complementarity, and the residual variation: some further results. *American Economic Review*, Vol. 62, pp. 747–751.

Pigou, A.C. (1910). A method of determining the numerical value of elasticities of demand. *Economic Journal*, Vol. 20, pp. 636–640.

Pollak, R.A. and T.J. Wales (1969). Estimation of the linear expenditure system. *Econometrica*, Vol. 37, pp. 611–628.

Powell, A.A. (1965). Post-war consumption in Canada: a first look at the aggregates. *Canadian Journal of Economics and Political Science*, Vol. 31, pp. 559–565.

Powell, A.A. (1966). A complete system of consumer demand for the Australian economy fitted by a model of additive preferences. *Econometrica*, Vol. 34, pp. 661–675.

Powell, A.A., T. van Hoa, and R.H. Wilson (1968). A multi-sectoral analysis of consumer demand in the post-war period. *Southern Economic Journal*, Vol. 35, pp. 109–120.

Prais, S.J. (1959). A comment. *Econometrica*, Vol. 27, pp. 127–129.

Rao, C.R. (1952). *Advanced Statistical Methods in Biometric Research*. John Wiley, New York; Chapman and Hall, London.

Robinson, J.V. (1960). *Exercises in Economic Analysis*. Macmillan, London.

Roy, R. (1942). *De l'utilité, contribution à la théorie des choix*. Hermann, Paris.

Samuelson, P.A. (1947–48). Some implications of linearity. *Review of Economic Studies*, Vol. 15, pp. 88–90.

Samuelson, P.A. (1950). The problem of integrability in utility theory. *Economica*, Vol. 17, pp. 355–385.

Schultz, H. (1928). *Statistical Laws of Demand and Supply with Special Application to Sugar*. Chicago University Press.

Schultz, H. (1938). *The Theory and Measurement of Demand.* Chicago University Press.

Sibson, R. (1972). Order invariant methods for data analysis. *Journal of the Royal Statistical Society, Series B*, Vol. 34, pp. 311–337.

Slutsky, E. (1915). Sulla teoria del bilancio del consomatore. *Giornale degli Economisti*, Vol. 51, pp. 1–26. (English trans. in *Readings in Price Theory*, G.J. Stigler and K.E. Boulding (eds.), Chicago University Press, 1952.)

Solari, L. (1971). *Théorie des choix et fonctions de consommation semi-agrégées*. Librarie Droz, Geneva.

Somermeyer, W.H., G.M. Hilhorot and J.W.W.A. Wit (1962). A method of estimating price and income elasticities from time series and its application to consumers' expenditures in the Netherlands, 1949–1959. Netherlands Central Bureau of Statistics, Statistical Studies, No. 13, mimeo.

Somermeyer, W.H. and A. Langhout (1972). Shapes of Engel curves and demand curves: implications of the expenditure allocation model applied to Dutch data. *European Economic Review*, Vol. 3, pp. 351–386.

Sonnenschein, H.F. (1972). Market excess demand functions. *Econometrica*, Vol. 40, pp. 549–563.

Sonnenschein, H. (1973). Do Walras' identity and continuity characterize the class of community excess demand functions? *Journal of Economic Theory*, Vol. 6, pp. 345–354.

Stone, J.R.N. (1954). *The Measurement of Consumers' Expenditure and Behaviour in the United Kingdom, 1920–1938, Vol. I.* Cambridge University Press.

Stone, J.R.N. (1954). Linear expenditure systems and demand analysis: an application to the pattern of British demand. *Economic Journal*, Vol. 64, pp. 511–527.

Stone, J.R.N. (1965). Models for demand projections. pp. 271–290 in *Essays on Econometrics and Planning*, C. Rao (ed.), Pergamon, Oxford.

Stone, J.R.N. (1964). Private saving in Britain, past, present and future. *The Manchester School of Economic and Social Studies*, Vol. 32, pp. 79–112.

Stone, J.R.N. (1966). Spending and saving in relation to income and wealth. *L'Industria*, No. 4, pp. 1–29.

Stone, J.R.N. (1973). Personal spending and saving in postwar Britain. pp. 75–98 in Bos, H.C., H. Linnemann, and P. de Wolff, (eds.) *Economic Structure and Development: Essays in honour of Jan Tinbergen*. North-Holland.

Stone, J.R.N. and G. Croft-Murray (1959). *Social Accounting and Economic Models.* Bowes and Bowes, London.

Stone, J.R.N., J.A.C. Brown and D.A. Rowe (1964). Demand analysis and projections for Britain 1900–1970: a study in method. pp. 200–225 in *Europe's Future Consumption*, J. Sandee (ed.) North-Holland.

Stone, J.R.N. and D.A. Rowe (1962). A post-war expenditure function. *The Manchester School of Economic and Social Studies*, Vol. 30, pp. 187–201.

Strotz, R.H. (1957). The empirical implications of a utility tree. *Econometrica*, Vol. 25, pp. 269–280.

Strotz, R.H. (1959). The utility tree – a correction and further appraisal. *Econometrica*, Vol. 27, pp. 482–488.

Summers, R. (1959). A note on least squares bias in household expenditure analysis. *Econometrica*, Vol. 27, pp. 121–126.

Taylor, L.D. and D. Weiserbs (1972). On the estimation of dynamic demand functions. *Review of Economics and Statistics*, Vol. 54, pp. 459–465.

Theil, H. (1971a). *Principles of Econometrics*. North-Holland, Amsterdam.

Theil, H. (1971b). An economic theory of the second moments of disturbances of behavioural equations. *American Economic Review*, Vol. 61, pp. 190–194.

Theil, H. (1973). A theory of rational random behaviour. Center for Mathematical Studies in Business and Economics, University of Chicago, Report 7327, mimeo.

Theil, H. and H. Neudecker (1957–8). Substitution, complementarity, and residual variation around Engel curves. *Review of Economic Studies*, Vol. 25, pp. 114–123.

van Hoa, T. (1968). Inter-regional elasticities and aggregation bias: a study of consumer demand in Australia. *Australian Economic Papers*, Vol. 7, pp. 206–226.

van Hoa, T. (1969). Additive preferences and cost-of-living indexes: an empirical study of Australian consumers' welfare. *Economic Record*, Vol. 45, pp. 432–440.

Wit, J.W.W.A. (1960). Income elasticities in 1935/36 and 1951 in the Netherlands: an application of a model for income spending. Netherlands Central Bureau of Statistics, Statistical Studies, No. 10, mimeo.

Wold, H. (1953). *Demand Analysis*. Assisted by L. Jureen. Almqvist and Wiksells, Uppsala.

Working, E.J. (1927). What do statistical demand curves show? *Quarterly Journal of Economics*, Vol. 41, pp. 212–235.

Yoshihara, K. (1969). Demand functions: an application to the Japanese expenditure pattern. *Econometrica*, Vol. 37, pp. 257–274.

Yule, G.U. (1926). Why do we sometimes get nonsense correlations between time-series? *Journal of the Royal Statistical Society*, Vol. 89, pp. 1–64.

INDEX

AUTHORS

SUBJECTS

COMMODITIES